Lessons from
MOUNT KILIMANJARO

Lessons from MOUNT KILIMANJARO

SCHOOLING, COMMUNITY, AND GENDER IN EAST AFRICA

AMY STAMBACH

ROUTLEDGE
NEW YORK   LONDON

Published in 2000 by
Routledge
29 West 35th Street
New York, NY 10001

Published in Great Britain by
Routledge
11 New Fetter Lane
London EC4P 4EE

Copyright © 2000 by Routledge

Printed in the United States of America on acid-free paper.

Library of Congress Cataloging-in-Publication Data

Stambach, Amy, 1966–
    Lessons from Mount Kilimanjaro: schooling, community, and gender in East Africa / Amy Stambach.
        p.cm.
    Includes bibliographical references (p.) and index.
    ISBN 0-415-92582-7 (hb) — ISBN 0-415-92583-5 (pb)
    1. Education—Social aspects—Tanzania—Kilimanjaro Region. 2. Sex discrimination in education—Tanzania—Kilimanjaro Region. 3. Educational anthropology—Tanzania—Kilimanjaro Region. I. Title.
LA1844.K54 S72 2000
306.43'09678'26—dc21   00-026956

For Matthew and Isaac

CONTENTS

4

"EDUCATION IS MY HUSBAND"
GENERATIONAL TRANSFORMATIONS

5

"BOYS, PRESERVE YOUR BULLETS; GIRLS, LOCK YOUR BOXES"
GENDERED MESSAGES IN CLASSES AND THE CURRICULUM

6

"THINGS WITH SOCKS"

7

"MOUNTAINS NEVER MEET BUT PEOPLE DO"

ILLUSTRATIONS

ACKNOWLEDGMENTS

I AM GRATEFUL to many people living on Mount Kilimanjaro who shared a part of their lives with me. The lessons they conveyed go well beyond what I could ever hope to represent in a book. In particular, the challenges of field research were made all the more interesting and enjoyable thanks to the friendship, advice, and hospitality extended to me by Mr. and Mrs. Clement Kwayu, Mama and Baba Tumsifu, Amini Uronu, Mama Nassiri, Geoffrey and Blandina Sawayael, Janet and Jeremy LeFroy, Sarah Cottingham, Shoo, John Ntiro, Mama Agnes, Mama Esther, Justine Sarakana, and Mdouah. Students, teachers, and parents who were involved in the secondary schools and villages where I worked taught me that learning is indeed a lifelong process. I cannot name here all of the people who generously answered my questions and spoke with me—there are too many and I am bound to confidentiality—but I hope their comments and concerns find some expression in the following pages. I alone am responsible for whatever errors or intellectual weakness this book demonstrates.

I must mention with special gratitude Marshall Z. Kwayu and Sarah S. Kwayu, who patiently and expertly educated me along the way and who saved me from many wrong turns and social blunders. My memories of living and working with them have become some of the most moving and transformative of my life.

In the course of writing this book, I have learned how intellectually indebted researchers are to their academic predecessors. In my case, Donna Kerner, Professor of Sociology and Anthropology at Wheaton College, Massachusetts, gave me a running start on this research; for this, I am immensely grateful. Donna's guidance in the field and her close reading of my work have made this a better book. I am also indebted to George A. Malekela at the University of Dar es Salaam for first suggesting that I study schooling on Mount Kilimanjaro and for providing me with friendship and collegiality throughout the years.

I first traveled to Tanzania in 1990 as part of a language study program sponsored by Fulbright-Hays. In 1991, I received funding from the Spencer Foundation to conduct research on the cultural context of East African schooling. In 1996, the Andrew W. Mellon Foundation and the Pennsylvania State University Center for the Study of Child and Adolescent Development provided funding for follow-up research on schooling, gender, and age-related transformations. Most recently, the National Academy of Education has awarded me a fellowship that has assisted me in making final edits and in preparing me to return to Tanzania to conduct further research. I am grateful to these institutions for their support and to the Tanzania Commission for Science and Technology (COSTECH) for granting me permission to conduct research in Kilimanjaro Region.

As a graduate of the University of Chicago's Department of Anthropology, I owe a debt of gratitude to many people who are there or who were there during my graduate days, when my plans for researching education in East Africa first took shape: Andrew Apter, Ralph Austen, Jean Comaroff, Marilyn Ivy, Marshall Sahlins, Terence Turner, and George Stocking. I am especially grateful to John Comaroff for his mentoring throughout the years; his dedication to his students sets the standards that I hope to live up to.

Many friends and colleagues read earlier versions of this book—sometimes in the form of conference papers—and offered crucial suggestions for revisions at various stages. My thanks to Katherine Anderson-Levitt, Misty Bastian, Marianne Bloch, Patricia Draper, Deborah Durham, Frederick Erickson, Janise Hurtig, Clement Kwayu, Jean Lave, Pier Larson, Stacey Lee, Bradley A. Levinson, Sheryl McCurdy, Lioba Moshi, Karen A. Porter, Deborah Reed-Danahay, Ladi Semali, Moira Urich, Fran Vavrus, and Brad Weiss. Their comments and suggestions have been immensely useful. I only wish I could have incorporated everything they suggested.

Flora Mbasha Popenoe, Joyce Lyimo, and Lucy Mule translated and transcribed hours of interview tapes from Kiswahili and Kimachame into English, and Suzanne Rosenblith, Natalie Crow, and Elizabeth Gross assisted at various stages. I am grateful to them for their help. I would also like to thank students and colleagues in the Department of Educational

Policy Studies at the University of Wisconsin, Madison. This book has benefited greatly from the readings of students in "701."

Ilene Kalish, Jennifer Hirshlag, and Jeni Kate Spear of Routledge have been absolutely terrific to work with—my thanks to them for offering editorial advice and direction.

Finally, I would like to thank Matthew Bershady for talking with me about this project all along the way. His insight, patience, and sense of good humor have been crucial to this study. It is to him and to our child, Isaac Henry, that I dedicate this work.

Portions of this work have been previously published.

"Seeded in the Market Economy: Schooling and Social Transformations on Mount Kilimanjaro," in *Anthropology and Education Quarterly* 27(4):1–23, is now part of Chapter 2.

"'Education is My Husband': Marriage, Gender, and Reproduction in Northern Tanzania," in *Women and Education in Sub-Saharan Africa*, edited by Marianne Bloch, Josephine A. Beoku-Betts, and B. Robert Tabachnick (Boulder, CO: Lynne Rienner Press, 1998), is now part of Chapter 4.

"'Here in Africa, We Teach, Students Listen': Lessons About Culture from Tanzania," *Journal of Curriculum and Supervision* 9(4):368–385, is now part of Chapter 5.

"WHAT EDUCATED YOUTH DO THESE DAYS"

DIVERGENT VIEWS OF SECONDARY SCHOOLING

"Why are we selling our land and cows to send our children to secondary school? I really don't understand it," asserted Joshua Makia, a seventy-year-old man living on Mount Kilimanjaro.

"Yes," responded Mzee Lema, "we've given up everything so that our sons—even our daughters!—can go to school."

October 1991

"These educated girls think they can come back and rule the roost! We pay for their uniforms and school fees, and then they come and tell us we are no good, that we are backward and traditional."

Mama Angela, mother of a secondary school graduate,
living on Mount Kilimanjaro. January 1993

"Education is the best thing we can give our sons and daughters. *Without* education, our children are nothing. *With* education, they can talk to the world. They can get jobs and move out of the village." *They* can get jobs and move out of the village.

Baba Elimbora, father of three secondary school students,
who lives on Mount Kilimanjaro and works
much of the year in Nairobi, Kenya. October 1996

1

Schools provide one of the clearest and most illuminating windows into the complexities and contradictions of cultural change. Whether it is a new institution built at the foot of Mount Kilimanjaro or a charter school established in the United States, schools condense a myriad of ideas about gender, generation, history, and culture. Disagreements about schooling are sometimes profound, as when parents privately pull children from classes, or students quietly resist their teachers' lessons. But regardless of the degree, debates about education provide a lens into social life beyond classrooms. They help us understand the connections people make between textbooks and the wider society, and they illustrate that the meaning and scope of schooling is often different from what is detailed in curricula and policies.

It was with this knowledge about the centrality of schooling in social life that I chose to study education on Mount Kilimanjaro. I was drawn to Mount Kilimanjaro because I had heard that the Tanzanian government had been using schooling for nearly three decades to develop a new national culture. What, I wondered, was the government doing in schools to bring so many different people into a common domain? What was the official idea of "culture" and how were people responding to it? I was also intrigued by the many reports I had read in U.S. newspapers about international agencies providing educational services to "poor countries" overseas. Many of these projects focused on teaching girls how to improve their lives and gain economic autonomy.

> The Clinton Administration will announce on Wednesday [at a United Nations conference in Copenhagen] the creation of a program to help keep girls in schools in Africa, Asia, and Latin America. . . .
>
> "In some countries, especially as they reach adolescence, girls don't attend school because parents fear they are not safe," Dr. Daulaire [chief policy adviser to the administrator of the U.S. Agency for International Development] said.
>
> Teachers will be trained to accept and integrate girls into a classroom where they might normally be ignored. . . . [New York Times, March 8, 1995, p. 12]

How did such programs fit into the government's plans to fashion an autonomous national culture through education? How did they fit in with local views about what educated girls and boys ought to learn and become? Reports on schooling presented a "school-to-the-rescue" model of education, one in which schooling transformed "traditional beliefs" into "modern practices."

I wondered how the school could be so much to so many different people. When I arrived on Mount Kilimanjaro, I encountered many more ideas about what school is and ought to be. To some people, schooling signified the demise of what they saw and valued as traditional culture. It raised concern about corrosive, Western influences on indigenous Chagga society, and it interfered with what some people saw as conventional relationships between men and women. Some Tanzanians, for instance, said that school-educated girls were undermining the norms that structured social life and everyday interactions—that they were contributing to economic decline and underdevelopment by not fulfilling their domestic duties. To others, the same institution was a sign of social progress. It attested to the possibility that anybody—rich or poor, male or female, old or young—could become educated and move up the social ladder, and that "the poor" could be lifted from a substandard of poverty to a higher social and economic level.

One of the issues most hotly discussed on Mount Kilimanjaro had to do with gendered and age-related social and cultural changes. Schooling was seen as reframing the ways many people thought children ought to interact with adults and as disrupting appropriate gendered relations among and between Chagga men and women (Mzee Lema's view, for instance, quoted above). Other people, however, including Baba Elimbora (the last of those quoted above) thought education helped people "talk to the world." Schooling, in their views, was a desirable institution, one through which "modern families" could be created, nurtured, and reproduced.

Taken together, arguments such as Mzee Lema's and Baba Elimbora's suggest that, no matter one's point of view, schools are often pivotal social institutions around which the configuration of society as a whole is imagined, contested, and transformed, and that schooling provides one of the clearest institutions for observing debates about culture, generation, gender, and history.

Understanding this multifaceted character of secondary schooling—as a sign of cultural demise and of economic reinvigoration, of state control and international development, of utopian ideals and social conflicts—led me down conceptual paths that I initially thought were unrelated to schools. It involved me in discussions about the symbolism of local foods, the mean-ings of lineage, inheritance, and marriage, and the significance of circumcision and initiation. It took me to many places and people that ostensibly had nothing to do with education: ritual specialists, lineage elders, church officials, even the singer Michael Jackson. And it helped me reflect on some of the central issues in the anthropology of education and gender—especially the ways that relations of power and authority are shaped through and socially attributed to schooling.

Schooling, I came to see, marked the definition, impact, and reshaping of new forms of gendered and generational differences. It corresponded with the division of labor along novel social lines that often marginalized partic-ular groups from economic and political resources, and it coincided with the creation of a sharp dichotomy between "traditional beliefs" and "modern practices." But it also contained a *constructive* mode that provided a lan-guage for identifying and strengthening relationships among various social groups, including educated women who sought to establish lives beyond the immediate social and economic control of fathers and brothers.

I was interested in exploring the positive outcomes and the seeming con-tradictions that schools condensed, for it seemed that the top-down transforming power of schools over society had been overemphasized in educational reports. I wanted to work in an anthropological vein, to see how schools express broad transformations within families and how beliefs and practices that constitute schooling also constitute broader relations in con-temporary social life. What better place to look at social manifestations of age, gender, and culture, I thought, than in an institution—the school—that models ideas about identity for younger generations? What better place to think about the macro-organization of societies than in institutions that claim to be microcosms of them?

Like most anthropologists, I have set out to write an ethnography that moves beyond institutional and geographic locations. To be sure, my focus is schooling on Mount Kilimanjaro, but it also includes the cultural ways in which schools and society reflect and act upon one another. In this regard, I am committed to something Clifford Geertz once said in a famous passage: that anthropologists don't study local places *per se*, they study *in* local places (1973:22), and, elsewhere (Geertz 1994), that an anthropological study of "foreign cultures" provides us with a way for thinking about alter-natives *for* ourselves, not alternatives *to* who we are. Distinctions between "to" and "for," and between "in" and "about" a place, stimulate reflection on the meaning of self and other. They help us think about the processes by which educational institutions—particularly schools—model and reflect these distinctions for particular cadres of society. I began this study in the spirit of explaining the many, often contradictory ways age and gender are formulated in connection with schooling, and it is in this spirit that I offer the following description of life on Mount Kilimanjaro—not, in the first instance, as a picture of what schooling on Mount Kilimanjaro is all about, but as a glimpse of some of the ways we, as human beings, variably organize social life around and through educational institutions.

AN ILLUSTRATION FROM VILLAGE LIFE

The core of this work is based on fieldwork conducted across more than half a decade, from language study in the summer of 1990 to field research from 1991 to early 1993, and again in October 1996. I would like to begin the ethnography by describing some of the setting in which I am situating my argument. I present first an episode from a household where I lived during the first few months of my stay and where I observed the changing faces of students as they went about their daily lives. I then set out the conceptual issues that inform the narrative of this study and provide an overview of the location, village, and school where much of this study is based. I conclude this chapter with a synopsis of later chapters, outlining briefly the overarching themes and arguments of this work.

Before moving to a rented house in the village, I lived for two months in a household with seven children and two parents. Three of these children were students at Mkufi Secondary School, the school that serves as the centerpiece of my analysis. The oldest of these students was Stellah Mbasa, my eventual assistant, friend, confidante, and housemate.[1] At home, children's operative mode (at least in the presence of their parents) was usually one of deference to adults. Students—particularly older girls—kept the basic operations of the household going. Every morning they put on their clothes to the loud shouts of Mama Elimbora[2]—"Stellah! Catherine! Elimbora! Lilian! Eudora! Kivawafo! Elingaya!" Mama Elimbora would call each of them in turn. Slowly at first, the oldest girls dressed, fetched water, washed clothes, and mopped interior floors. Boys in the household were charged with feeding the guinea fowl and watering the vegetable garden and flowers.

Morning duties were in general less onerous than what was expected of children after school. At the end of the day, Stellah and Catherine were supposed to cook dinner, Elimbora to tend to her younger brothers. Male cousins in the neighboring house, some of whom ate meals with this extended family, were tasked with the project of cutting grass and cleaning and feeding the goat and her kids. This was the plan, though not always the practice: children were often looking instead for some diversion.

In the afternoon hours, before these children's parents came home, the "boom box" came out of the locked cupboard, and Bobbie Brown, Black Box, and Michael Jackson tapes were played over and over again, often to the whine of straining batteries. The doors were flung open—windows too—so that neighboring friends might hear and join the party. To me, these were familiar signs of adolescent culture, flirtations with freedom and innocent rebellion. In fact, I welcomed this time in the late afternoon when I felt I could relax and connect with the songs and scenario. The children told me to "make myself at home" (*jisikie nyumbani*[3]), but the neighbors—adults and other youth in the community—had mixed opinions about the afternoon brouhaha.

Mama Lucky, who lived catty-corner from the Mbasas and who had married one of Mr. Mbasa's father's brother's sons,[4] loosely endorsed the afternoon release, calling it "what educated youth do these days." She said she was rather amused by the chaotic dancing when she came one day to collect her daughter, Lucky. Lucky was one of the quieter Form 2 students but a ready participant in this "disco" culture.[5] The neighborhood boy who lived across the road said he too was intrigued by the students' loud music. Like a fraction—about 5 percent[6]—of the children in the area, he had quit school at Standard IV and spent most of his days farming and tending to livestock. He never joined the celebrations inside the house but instead hung around the main road and watched.

Less appreciative, Bwana Mafue, an itinerant worker, scoffed at the music when he came to the door looking for Baba Elimbora. Muttering that such dancing and loudness was disrespectful and that these girls were behaving inappropriately, he attributed the "nonsense" (*ujinga*) to Western education (*elimu ya kizungu*) and condemned schools for ruining African women. His view that schooling was particularly damaging to women—and to a patrilineal social order in which inheritance is reckoned through male lines—was shared by several others in the community, including Bibi Lenga, a ninety-year-old woman who lived across the road in a small wattle-and-daub house.

Bibi Lenga said quite firmly that "girls who danced this way will never get married or have good husbands." She clarified that the sexual allure of the song lyrics was not the problem. (I translated the lyrics the children were singing and asked if they offended; she said not.) At issue was the general revelry—an indication, she said, that the girls' parents had no authority. If parents could not control their daughters, why would men want to marry them? If educated girls were so proud of themselves that they could defy understandings about social deference, how would they behave in a married setting in which they would be expected (according to Bibi Lenga) to submit to husbands' authority? Both she and Bwana Mafue suggested that schooling contributed to girls' moral decline, and their comments clued me in to some of the ways educated young women, more so than young men, were construed through some lines of social discourse as a threat to the normative order and Chagga tradition.

Their comments provided an early theme: that of the emblematic value of schooling as a means for explaining social changes between men and women and between younger and older generations. And they gave concrete form—in the lives of these students and girls—to the general sentiment that school-educated girls were too independent and that youth in general were straining traditions.

Yet school-educated girls and their male counterparts did not see themselves this way. The girls in the Mbasa household typically described themselves as "educated" and "developed," and they described Bibi Lenga and others who had not attended school as "backward" and "superstitious." I often heard students talk about unschooled people in derisive terms, even as they also respected elders in other contexts for the social powers old people embodied. Uneducated people were responsible, many students put it, for "holding us back from achieving modernity" and for "keeping us in the bush" instead of "helping us get jobs and moving to the city." According to some students, it was not *they* who threatened custom, but "ignorant people" who had not gone to school and who, as a consequence, did not know how to adapt their culture to "modern ways."

Students' views that old people held them back were manifest in many settings, including situations in which students *avoided* unschooled elders whom they feared might curse (*laani*) or jinx (*nuksi*) them. Chief among students' critics were elders who thought students were "showing off" and trying to be "bigger than themselves." Some old people were especially critical of schoolgirls who wore stylish clothing and makeup and had salon-styled hair. Others felt that fashionably dressed girls were respectable yet too assertive in their independence.

Especially censorious were some members of the community who self-identified as "born-again Christians"—religious persons who, as a whole, tended to be school-educated themselves but who sometimes questioned the moral implications of students' material culture.[7] Among this group were these students' paternal uncle and his wife, who lived adjacent to Baba and Mama Elimbora. Like some village elders, this couple condemned loud music and disco dancing. Their opposition was not to dancing and music *per se* but to the moral values they believed students' interests signified. When the students' uncle and aunt came home in the evening, the Mbasa children would quickly change their tune. For even though they lived next door, members of this extended family interacted fluidly with one another. Quick as a flash, when Stellah and the others heard the uncle's pickup truck rumbling down the road, they would shut down the party, put on a new face, and reflect another educated identity. The music would go off, the furniture would be straightened, and water would be put on to boil for tea. At home in the morning and in the course of the school day, the Mbasa children would defer to elders' authority. They would acknowledge the wisdom of elders and teachers and obey the commands of parents at home. They would even formally proclaim themselves born-again Christians in appropriate settings. Yet they would continue to dance and sing to Bobby Brown tapes when they were in other places.

The multiplicities of students' identities and views were not at all lost on some of them. When I mentioned to Elimbora that dancing to loud music seemed to go against the values she said that she espoused as a "Born Again," Elimbora answered that "school-educated people enjoy traditional *and* foreign things." She argued that "born-again Christians were not 'either/or'"—meaning they neither subscribed to Western-Christian ways, nor embraced all of the beliefs associated with African grandparents. She noted that much of the distinction older people made between "local tradition" and "modern schooling" was a product of their *own* educational experiences that saw the two as incompatible—a view that attests to the combinatory power of schooling and local culture to produce conceptual categories. For Elimbora's characterization of elders' views about what is old and new was itself an education-institutional rescripting of a local history and culture that did not specifically package "education" with "learning," or "old age" with "tradition and custom." Her later comment—that people who thought schoolgirls were immoral were themselves "ignorant and uneducated"—again indicated that schooling and culture together construed "ignorance" and "differences" in specific ways.

Elimbora later asserted, without any prompting, that schools "teach us about foreign things," and that one of the reasons Tanzanian students "danced American" was "because school-educated people appreciate foreign culture." She pointed to her own grandfather's radio and telephone as further evidence of a schooled, material culture (her grandfather had been a teacher at a local school). And she noted that her own style of "Western dress," as she called it, contrasted with most village women; Elimbora wore European- and American-made clothing that she bought at the popular used-clothing market in Moshi Town. To Elimbora, new fashions, new music, new forms of speech—all were emblematic markers of a school-educated and "modern" (*wa kisasa*) person. To her, they were constructive signs that indicated economic change and social progress. Yet these very items signaled, to other people, students' immorality and material pretensions.

As this episode at the Mbasa household illustrates, schools are often regarded as containing the possibility for social change. Whether on Mount Kilimanjaro or elsewhere in the world, schools stand for the possibility of creating new social forms. They offer new ideas and practical solutions for moving people beyond their past, even as they help to establish a conceptual antinomy between "tradition" and "modernity."

CONCEPTUAL ISSUES: THEORIZING MODERNITY, GENDER, AND GENERATION

Identifying "modernity" is a difficult project, for "the modern" emerges, in a rather immaterial way, through the symbolic production of "customary practice," modernity's conceptual opposite. Modernity and tradition, as many have discussed (e.g., Appadurai 1996; Comaroff and Comaroff 1993:xi–xv; Watts 1992), are experienced by various groups and individuals very differently. Sally Falk Moore notes (1996b:603) that modernity has typically been discussed in academic circles either in connection with a foundational order—"tradition" (e.g., Habermas 1979; Weber 1968)—or in relation to a pastiche of traditional themes that form the core of a "post-modernity" (e.g., Benhabib 1992; Rabinow 1986). An older anthropology has examined "traditional culture" while a more recent line has looked at the "multicultural."

My objective in this work is to address neither the realities of past forms nor the intricacies of a postmodernity. Instead, my focus is on what I have found to be a more ethnographically answerable question: How do collective ideas about what is modern and traditional emerge in connection with people's understandings of schooling? I address this question through a discussion of my observations of social life on Mount Kilimanjaro, particularly through an analysis of the ways age and gender are multiply formulated. For what I found in my work with people in Machame is that gender and generation underlay home and school tensions: women's and men's different social positions fuel debates about fairness and equity. Similarly, older people view students as subordinates who need to be recipients of knowledge, while the school system elevates students as capable of learning and thereby as capable of transforming society.[8]

One of the operational assumptions found in school policies and curricula, I found, is a commitment to "improving" old social forms and to moving people on to a "better world" through a system of classroom instruction and examinations. On the face of it, a diverse literature on schooling is extremely useful for understanding such operational assumptions (see, for examples, Adamchak and Ntseane 1992; Biraimah 1989; Elliott and Kelly 1980; House-Midamba 1990; Meekers 1994). Much of this literature examines the impact of schooling on indigenous African values and demonstrates how students variously respond to and use schooling to create new social forms. Yet some of this work turns on the view that schools themselves are the main engines of social change, and some of it does not consider how people collectively invest schools with the cultural capacity to change social relations.

The view that schooling changes social life—known in the development and educational literature as "modernization theory"—is an optimistic model of socially planned change that is often incorporated into international development policies. Modernization views maintain that schooling is a culturally homogenizing process (see, for examples, Bendix 1964; Inkeles 1998; Inkeles and Smith 1974; World Bank 1988). Pedagogy, seen from within this view, is a matter of transmitting knowledge from "more" to "less" educated groups and of assisting underdeveloped peoples and countries in securing basic needs (food, shelter, employment, a certain level of infrastructure). Modernization approaches, or what I, with tongue in cheek, call "school-to-the-rescue models," posit that with the right combination of raw materials and human capital, poverty can be eradicated and countries may thrive. The model puts to the test in principle an old Frazerian notion (Frazer 1890) that certain peoples fare less well with "reality" not because they are cognitively "deficient" but because they lack the information and resources they need in order to think and act effectively.[9]

I find modernization approaches and policies that come out of them thought-provoking and insightful, particularly for the ways they theorize what *appears* to be the standardization of culture through education. But like others (e.g., Levinson and Holland 1996), I question their general level of abstractness and their initial starting points. At root, school-to-the-rescue models turn upon a particular assumption that "becoming modern" stems from outside cultural forces, mostly from Western states, and that modernity is a unidirectional process that moves people toward a common end. I did not always see these connections in my work, nor did I see all "educated persons" being culturally produced in the same way.

The modernization literature that I had originally been working from predicted greater empowerment for underprivileged groups. Its idea was that more information and access to knowledge would provide historically disadvantaged groups, including women, with new economic opportunities and greater market access. While such was in some regards a goal that was achieved, the social-reconstructive dynamics of education were more diffuse than could have been foreseen. Schooling *did* economically advance some underprivileged groups, though in ways that often created new hierarchies.

When researchers have looked at social differences and hierarchies (as when they have looked at alliances that have formed between wealthy elite and state education ministers, e.g., Fuller 1991), many have focused primarily on class and economics and on the class-polarizing effects of higher education. Theories of "the educated person" have focused on the ways people are constructed as basically nongendered adults. They have equated "education" with, strictly speaking, "what goes on in the school" and have not considered the ways a person may be transformed through schooling or redefined in terms of age, gender, ethnicity, or religion—even in terms of the other students with whom she or he has schooled. Neither have they considered that women and men may be differently constituted as educated adults or that schools may as well *de*construct educated identities even as they redefine them.

To be sure, anthropologists have produced numerous studies of gender, personhood, and generational transformations in Africa.[10] And several working at the crossroads of education and anthropology have discussed the importance of culture for understanding African schooling. Robert Serpell (1993), for instance, has illustrated vividly that education goes beyond that which is spelled out in the school curriculum, and D. A. Masolo (1994) and V. Y. Mudimbe (1988) have demonstrated that African knowledge emerges out of African history and culture, not necessarily out of schooling. However, except for several insightful articles,[11] there has been to my knowledge no focused look at the cultural context of schooling in the anthropological and education literature on gender and social relations in Africa. There has been no extended look at the ways in which what goes on *inside* schools is related to what goes on in the greater outside. In short, the school—and education—are glaringly absent from anthropological works on culture; and "culture," as a theoretical framework for linking educational institutions to marriage, kinship, and inheritance, is strikingly absent from works on education.[12]

My goal in this work is to bring considerations of age and gender into an anthropological investigation of education in East Africa. I move away from the ongoing dialogue in philosophy, psychology, sociology, and education about how gender and generation shape what men and women know,[13] and focus instead on the historical, political, and social conditions that culturally produce conceptualizations of gender, age, and education. Drawing upon the work of other anthropologists who have successfully described schooling in connection with cultural models of community, nationality, gender, and the family (e.g., Hall 1995; Holland and Eisenhart 1990; Lacey 1970; Luykx 1999; Peshkin 1972; Reed-Danahay 1996), I further the classical anthropological tradition here of understanding "schooling" in historical and cultural context. To this end, I have shaped this work to speak not only to readers interested in African culture—students and scholars of Africa, potential future teachers on the subcontinent, people who live and work in Africa and abroad—but also to wider discourses in gender studies, anthropology, education, and international studies.

Over the past two decades, anthropologists of gender have made contributions that bear directly on education, although as noted, "education" has not always been a focus of their analyses. Anthropological studies of gender have moved from looking at women vis-à-vis marriage, sexuality, and reproduction (e.g., Lévi-Strauss 1969, 1971; Leach 1965) to analyzing local critiques and dissatisfactions with prevalent gender arrangements (e.g., Abu-Lughod 1990; Tsing 1993). The focus has changed from perpetuating Western assumptions regarding gender by focusing primarily on women in connection with the private domain and men in connection with "the public" (e.g., Ortner 1974; Rosaldo 1974), to exploring how constructions of gender fluctuate depending on the social situation (e.g., Kondo 1990; Shire 1994). And the field has moved from focusing on the "exchange of women in marriage" (e.g., Evans-Pritchard 1951; Lévi-Strauss 1969, 1971) to the many ways women and men assert rights of authority over spouses, sexual/domestic partners, and their children (e.g., Bledsoe 1990; Hodgson and McCurdy 1996).

What I find particularly interesting is that, even as anthropological analyses have become more nuanced in theorizing transformations and identity, many of the people whom anthropologists study have begun to talk increasingly as though gender and age were *things*. Gender has been taken out of the realm of unarticulated experience and transformed into a public discourse. It has been brought into the open through a political economy of development in which gender and sexuality have been the subject of state control and consumer marketing. And it has been regulated through institutions such as the school, where the rules of discipline, routine, and teacher-student interactions presuppose that gender is synonymous with sexual dimorphism. On Mount Kilimanjaro, as in many places, gender is routinely (though not exclusively) seen as having to do with the sexual division of labor between girls and boys. Girls have a right and responsibility to do "this," boys a right and responsibility to do "that." Girls ought to work and study in order to produce "this," boys ought to do so in order to get "that." Frequently the "this" and the "that" are conceptually divided between two social institutions, home and school. They are either couched in terms of what boys and girls *who go to school* will get in the way of future jobs (which is in practice frequently very little), or they are presented in terms of what boys and girls *who learn their lessons at home* will get in the way of local capital: blessings, children, ritual power, and (though less frequently these days) land.

Age is also often reified—it is frequently treated as though it were a *thing*. In educational settings, such as schools or religious programs, youth are often positioned as recipients of knowledge, as subordinates within a formalized social structure, persons supposedly waiting for information to be given to them. Youth in school settings are typically viewed as persons to whom information and knowledge is transmitted. Youth are viewed as capable of being educated, of being transformed socially through state-sponsored schooling. This top-down official view gives the illusion of making "youth" look like it is increasingly a standardized category—more and more like what youth in any part of the world might look like to a casual observer. However, the formalized structure of the setting should not be mistaken for its internal dynamics. As we will see of students in secondary schools on the mountain, broader systems of relations contribute to the social production of youth as a category. Students' peer groups and popular culture cut across what elders and teachers openly teach.

Schooling has been instrumental in objectifying gender and generation as social categories and in bringing discussion about age and gender into everyday debates about education. In its focus on autonomy and progress, competition and rationality (see Apple 1993; Corrigan and Sayer 1985; Jacoby 1994), schooling constantly reminds us—and demands—that the *individual* is the fundamental unit of social interaction. And in its focus on rights and identities, on self-assertion and autonomy, contemporary school discourses guarantee us each a gender, typically drawn along sex dimorphic male/female lines,with different implications for our roles in society. Because the school is integrally connected to the other institutions that create new, ever-changing, "modern" subjects (Anderson 1983:16), it frequently serves as a convenient cultural imaginary for believing everyone is becoming more alike. The school is often seen, at least from a distanced, often policy-oriented, perspective, to be the Great Leveler of Social Difference.

But is it? If the school has the common effect of projecting the particular in universalizing terms, what are the relative logics of these forms, or are they also the same? Are the operations of schooling so hegemonic that they truly do erase local practices? Or are cultural logics so steadfastly firm and resilient that not even schooling can rout indigenous beliefs (Bloch 1993)?

My point of entrée into these complicated questions is people's manifold concerns about age and gender. Throughout this work, I contend that to understand changing modes of identities—and indeed the very processes by which identities are objectified—it is necessary to pay greater attention to debates surrounding schooling. *How* culture is manifest is a complicated process that often involves deciphering contradictory schemes (Bourdieu 1977:72). But that people living on Mount Kilimanjaro variously defined it to me in terms of a special symbolic domain (including the lineage, language, dress, food, and custom) is in part a consequence of the reifying categories of identity that are woven into the contemporary discourses of the school. As McRobbie (1994:178) and Bourdieu (1984) have pointed out in very different ways, schools are arenas where shared age-specific experiences among young people allow us to talk meaningfully about gender and generation.

In what follows, I turn to the ethnographic time and place of this work—Machame, Ndala Village, and Mkufi Secondary School in the early to mid-1990s—and to how the history of schooling informs contemporary events, including the recent expansion of secondary schooling in Tanzania. The stage has hopefully been set for an ethnography that is about neither "modern schooling" nor "African tradition." Rather, this work examines the ways people construct and explain differences in terms of the two and how, in so doing, they classify the natural world according to cultural ideas about identity and human difference.

LOCATIONS: MACHAME, NDALA VILLAGE, AND MKUFI SECONDARY SCHOOL

Historically, the people of Machame trace their ancestry to migrations from Shambaai territories in the south and Meru territories in the west.[14] Older ethnographies record that two brothers, Mashami and Nro, fought at the foot of Mount Meru (near present-day Arusha) and as a result went their separate ways (Dundas 1924; Stahl 1964), though few people I met spoke of this today. Mashami migrated east to the western slopes of Mount Kilimanjaro; Nro remained in Meru.

Schooling figured centrally in the colonial history of Machame. In the late nineteenth century, local chiefs (*mangi* in Kimachame)—not only in Machame but in neighboring Chagga chiefdoms—were adept in coaxing European missionaries to settle on the mountain. Their intentions, as recorded by scholars and local historians, were to monitor and control

Europeans' activities while simultaneously learning about and gradually gaining expertise in the burgeoning coffee industry (Lawuo 1984; Lema 1969). Through the British system of indirect rule, people on the mountain developed an extensive school system funded through taxes collected from coffee revenues, and they established cooperative societies that provided farmers with fertilizers and farming tips and connected the region to international markets. Schools and cooperatives, as well as private businesses, were all brought under government control by the early 1970s, and the limited autonomy people had in governing themselves locally during the colonial era was brought to an end shortly after independence, in 1961.[15]

Many people living in Machame today consider themselves part of a larger cultural group, "Chagga." Although this ethnic label is largely a reflection of colonial census categories, the population shares a cultural history that extends through three centuries of intermarriage, warfare, and trade networks. This cultural history is today a key component of regional identity, and it facilitates the sentiment among people in Machame that they are culturally connected to a broader community. The label "Machame" refers to the territory ruled at the turn of the century by a hereditary chief (*mangi*) who controlled regional trade and oversaw the distribution of land and food in exchange for the clientage of members of nonroyal lineages. Machame is not an official administrative unit, although many people speak about it as such today.

With a population of about 70,600 in 1996,[16] Machame is one of the most densely settled nonurban areas in Tanzania. Despite its proximity to Moshi Town, Machame is geographically and culturally distinct from the regional capital in several ways. It is located on the slopes of the mountain, away from the dry, dusty plain below (Illustration 1). The mountain is lush with banana trees and coffee shrubs, and the air is cooler and damper at higher altitudes than in the lowlands near Moshi. Unlike in Moshi, land in Machame is identified culturally with Chagga history and ritual life. Past generations are buried in banana groves that surround Chagga houses on the mountain, and rites of passage and rites of intensification are associated with sacred groves.

Traveling to or from Machame to Moshi is, these days, easy enough by truck, bus, or car. Although people say that in the past it took them an entire day to walk to Moshi, today the distance can be driven in a matter of thirty or forty minutes. Dozens of minivans ply the tarmac road that leads from Foo (a village at the geographical height of the paved road in

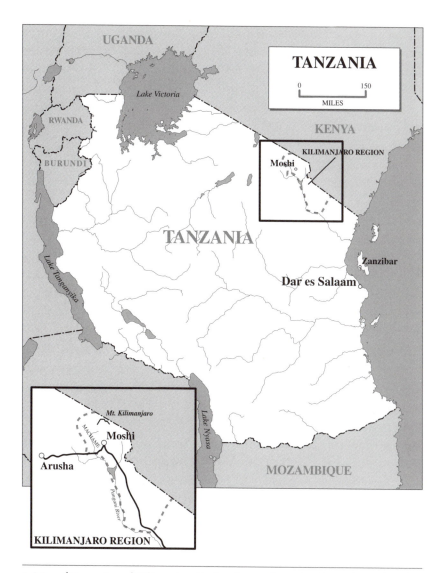

1. Map of Tanzania and Kilimanjaro Region. Insert shows Machame, located to the west of Moshi.

Machame) down the mountain, through several villages (including Ndala), and ultimately to Moshi, a bustling town of approximately 110,000 people in the early to mid-1990s. People come and go along this road to jobs in Moshi, to their lowland farms, to markets in Moshi, or to the Moshi bus stop where they then catch buses to further points such as Arusha, Mombasa,

Nairobi, and Dar es Salaam. Many people who work in town commute on a daily basis, giving Machame, in contrast to some other areas on the mountain, a bit of a suburban feel—yet with nothing of the American strip-mall sprawl.

Ndala, one of several geographically contiguous villages in Machame, had a population of about 7,000 residents in 1992. By 1996 this figure had grown to approximately 7,400.[17] Of these people, several different clans (*ukoo*) are the most prominently represented, including among the largest, Kwayu, Mafue, Nkya, Massawe, and Mbowe.[18] According to local accounts of the area's history, Ndala was populated by people who could not inherit land in other areas of the mountain and who moved down the slopes to places like Ndala where land was less densely populated and uncultivated. Kwayus came from the northwest, just over a major river. People of the Mafue clan came from the area to the north, and people of the Mbowe clan came from the east, from an area just on the border of Machame. Nkya and Massawe both originated in Kyalia and Nkuu, and the branches in Ndala are regarded as offshoots of lineages from the north.

Administrative divisions within Ndala divide the area into seven subvillages (*kitongoji* in Kimachame). There is no densely settled central village area in Ndala. Rather, the population is fairly evenly distributed, and people socialize in bars and shops that dot the village. A few shops line a quarter-mile stretch of the tarmac road that cuts through the village, and two mosques and four churches mark the area, the largest of which are visible from the tarmac road. Together, two Evangelical Lutheran churches seat about 2,500 people, Assembly of God and Catholic churches another 500 people between them,[19] and the largest mosque, a converted bungalow (once the house of a colonial settler), provides space for about three dozen men.

Today, as in the past, church and school are intricately connected, and Muslim leaders are increasingly playing a role in defining what goes on in church-sponsored schools. Mkufi Secondary School, where I focused most of my observations, is managed through the Evangelical Lutheran Church of Tanzania. Responsible for hiring and firing teachers and for building and maintaining the school buildings, the church provides only a minimum of funds; most of the financing for the school comes from private donations and students' school fees. Despite its religious affiliation, Mkufi conforms in principle to the standards set out by the Ministry of Education for all secondary schools in Tanzania, both government and private. At the time of my research, it was one of approximately 300 private secondary schools in the country (Ministry of Education and Culture 1992a:8).

Mkufi Secondary School was built on the burial site of a colonial settler, thirteen miles west of the regional capital, Moshi, and at the very foot of Mount Kilimanjaro. The name itself, Mkufi, means literally "a place where there are large trees" (though I have given it a pseudonym here). The school board had hoped to build on the other side of the road, under the shade of a stand of evergreens, but instead was forced to build near the settler's grave, where the land was less desirable but cost the school board nothing, and where the school could have access to thirty acres of land from the adjacent state-run coffee farm. Few people living in the area remember Mkufi as the site of a European settler's grave. Most see it as the place where the village worked hard to build and staff a new secondary school. Only during the last few years, and despite the dry, rocky soil, has Mkufi flourished to include a vegetable garden, a maize and bean farm, three classroom buildings, a cookhouse, and a library surrounded with white painted rocks and flowers. Yet the construction of Mkufi on dry, desolate land attests to the way once barren and uninhabited areas have been revalued and put to new use. Neighbors have staked the boundaries of their banana groves closer and closer to the school compound and have planted banana trees and dug irrigation channels to the northeast of the school. These activities mark a vested interest in the land on and around the school compound and reveal one way the school has contributed to local revitalization.

Several Lutheran and Muslim businessmen and leaders from Ndala and two other villages financed the construction of Mkufi in 1988. According to the school chairman, no children from these villages had been selected for government secondary school that year, and leaders within the communities had to take action if they were to see their children educated.[20] The founders' goal of making Mkufi "one of the best schools in the country" inspired hope among residents of contributing villages that their area would be known for its fine education. The original proposal, approved by the Ministry of Education and Culture in 1989, declared that the purpose of setting up the school was to "give the students [a] practical education" (Project Proposal 1989:2–3). According to the proposal (as with other blueprints for Tanzanian education—see Nyerere 1967), the aim of education was to teach students how to reinvest practical skills into the local economy.

Beginning in the mid-1980s, the government made it increasingly possible for communities to use private funding to establish their own secondary schools. Until then, the growth of the private sector had been discouraged and emphasis had been placed firmly on supporting government institutions. But policy changes and pressure from parents to make more schools available for their children resulted in what appear—at least in terms of numbers—to be significant changes in the educational system. Between 1986 and 1991, Form 1 intake doubled nationally (Ministry of Education and Culture 1992b:14–15), and the number of students enrolled in private secondary schools began to exceed that of students enrolled in government secondary schools. With the exception of years 1990 and 1993, girls' enrollment rates nationwide between 1986 and 1996 grew faster than boys'—sometimes more than twice as much annually.[21]

The rapid growth of secondary schooling was interpreted by many on the mountain to be an indication that the objectives of policies were being put into effect and that the community was prospering. Building private secondary schools was recognized as one way to increase the chances that some students would do well—at least in terms of having the opportunity to continue beyond Standard VII. By creating more spaces, educators enabled more and more students to succeed—at least within a system that defined success in terms of matriculation.

But even so, given that so many students dropped out or failed in the course of secondary schooling and were not necessarily "squeezed out" by unavailability of places,[22] the question persists: What is the purpose of this education? Why, in light of the high rates of failure, do people nonetheless work so hard to be admitted? Is secondary schooling a credentialing process in which students earn certificates of participation that then qualify them for employment, as Ronald Dore classically described (Dore 1976)? Or are schools "holding tanks" where primary graduates have a chance to grow up and become full adults before going on to marry and start families of their own, as founders of Mkufi Secondary School argue in their proposal to the Ministry of Education and Culture? What do people hope to get out of education? Again, what is secondary schooling all about?

Schooling, as the quotes at the opening of this chapter begin to illustrate, is not always about reading, writing, or arithmetic, but includes a range of concerns that extend well beyond the walls of the classroom and beyond what the curriculum is designed to instill. Judging from what I encountered in Ndala Village, schooling has as much if not more to do with the structuring of gendered and age-related differences as it does with conveying a body of information from one generation to the next. Having the opportunity to continue in secondary school is at one level a mark of educational success. Being there, advancing within the system, is a way of advancing socially and, in the eyes of many people in Machame, is more desirable than simply finishing primary school and remaining at home to farm. Schooling from this perspective is seen by many people living on the mountain as a means of escaping "tradition," a way of moving off the land and into the cash economy. This is not to say that schools erase tradition; schools re-create and preserve tradition as a "fixed past." But it is to say that for girls and boys, the opportunities are not always the same, and their decisions to matriculate through the system ramify with the social order in different ways.

"A Person Living in a Foreign Place Should Not Question Everything She Sees": Reflections on Fieldwork

Finally, and before I discuss these different ramifications from various angles in the chapters that follow, I would like to say something about the practical ways in which I carried out research. The story of how I came to work in Machame and my own reflections on the process provide some background for thinking about the paradoxes of schools as social institutions. As the following discussion illustrates, cultural notions of education, and anthropologists' own education as researchers in the field, are often difficult to separate. The research we conduct—or read about, for that matter—is as much a part of our own ongoing education as it is about schooling in other places. As such, ethnographies of education are, I believe, extremely fascinating to read about—and to write.

While conducting preliminary research in Tanzania some thirteen months before my longest stay, I contacted an administrator within the Lutheran Church in the regional capital, Moshi, and expressed an interest in studying the role of the Church in secondary schooling. I had hoped to teach as part of the project, both as a way of rooting myself for a full academic year at one institution while visiting and observing other schools and of providing a service to local communities. The church administrator was interested and offered me a position at a recently built secondary school. We agreed that I would teach part time and that in exchange the school would provide housing for me. The details of the arrangement were left to be worked out by mail in the intervening months, and when I returned to Kilimanjaro a few months later, a secondary school had been selected that was, in the church administrator's view, "equipped for European visitors."

Mkufi Secondary School in Machame, where I was to gather most of the data that serve as sources for the descriptions and analyses in this study, became my primary workplace for the next year and a half and again in 1996. Visits to other schools, and my closer familiarity with an all-girls school in Machame near the house where I lived part of the time, were to provide a framework for thinking about the routines (especially of schooling) that contributed to the formation of educated persons.

When I first arrived, notebook in hand, I was surprised to see that many people had a preconceived role into which I, an Anglo-American researcher, could be placed. Already some people were mistaking me for a missionary and citing biblical verses in the course of conversation, rather than typical Kimachame, Kiswahili, or even English phrases. Others treated me like a Peace Corps volunteer, with a mixture of disbelief, cautious skepticism, and respect.[23] A couple of students at recess at a local primary school ran toward me one afternoon, shouting "Jimmy Carter! Jimmy Carter!"[24] and greeting me with the standard student salutation, "Good morning, sir!" Clearly there had been "white Europeans" (*wazungu*) here before, and whether or not they had been men or women, they had been culturally codified, by some at least, as symbolically "male." I was initially but another representative of them and another "sir" with whom these students communicated.[25] Despite my reservations, I had a hunch that initial receptions of me as a missionary or Peace Corps volunteer might prove insightful. Local representations of Machame as "a little Europe" and as "the most developed rural area in Tanzania" promised to reveal something about the history and culture of schooling in the community and of the national and international connections it evoked—especially around gender—for these Tanzanian students. Anticipating this, I decided to stay.

At first I was treated with kid gloves. Teachers greeted me with heightened formality that reflected social distance—"Good morning, Madam. I am so happy to see you today"—and the school cook poured and stirred my morning cup of tea. I tried unsuccessfully to dispense with these rituals (I was not used to them) and in an effort one day to make small talk, I asked

Mr. Munuo, the mathematics teacher, where he had been that morning. I thought perhaps he had traveled to town for an appointment or to attend to family matters, but as with so many things early in my stay, I was mistaken. Teachers in the room were suddenly quiet, and Mr. Uroki, the English master, reiterated my question, noting that Mr. Munuo had missed his morning classes. "Why do you want to know, Mr. Uroki? Do I always ask you your whereabouts? What is this, that you need to know where I have been?" Although Mr. Munuo focused his attention on Mr. Uroki and strained to remain polite, he was clearly speaking to me. It was obvious that this was not small talk, but that I had breached a sensitive issue.

Social relations on Mount Kilimanjaro (as in many places around the world) are often constructed through indirect speech, and questions about a person's whereabouts are sometimes highly sensitive. Yet I did not know, at first, how serious this was. "Umetoka wapi?"—where have you been?—is, I came to learn later, tantamount in some social contexts to accusing someone of illicit conduct, and not a friendly opening question as I had come to know it from my North American experience. People rarely ask it of one another, unless they intend to embarrass someone or are sure that they know where the person has been and that it is acceptable to mention it. Knowing when to speak and when to keep quiet is often a matter of knowing what is socially valued and of knowing the rank and status of the person to whom one is speaking. People frequently pulled me aside to tell me things about other people, and it was through these heavy whispers that I began to understand ways in which knowledge and meaning were entailed in a rich network of constantly changing social relations.

Clearly there were personal and social dynamics behind the workplace routines (and teachers' diversions from these routines) that I did not yet understand. It was Mr. Uroki who gradually socialized me into the inseparable worlds of the school and village and who prevented me from making many more blunders. "Don't walk home with the students," he advised me. "Teachers must maintain their social distance or else what will they [students, other teachers, villagers] think of us?" Mr. Uroki quickly became my teacher, friend, and boss. His implication here was that I must work consciously toward developing a socially mature, adult image and that, despite my comparatively young age (I was closer in age to the students than to the teachers), I should work on allying myself with older persons of authority. Other tips he offered were less direct. As head of the English department with a certificate of teaching from the state, Mr. Uroki was in a position to supervise my work in the classroom. More than once he lingered outside the room where I was teaching and later pulled me aside to give me pointers.

After a few weeks, I invited Mr. Uroki inside to observe, rather than to stand by the window. But he scoffed, first denying that he was listening to my lessons and then noting that by observing students "secretly," he could assess how they (and I, I thought) really behaved.

His implication—that observation had to be done covertly—contradicted the professional code of ethics that governed my anthropological research—about the open and transparent nature of fieldwork and about the accountability of observers to those whom they observed. This was not an immediate conflict for me, for Mr. Uroki was observing *me*, and I could for a time "let him observe by his values, me by mine." But he and others soon began suggesting ways I might improve my own research. "Don't tell people who sent you here. They will think you're a spy." Or, "You don't have the same last name as your husband, do you? Are you really married? Don't tell your students this. Just have them call you Mrs. Stambach." But hadn't I just written a "Human Subjects' Rights"[26] statement in which I had affirmed my belief in the necessity of conducting research openly? And hadn't I agreed to make my identity and project known, even to people who were not necessarily interested in what I was doing?

Negotiating different cultural views about observation and self-identity—one of the more delicate tasks in the months to come—became in itself an exercise in learning about how power and knowledge are configured in this part of the world. Coming to terms with the ethical and methodological issues behind such negotiations was never easy, and in part I came to understand the knowledge/power/identity nexus in terms of some of the many pithy and ultimately contradictory aphorisms that people constantly iterate in conversation.

One aphorism, originally described to me as a saying taught to girls who are about to marry, had multiple meanings depending on the context, making it useful in many settings. The saying was a long one. "A person who lives in a foreign place should not question the things she sees, but upon returning to her natal household, may comment all she wants."[27] The aphorism has age-related and gendered meanings, depending on the person to whom it is directed. When said to young brides, it is often used to remind them that, as newly incorporated affines within their husbands' patriline, they must keep their mouths shut and reserve comment until they return home to visit their parents. When directed to men, the saying is generally used to remind them that although men have the social right to speak critically about their own households and families, they are not in positions to speak critically of others'. Men are granted the privilege of commanding and directing the activities of women and children who reside with them but are not permitted to intervene in others' household affairs.

As I eventually learned, "a person who lives in a foreign place should not question the things she sees, but upon returning to her own household, may comment all she wants" is hardly license to return home and make a ruckus, nor is it permission to reveal the intimacies and enigmas of people among whom a "stranger" has lived. Indeed, a second interpretation of the saying ridicules those who spread rumors from place to place. When said sarcastically, it makes fun of the fool who runs home to safe territory and criticizes things seen elsewhere. It mocks the person who does not have the gall to speak her or his mind openly. It also chastises the irresponsible anthropologist who reports "strange" beliefs and practices without putting them in context. The implication is that the "tattletale" is not able to manage information responsibly but instead goes behind people's backs and gossips. This fuller meaning points to the wisdom of reserving comment for appropriate occasions and audiences and to the foresight to listen without speaking, to observe for a time without commenting, and to convey information in measured ways. It presents a complicated view of, again, the way identity and disclosure are dealt with in Machame and more broadly of the way everyday conversation is given meaning within a context of what is considered important—or not—to know.

As with the phrase I asked Mr. Munuo—*umetoka wapi?* (where have you been)—"a person who lives in a foreign place" provides evidence of the ways self and knowledge are carefully concealed and revealed on Mount Kilimanjaro. Understanding the implications of such phrases and exchanges are important both to the production of this work and for understanding the comparative significance of schooling on Mount Kilimanjaro. Local sayings remind an ethnographer such as myself that people are aware of what others say about them, and that whatever an ethnographer writes "upon returning" is open to reinterpretation by those of "another patriline." Such, I believe, is one of the necessary and rewarding aspects of writing ethnography today. Gone are the days, if ever they existed, when an anthropologist sees her analysis as completely objective. Instead, ethnography—an educational genre in its own right—is a two-way street, a process by which all people involved are culturally transformed.[28]

In practical terms, most of my time—at least three days a week—was spent observing classes and teaching English at Mkufi. I lived and worked in Machame (in Hai District) as anthropologist and part-time teacher. I spent two days a week conducting informal interviews and household surveys in the surrounding community and visiting other secondary schools in Kilimanjaro Region. I collected survey information pertaining to people's educational backgrounds, occupations, and household resources. I also had many interviews and conversations with men, women, and children in the course of conducting our everyday activities. These conversations, most of them conducted in either Kiswahili or English, provided me with greatest insight into local views about social life and schooling.

Inside the school, my closest affiliations were with the teachers and the headmaster. I heeded the advice of Mr. Uroki regarding not socializing with students (he made it difficult for me to do otherwise). And I listened to and engaged with teachers' heated debates about the significance of schooling. I was constantly struck by the passion and insight teachers brought to staff room discussions about education, and I noted several times in my field notes that they were more politically informed about international issues in general than teachers I knew in the United States. I engaged with students in class and on school grounds, either in the course of teaching or observing. I came to know an entire school of students and was able to watch their interactions throughout the year. Because I was teaching Form 2 and 3 students, my connections with them were the greatest. I knew many of their parents, siblings, and other relatives, and something about their desires and aspirations.

My identity as a teacher was both advantageous and, at times, a problem. It incorporated me quickly into the community yet identified me with the educated elite (an identification perhaps unavoidable even if I had not been teaching). It also put me in a sometimes compromising position between conducting "objective" research and engaging in participation, as when asked by teachers to evaluate and discipline students in my classroom. Dilemmas notwithstanding, my teaching role was invaluable for eliciting constant conversations about the value of schooling in Machame and for understanding how people linked a part of their local history and culture to the European introduction of formal schooling. While I recognize that I held considerable power over students as their teacher in the classroom, I nonetheless hope to have conveyed their stories in an honest and recognizable way while protecting their confidentiality.

Outside of schools, my closest affiliations were with upwardly aspiring Chagga, many of whom identified with the school and the Lutheran Church. I thus present a picture of schooling and Chagga culture in the following pages that is weighted toward perspectives that were identified as Christian on the mountain. I also present a picture of social life that emphasizes girls' and women's diverse views. For although I interviewed roughly as many men as women in the course of conducting household surveys, and although I had many insightful conversations with men, much of my time was spent in the company of women, with whom I talked about more intimate and idiosyncratic matters. Many of my contacts were neighborhood women in both Ndala and Foo villages. The wife of the owner of the house where I eventually lived in Foo Village, for example, was a constant source of support and conversation, and she, Stellah, and other neighbors socialized me into the world of cooking, talking, farming, and attending births, wedding, and funerals. Likewise, the wife of the chairman of Mkufi Secondary School—Mrs. Mbasa, in whose house I lived for the first two months of my stay in Machame and to whose house I returned frequently for ritual events and overnight stays—provided me with social and personal support and incorporated me into family life to such an extent that by the end of my stay I was sharing beds with their children and serving and cleaning up after guests and strangers whom they welcomed into their house. This incorporation not only provided me with a sense of well-being and gratitude, it also gave me an appreciation for the dynamics—mostly jovial, sometimes fraught—of family life.

Additionally, I spent a great deal of time with Lameck Mbasa, younger brother of the chairman of the school board and veteran fieldworker on other research projects in Tanzania.[29] Lameck and I conducted household and school surveys and, in the course of the many months I spent in Machame, had many conversations about the history and culture of social life there. On numerous occasions, after finishing our day's work we would drop into a local restaurant (*mkahawa*) for roasted meat and drink and would spend the time talking about the people whom we had met and interviewed that day. Lameck's personal knowledge about these people and their positions was invaluable for helping me understand many of the social dynamics that were not obvious to a new visitor. And his abilities to reflect on his perspective within the context of others' in the community provided some insight for me into men's views about land, lineage, and the role of schooling in effecting transformations in men's positions. At the same time, and as with Stellah, my understandings were shaped to a great extent by his views and provided if not an overly partial view of life in Machame, at least a starting point for understanding and formulating my own ideas about the social and cultural composition of the community.

In the end, I came to view the ways people reacted to and treated my relatively brief stay in Machame as a means of understanding how people living on Mount Kilimanjaro think about what it means to be educated. I also came to see that local ideas about "foreign places" and "natal homes" constitute particular cultural expressions of the ways gender relations and social reproduction are shaped in connection with education. Aphoristic knowledge was frequently put to use to *re*make the values embedded in aphorisms. That is, pithy sayings bandied about in everyday speech were often used to criticize conventional wisdom. In this regard, I found Mr. Uroki's and others' lessons to be particularly relevant for thinking about the attitudes surrounding education. If it was regarded as so extremely important for a person like me "not to question the things she sees, but upon returning home, to comment as much as she wants," how must it be for students who sit in class but do not understand what the teacher is saying? Or who disagree with what is being taught and have other ideas? Are students permitted to be critical and inquisitive in class? Or do they too have to wait until they return home to question, analyze, and digest what they have seen and learned at school? Is there a distinction between home and school life, or is this divide a fluid one? Over and over, these were concerns and questions I heard students, teachers, and parents ask, and ones that were to arise as I fine-tuned my eyes and ears to people's interactions and arguments about schools' mediation of home and community.

So, to conclude this chapter, I have spelled out so far the central problematic of the study and provided information on the methodology and research techniques. I have focused on my early impressions of some students' everyday lives and on my early fieldwork experiences in order to emphasize that the place of departure for any ethnographic study—like any educational journey—is always one's own situated perspective. In the following chapters, I look at the social issues surrounding debates about secondary schooling. In Chapter 2, I examine social life on the mountain and look at how schooling is framed as a contemporary form of inheritance. I discuss some of the visible signs Chagga refer to as indicators of their way of life, and I examine the socially prominent view that lineage lands and schools symbolically interrelate. In Chapter 3, I delve more deeply into a discussion of social life, and I examine how contemporary accounts of female circumcision and initiation relate to school materials. The point of Chapters 2 and 3 together is to provide basic information on the structure and organization of social life and to illustrate the gendered and generational transformations that people identify with secondary schooling.

Chapter 4 provides a narrative account of three female protagonists who, as secondary school-leavers, self-identify as "modern women," or what they call "city sisters." It takes as a central problematic the increasingly popular view among young women graduates that schooling ought to substitute for marriage, and it unpacks the cultural reasoning behind their arguments, showing how schooling plays into their future plans. Chapter 5 moves into the schools themselves and examines the curriculum and various messages embedded in select lessons. In combination with Chapter 6, it looks at some of the "modern" signifiers of student culture that are being produced via music videos, imported clothing, and the media. Chapter 7 draws the several themes of the ethnography together and closes with thoughts about the culturally endowed capacity of education to objectify sensibilities about self and other.

2

SCHOOLING, INHERITANCE,

AND BANANA GROVES

SIGNS AND SYMBOLS OF LOCAL LIFE

Any parent who loves a child is a parent who will do everything possible, if it is to sell their banana grove, if it is to sell a cow, if it is to sell a shirt, if it is to sell a dress, so that the parent can pass on education to the child. If you give monetary inheritance, it will run out quickly and burglars may take it. If you pass on a house, the house may collapse, and so on. If you give even cars, some will cause accidents in the road and the children will be written off.

There is no inheritance, we do not have any valuable inheritance that we can give our children that is more valuable than education. Education is a special type of inheritance. Education will not grow old, [there are] no burglars who can take education from our children's brains, there is no, no, I do not know what will take [it] away. If your child is educated, you have everything that can benefit that child in life.

Excerpt from a secondary school
graduation speech.
December 1992

I BEGAN my research at the end of a school year and so started out by listening to many graduation speeches. A common theme explored by many speakers was the connection between inheritance and education. As in the excerpt above, many spoke at length about passing on an inheritance to their children, and many speakers spent a great deal of time emphasizing the importance of education.

Still new on the project, I turned to Mr. Uroki for insight into speakers' themes. I recognized from having read older ethnographies (Gutmann 1932; S. F. Moore 1986; Raum 1940) that patrilineal (father-to-son) inheritance in the form of banana groves had been a central component of social reproduction on the mountain for many generations. I wondered if, in contemporary times, when people were speaking of schooling as "inheritance," girls were not also gaining something new by "inheriting" an education. Mr. Uroki did not address my questions directly but gave me a cryptic reply. "Well," he said, seeming at times to have a better grasp of my own project than I, "if you want to study Chagga culture you have to look into the banana grove. But don't forget heifers and banana beer [*mbege*]. That is how we make our life." To him and others with whom we sat drinking *mbege*, there was an obvious connection among these media—a connection that captured something that was fundamentally and essentially Chagga to these men and women. Mr. Uroki said little more at the time about what that connection might be, but he did not forget that he had assigned me the task of working through this exercise.

Some weeks later, while celebrating the marriage of our neighbors, Samueli and Monica, Mr. Uroki held up a calabash of banana beer and pointed to the roasted meat. In front of this audience of Chagga male elders, he tested me, "What is this?" When I answered the obvious, "*Mbege na nyama*— banana beer and meat," he scowled, for I had answered the wrong thing.

Since being quizzed publicly, I have been mulling over the interrelationship of land, livestock, and banana groves, and over the connections graduation speakers have made between inheritance and schooling. I have come up with an answer to Mr. Uroki's question that reflects more appropriately, I believe, the cultural significance of these media and unravels a knot of tensions many describe as existing between "Chagga elders" and "school-educated youth" today. Part of the answer, and part of understanding parallels between schools and land, involves delving into the symbolic representations of the banana grove (called the *kihamba* in Kimachame; see Illustration 2). For as a wealth of ethnographic literature points out, and as I heard reiterated many times, the banana grove is instrumental in symbolizing gender and generational transformations on Mount Kilimanjaro.[1] It

2. A residence in Machame. The entire compound sits on a quarter square acre of kihamba (banana grove) land, visible in the background.

figures into popular conceptualizations of youth and into cultural discourses about human development. It also serves as a collective symbol of patrilineality and masculinity that has more recently been extended to some school-educated women on Mount Kilimanjaro. It was with an eye toward understanding the place of the school in imaging people's ideas about gender, generation, and culture that I began to look at the banana grove and think about the social relations inscribed in it.

Babu Munissi's Desiccated Trees: Banana Groves and the Signs of Social Difference

About two months into my field research I moved to a house roughly nine kilometers up the mountain. Stellah Mbasa, whom I introduced in the previous chapter, accompanied me, and for much of the next twelve months she and I lived with Mama Claudia, wife of the owner of a house that Mkufi Secondary School rented for teachers. At the back of the house, about twenty yards from the porch, was a faltering, desiccated banana grove. The trees were scruffy and fruit was minimal. The grove had not been well attended. One day, a temporary, hired worker (*kibarua*) began to cultivate and irrigate the dying grove. Sixteen years old and in search of paid employment, he had come from Mwanza (a midsized Tanzanian city on Lake Victoria). Babu Munissi, whose grove this was, had hired this boy to "clean" the trees and bring them back to life. "I want that grove to grow great big bananas. Otherwise my brother's son or grandson will take this land," Babu Munissi said, alluding to the fact that untilled land was subject to claim by male relatives. Babu's own grandson, fifteen-year-old Solomon, could technically have cleared the weeds. And his granddaughter, Aikande, could have harvested the fruit and trimmed the trees. But both of them were going to secondary school and had no time to bother with farming. So Babu decided to "hire out."

Seeing the hired stranger tilling the grove when Solomon, Aikande, and others their age were going to secondary school prompted me to think further about the changing significance of banana cultivation in connection with secondary schooling. Bruno Gutmann, German missionary and anthropologist, noted more than sixty years ago that boys were taught during ritual initiation that "if you look to the earth, you would see the bones of men" (Gutmann 1932:304). Otto Raum, an early ethnographer, mentioned that Chagga children were taught riddles about wealth and lineality: "Father has a cowskin that cannot be lent: the yard." And "Father left me a bowl from which I have been eating ever since: the irrigation canal" (Raum 1940:219)—canals run throughout the grove, channeling running waters from the snowcapped mountain to banana trees. These and other sayings captured some of the reverant language people used to talk about the land and pushed me to examine how social relations today are projected onto and through the grove.

I had heard many people talk about the grove as a site of power much as some talked about the school today, and I had heard the school and the grove pitted as antinomies—one could *not* make a claim to one *and* still retain the other.

I began by asking Babu Munissi about banana cultivation. For he not only knew about this particular grove but had more than eight decades of insight into farming. I also spoke with many women and men who, in the course of discussing schooling, frequently lapsed into reciting rules about agriculture. Time after time the normative picture presented was one in which youngest sons inherited their fathers' houses and the banana groves immediately surrounding them, and oldest sons inherited banana groves farther away from fathers' houses.[2] In cases where the banana grove had been passed down from father to son (that is, through the patriline), people were keen to describe predecessors who had cultivated and lived on the land. In one case an old man described his great-great-grandfather who, he said, had been in charge of keeping the irrigation channels (*mifereji*) clean. This person had been able to augment the number of his trees by ritually maintaining and purifying the irrigated water.[3] In another case, an old man described the once barren land surrounding his banana grove and attributed the now hardy and laden trees to the efforts of his grandfather.

The fruit—which was typically harvested by girls and women—was easily cut with *nndo* (in Kimachame, a special knife tied to a long pole with banana tree fibers) and stored in the cattle stall or in the house until the bananas were ready to be used. Throughout the year, girls and women were responsible for trimming and harvesting fruit from the trees. During January and February, they cut and tore off sheaths from around the base of the banana tree and used them to repair leaky roofs and cattle stalls. Boys and men weekly hauled manure from cattle stalls to banana groves and spread it around the trees. Boys also constructed and maintained the irrigation network. Older men supervised boys in building bridges, tunnels, and channels. Bridges were usually made of banana stalks or bamboo, and channels were typically stopped up with bunches of dried leaves. The distribution system followed a semiregular pattern, with usufruct dependent on farmers' participation in regular maintenance. According to a Form 3 student, who described the irrigation system in an essay, "Those who do not attend [regular meetings on irrigation] must pay money unless they have special reasons. If they do not pay, they are not allowed to irrigate their farms."

Babu Munissi and many of his age-mates declared that hard work in the banana grove pays off. "Do you see my wife over there?" Babu Munissi asked me one day. "She is stronger than any of these young women who work in offices in town." Babu Munissi attributed his wife's strength to her having worked many long days in the grove. He also attributed his own longevity and keen wit to having eaten the fruits of his own trees. Some of the banana varieties that grew on the mountain, he said, were more fit for men to eat than for women.[4] *Mishare nlelembwe, msusu,* and *itoki,* for instance, were especially good varieties for making what he called "male foods." *Inanambo*, in contrast, was a banana variety that he thought good for making banana soup (*mitori*), eaten by women after childbirth.

At the time of my work, a group of Chagga men were uprooting certain varieties of trees. *Finangwa* and *ilalyi* were declared unfit by some members of the Lutheran Church on the grounds that the fruit they bore was sometimes used for making beer, and that beer drinking led to fornication. In Babu's view, these trees—and beer—were essential to good health and longevity, yet some Chagga men were keeping their land pure by cultivating only certain varieties. At times, abstemious Christians spoke about their own spirituality in terms of the grove and of banana tree products. Unbaptized people were "green banana basts," they said; churchgoing Christians were "dry, strong trees."[5] In linking the grove to banana beer production and the drinking of alcohol to youths' promiscuity, temperant church members attempted to reconstruct the image of the banana grove along lines that were in keeping with their views of Christianity. As with selling land, uprooting trees was an indication that land and social relationships represented through it were under increased scrutiny.

Yet not everybody uprooted their trees, nor did most people sell their land. When I asked why the land was so valuable despite the fact that it was rarely, if ever, sold, the most consistent answer I got was that "one of my sons can eventually build a house on it." Indeed, many banana groves were marked in Machame with partially built houses. Sometimes these structures consisted of only rudimentary foundations; they stood for years, unfinished and grown over with moss and weeds. However, even the most destitute of groves and houses remained important to families and individuals. The houses themselves were durable testaments to current and future claims. Despite graduation speakers' advice that people sell groves to send their children to school, very few people did. One family I knew was renting its grove to get money to send the daughter to school. Another had sold a quarter acre of land to pay for books, pens, school uniforms, and private tutoring. However, with a few exceptions, most people whom I asked responded adamantly "no!" To sell or lease inherited land was to risk loss of the goodwill of the ancestors buried there and to waste the staple foods from the trees.

What is it about the banana grove and land, I wondered, that made people speak so grandiloquently? Why did people talk about so many of their ordinary beliefs in terms of planting, cultivation, and cooking? Even graduation speakers compared the banana grove to the inheritance of education.

In the words of the speaker quoted above, "Education is a special type of inheritance. Education will not grow old. [There are] no burglars who can take education from our children's brains. There is no, no, I do not know what will take [it] away." His words resonated with what a university graduate who had been born on Mount Kilimanjaro said his father had told him: "'Schooling is your inheritance; I have no land to divide and give you,' implying that I had to do the best I could. I wasn't going to get anything more than schooling from my father." And they resonated with what a Chagga man said in a village on eastern Mount Kilimanjaro: "What we now give [a child] is education so that he or she can further himself or herself. If he or she has gotten this education, I think this is the inheritance he or she has gotten from us."[6]

Given the centrality of the banana grove to life on Mount Kilimanjaro, one might be tempted to say that the grove is a "total social phenomenon" in the Maussian sense (Mauss 1967)—that is, it expresses seemingly immutable and enduring legal, economic, and moral dimensions of Chagga life. For some people living on the mountain it is apparently so, yet not for everybody. Many people also described the grove as an *outmoded* symbol of tradition and history, and as an icon of underdevelopment and emerging class poverty. Babu Munissi and his age-mates, on the one hand, put the grove at the center of their universe. They valued the land both for the banana trees and for the social relations trees symbolized. But the graduation speaker, who equated inheritance with schooling, saw the grove as convertible, not static. For him, the significance was not the land itself, nor even the productive and reproductive relationships generated through groves. Rather, the important thing about land and the grove was that they could be sold and converted into schooling.

Over time, the banana grove has come to possess many distinct layers and cultural references. As Setel well puts it, the banana grove is "the lineage producer, agricultural producer, provider of material for shelter, and unit of political capital. It [is] first and foremost none of these, yet in the 'seamless whole' of its cultural topography and with shifting emphases, over time it has simultaneously been all of them" (Setel 1995:68). The grove and the school speak to almost everyone; they lie behind many aspects of Chagga sociality. Yet the school and the grove also reflect class distinctions, as is illustrated in the following description of a fund-raiser that followed the graduation speech. School and grove touch off debate about development, bring people together, and objectify social opportunity. Yet the binary between schooling and the banana grove also reflects the dynamics of social differentiation.

After the guest speaker who had called education "an inheritance" retired to join the other guests, an auctioneer stepped up to auction some goods. Among the wares were a cassette player, a radio, a woman's dress, and a large bunch of bananas. The last item drew jeers and laughter from some parents, who wondered aloud about the poor soul who had donated the produce. The auctioneer reprimanded that no item was too small, and just then a wealthy woman—a secondary school graduate—bought the bananas for a handsome sum. She commented to her sisters and neighbors in attendance that she was more respectful than they of tradition and custom.

When I later asked the woman, Mama Daudi, why she had paid so much for something she herself could grow on lineage land, she responded, in a characteristically cryptic way: "the dog always comes home to die." Her sister-in-law said that Mama Daudi was speaking aphoristically, based on the saying that, "no matter how far a person moves from home, that person will always return home to die."[7]

"What does she mean by that?" I asked.

"She knows that she has to do more than she is currently doing for the village, she has to pull us up just like everyone else."

"So she made a big thing of buying those bananas?"

"She's just trying to make up for what she's never done," she said, alluding to a perception that some of Mama Daudi's other relatives shared—that she had moved economically far and now had to "return home" and distribute her wealth.

This seemed plausible, though Mama Daudi's decision to buy the bananas seemed more complicated, judging from something Stellah said: that Mama Daudi did indeed lead a fast-paced, urban life but that she had also done a lot for the school, including getting the women's church auxiliary involved in sponsoring fund-raisers. Stellah suggested that Mama Daudi's sister-in-law was jealous and simply backbiting; in buying the bananas Mama Daudi was indicating that she still valued her local customs. Yet the difference between buying versus bringing them yourself was evidence to Stellah of status differences. Stellah said that Mama Daudi was not only school-educated but also rich. Chronologically younger than some of the male village leaders, she was in some situations, such as this, quite powerful. Even though, like everyone else, Mama Daudi grew bananas on patrilineal *kihamba* lands, here at this ceremony, she *bought* rather than *brought*, what amounted to an iconic condensation of Chagga tradition.

Mama Daudi herself said that she needed the bananas for cooking dinner, and indeed she served them a few days later at a ritual function for school board members. She prepared the bananas with meat to make a popular dish, *mishare tya nyama*, noting to several men eating heartily at the function that the bananas had come from the school auction. None of the guests at this function condemned the bananas. To the contrary, *mishare tya nyama* was a food that signified respect. Serving the dish linked the work of school board members with the institutions and rituals of enduring "Chagga-ness." For bananas and meat were served at weddings and funerals, name-giving ceremonies, and other rites of passage.

These two events—the graduation auction and the school board dinner—further illustrate some of the ways schooling and banana groves are brought into symbolic relation with one another. At one level, banana groves and schools symbolize different levels of sociality: *kihamba* land signifies tradition and custom; schooling signifies modernity and the commercial economy. Both the school and the banana grove provide an inheritance, though they orient people to what many perceive to be asymmetrical social systems—the former toward urban centers and international markets, the latter toward a system of affective relations in which social rank is predicated on agnatic hierarchy.

It seemed from preliminary observation that education, like land, was not only a practical resource that people approached with an eye for utility, but also a means for developing social networks that would benefit a person beyond years spent in school. With so much mixing of schools and groves, it seemed to me that I should look more closely at what schooling signified. I turned my attention next to what people said about school and the promises it held for children.

THE PROMISES OF SCHOOLING: DEVELOPMENT AND SYMBOLIC CAPITAL

Before arriving in Kilimanjaro, I had heard Tanzanian vendors, businesspeople, schoolteachers, and professors comment that "the schools on Mount Kilimanjaro are among the wealthiest in the country" and that "the Chagga had inherited some of the best colonial schools." Such stereotypes circulated widely outside Kilimanjaro Region. Many people I spoke with in Dar es Salaam believed schools in the north—and especially in Machame— were financially supported by foreign organizations and donor agencies. Some had nicknamed the people of Machame "Palestinians" (*Mapalestina*) for their tenacity (*ukali*) in struggling for better schooling. This name alerted me to the unusual extent to which some people in Machame were identified as "go-getters"—as Palestinians were seen by some people living on the mountain[8]—and I arrived on Mount Kilimanjaro expecting to see people virtually pushing one another aside for personal gain.

Once living in Machame, however, I was presented with a different picture. Many people contended that the comparatively high quality of schooling in Machame was not a result of Chagga cunning and deceit nor of aggressive competition. Rather, they said, it was evidence of hard work and diligent planning. The material resources many enjoyed were still less than what many felt they deserved. The response of one Chagga headmaster to my comment that some people in Dar es Salaam had described schools in Machame as comparatively well equipped was typical. "Yes," he said, "we are really showing that hard work pays off. We know the value of schooling, and we work to make sure our children get the best education they can." When I pressed further and indicated that some people in Dar es Salaam had suggested that Chagga had an unfair advantage (their argument was that missionaries had poured a lot of money into Kilimanjaro schools during and since colonial days) he answered, "What can we do about history? We have inherited what we have inherited. Other people are just jealous."

I later learned how profoundly jealousy (*wivu*) figured into local and national discourses of politics and power, and how fundamentally colonial history was associated with the availability and quality of schooling in Machame. What caught my attention at that moment, however, was the extent to which the headmaster, like many others I had met, regarded schools as highly visible markers of local—and regional—development. There was a kind of competition going on in Tanzania over access to secondary schooling, and if this competition was not as aggressive on Mount Kilimanjaro as people in Dar es Salaam had described it, it was nonetheless intense. Everyone, so it seemed, wanted well-qualified teachers, new textbooks, and basic amenities such as desks and chalk, and they wanted the chance to send their children to secondary school—not to be limited by the number of schools registered in their region.

Throughout my stay I was constantly amazed at the lengths to which some parents went to enroll children. It was not unusual for parents to travel from distant villages to speak with administrators or teachers and to offer administrators *hongo*—a bribe, in essence—as incentive for admitting academically underqualified children. One woman I met at Mkufi Secondary had walked several kilometers in the rain and then boarded the back of a pickup truck to ride from Nkwamangi Village to Ndala. She was hoping to meet with the headmaster to discuss possibilities for enrolling her son in Form 1 and had brought a "letter" (*barua*) that contained a few hundred extra shillings. Even the headmaster at a nearby secondary school was lobbying headmasters in Dar es Salaam in an attempt to enroll his son in a prestigious urban institution. (Ironically, he, like many people in Kilimanjaro Region, thought the schools in Dar es Salaam—even the private ones—were better than those in Kilimanjaro, the exact opposite of many people's views in Dar es Salaam.) The bursar at a nearby government school was looking to enroll his daughter at a secondary school in Nairobi. He, like many others who sent their children to Tanzanian day schools, thought Kenyan schools were academically better.

The ends to which many parents went to find placements for children suggest that some people regarded schools as having an inherent value, that they saw schools as embodying something good, and that they thought more prestigious schools paid off. It was not unusual for children from Machame to go to live with distant relatives. Because there were regional quotas at the time (only so many students from each region could enroll in government schools), parents would sometimes send children to live with aunts and uncles in less populated regions, where competition for secondary schooling was less intense. Mobilization of the extended kin network drew agnatic relations and the school into further relation with one another. Thus the daughter of a wealthy businessman in Machame was living with her uncle in Morogoro, and the son of a village government worker was studying with an older brother in Dodoma. As a Standard VI student, the daughter stood a better chance of being admitted into government secondary school than if she had been one of dozens who had passed the exam on Mount Kilimanjaro. And the village government worker said that if his son did not pass, his brother would continue to provide for him; he'd pay the high fees for private secondary school and would see that he got extra tutoring sessions.

Clearly, parents and relatives invested an awful lot in schooling, but what, exactly, were students expected to get out of the experience? What was the purpose of going to secondary school? What was schooling in this area all about? To understand this, I looked first to the school syllabus and to the areas of the curriculum that people touted as "successful." I found that the agricultural syllabus was widely described by parents and teachers as the cornerstone of secondary education. This was not surprising, given that emphasis on vocational schooling since early years of independence had been directed toward student farms (Nyerere 1967; Psacharopoulos and Loxley 1985). It also fitted appropriately with parents' emphasis on land cultivation and the banana grove as central to the high quality of social life. But what I found was that the syllabus itself portrayed the land and social relations produced on it in a manner that was quite different from the relationships people described as existing on Mount Kilimanjaro. Even though many pointed to agricultural science as important for their children's schooling and for connecting school lessons with village life, the values and precepts embedded in the agricultural science syllabus worked to change agrarian relations on the mountain. They did so in a way that sought to undermine the cultural logic of the *kihamba* regime rather than to innovate and build upon it, as some people I spoke with would have preferred the Ministry of Education and Culture do.

EDUCATION FOR SELF-RELIANCE AND THE AGRICULTURAL SCIENCE SYLLABUS

In an influential policy known as "Education for Self-Reliance" written six years after Tanzanian independence, Julius K. Nyerere, the first president of Tanzania, had asserted that students were to work on a farm or workshop and to manage and market the crops they produced. In so doing, they were supposed to practice the political philosophy of education for self-reliance.

> [A]ll schools, but especially secondary schools and other forms of higher education, must contribute to their own upkeep. They must

be economic communities as well as social and educational communities. Each school should have, as an integral part of it, a farm
or workshop which provides the food eaten by the community,
and makes some contribution to the total national income.

This is not a suggestion that a school farm or workshop should
be attached to every school for training purposes. It is a suggestion that every school should also be a farm; that the school
community should consist of people who are both teachers and
farmers, and pupils and farmers. ("Education for Self-Reliance,"
Nyerere 1967:283)

The objectives of agricultural science—to develop a respect for manual
labor among secondary school students—were clearly spelled out in the
syllabus, yet the subtext of many lessons on mechanization and technology
was that manual labor was backwards and primitive. Despite the call to
humble students—to make them honest laborers within the developing
nation—the agricultural science syllabus presented African traditional
ways, including agricultural production on the banana grove, as inferior to
mechanized technology. The syllabus reified a set of customs and beliefs
and contrasted "modern" knowledge with the Chagga *kihamba*. In doing
so, it contributed to the very tensions it claimed to overcome in order to
integrate students with pastoralists and villagers and to minimize the
development of an educated elite. I decided to look closely at the syllabus to
consider how culture and land were defined and represented there.

The agricultural science syllabus in use at most schools was published in
1977. In it, farming is presented as a subject through which to teach students fundamental principles of African socialism. The opening statement,
listed under "Aims and Objectives," notes that farming will convey to students an appreciation for the land and manual labor. Yet there is an
underlying message in the syllabus that cuts against its stated purpose. In
contrast to the goals laid out by Nyerere—that "the school community
should consist of people who are both teachers and farmers, and pupils and
farmers" (1967:283)—the syllabus presents farming as something "others"
do, something that differentiates students from their unschooled peers and
alienates them from the land.

Agriculture is described in the syllabus as a business and scientific
activity. When cooperative farming is discussed at all (usually in classes
labeled "Socialist Production"), the organization of workers is portrayed

as something that is governed by the state—not as something that exists traditionally among extended African families. To be sure, the syllabus mentions that the extended family (*wajamaa*) is an important component of development. Without kin networks, the state will fall flat and labor will have no social structure. The family in the syllabus, however, in contrast to what people describe as "family" on the mountain, is less a community organized around local leadership and village elders with its own valuable set of strategies than a community that needs to be reformed by students who have studied agriculture *scientifically*. One of the practical lessons Form 4 students are to learn involves "disseminating modern technology to the *wajamaa*" (p. 52). This topic implies that African families are in need of technology and assistance, not that they can provide innovative methods worthy for students to learn and apply. Beginning with lessons in Form 1, the syllabus presents agricultural science as a governmental, not familial, concern. Students are supposed to learn that state ownership of land influences the way "tribal tenure systems" have been revised, including the specific land tenure system of the *kihamba* lands on Mount Kilimanjaro. In Form 4 they are to learn that the interrelationship between agricultural extension officers and farmers contributes to higher levels of productivity. Classes on economic theory are to focus on "governmental regulations" and "state and parastatal production farms," not on the way land and production are valued in local, African terms (p. 31). "Youth" and "farmers" may both have some knowledge about how to cultivate the soil, but the orientation of students (as the agricultural science syllabus portrays it) is to the state and national production, not to the village and local concerns.

Agricultural science classes specifically target livestock practices and land tenure systems on Mount Kilimanjaro as "problematic." "Overpopulation on the slopes of Mount Kilimanjaro," the subject of the second topic to be taught to Form 1 students (p. 6), introduces the demographic issues of population density and overcrowding. Teachers are instructed to convey that "tribal tenure systems" (again, the Chagga *kihamba* is mentioned specifically) lead to "social fragmentation and overcrowding" and to the economic devaluation of land. In lessons on "problems encountered in the current land tenure arrangements," students are supposed to learn that in traditional contexts, land is subdivided to such an extreme that many Tanzanians are left homeless and are faced with economic hardships. The problem of overcrowding on the mountain lay in the rules of tribal land tenure; if only tradition could be revised, the syllabus asserts, the nation might develop toward the goal of self-reliance, and traditional land tenure problems might be resolved.

This is not to say that the agricultural science syllabus entirely *ignores* the importance of local culture. It raises the subject in certain contexts— usually, however, to disarm it. For throughout the syllabus, culture is the ever-present factor that agricultural science is supposed to improve. Students are supposed to learn that modern techniques can ultimately be combined with what their parents did, yet the language of the syllabus suggests that traditional farming carries a social stigma. One of the aims articulated in the syllabus is "to stimulate interest by showing in practical ways that agriculture, as an applied science is a dignified and paying occupation." Another is "to teach pupils by example the dignity of manual dexterity" (p. 2). But the language of the syllabus suggests something other than what is overtly stated. It would seem from these aims and objectives that banana grove farming is humiliating and dirty: that farming is seen as a menial task. It is something that—like the boy Babu Munissi hired—is better left to unschooled peers.

The language of the agricultural science syllabus, then, suggests two sides of a single coin. It presents agriculture as fundamental to African life and inseparable from rural development. Yet it also presents traditional farmers as "others" from whom "we" (students) must learn, even though farming is undignified. In this regard, farming, like culture, is presented in a particular way: as a reified set of practices and beliefs that needs to be attended to in the interest of national development. In treating farming as a thing that evolves in direct proportion to technology (more advanced societies use more advanced technology; less advanced societies use their hands and simple instruments), the syllabus implicitly alienates students from social symbolics of *kihamba* life. It integrates the banana grove and school by drawing attention to their similarities, but it directs the agricultural efforts of students toward the development of the state.

ANSWERING THE RIDDLE: HOW SCHOOLS AND GROVES SYMBOLICALLY INTERRELATE

In contrast to the syllabus, discourses of farming on Mount Kilimanjaro typically link agrarian production to the symbols and processes of social production, in particular to institutions of marriage and inheritance. Local visions often portray tradition and agriculture as *male* signifiers associated with lineage wealth; the *kihamba* land is a patrilineally inherited plot that contains graves of agnatic kin. Conventional wisdom on Mount Kilimanjaro seems to be that men are the natural proprietors of land. Men are identified with culture in the old-fashioned sense of the finer and higher aspects of human thought.[9] To give brief evidence of this: Mr. Uroki and his male age-mates demanded—and usually received—the largest servings of banana beer and meat. They spoke authoritatively about "their" land and said their sons would inherit banana groves.

If we step back from this microanalysis for a moment and reflect on what it means more generally to go to school in Machame or elsewhere, for that matter, it is worth noting preliminarily that schooling makes a profound difference in the ways people think about and organize their lives. It models changes in political organization, the division of labor, social stratification, economic exchange, and cultural differentiation. Schooling, like the banana grove, works its way into all levels of lineal and affinal relations. It structures the expenditure of human thought and energy by offering diverse social groups and individuals a conceptual language that covers many aspects of life. As such, the school, like the grove itself, is a useful—if incomplete—heuristic. Institutionally and symbolically, it models many relations within Chagga society; however, it does not do so in ways generally anticipated by educators or in school policies. It often effects, and comes to stand for, something other than what we see in school curricula.

This may seem an obvious point—that policies are not always implemented in practice as planned. But some research in the comparative sociology of education makes it sound as though the school is all-powerful and that people spend more time responding to than they do directing or redirecting the influences of schooling. In contrast to what Alex Inkeles has argued (1998:338), for instance, evidence I have presented here suggests that schooling does not lead necessarily or directly to the "massive abandonment of tradition." Rather, schooling insinuates a set of oppositions—modern/traditional; male/female; public/private, and so on—onto what people say and do. It does so through curricular structures, school policies, and social organization, not in any totalizing or systematic way but partially and gradually, in the process of structuring everyday interactions.

The view Inkeles and other modernization or school-to-the-rescue theorists espouse is that schools are unstoppable social engines that drive Third-World economic and political change (for examples, see Psacharopoulos 1995; Psacharopoulos and Loxley 1985; Resnick 1968). Such a view assumes that schools in the "Third World" are culturally "outside" and different from the local community and that school-educated persons are bearers of entirely other and more innovative styles. As discussion here has begun to show, schools in Machame *are* in practice to an extent viewed as "other," but they are endowed by many people locally with the capacity to convert and integrate foreign knowledge with local values. Schools are not wholly "European" institutions but are part and parcel of local operations. Parallels people draw between the school and the grove reflect the mediating effects of local cultural categories. To put it another way, schooling invariably works within a repertoire of practices and images that already bear out in what people say and do; official policies are viewed through a familiar lens. On Mount Kilimanjaro, this lens is best seen when focused upon the activities and rituals associated with the banana grove, for there—in, on, and through the grove—people most freely articulate the fault lines of social life.

Seen this way—as a transformation of sociocultural principles and precepts embedded in other signifying practices, including but not limited to inheritance—the picture of schooling presented so far in this work differs from status attainment models in major ways. It does so not least by conceptualizing success and educational outcomes in terms that have meaning locally. Much of the status attainment literature on schooling in Africa, and indeed worldwide, has used examinations and demographic statistics to measure student outcomes and academic success.[10] In contrast, my emphasis here is to look at what people consider success and education to be. Educational success in Machame is understood in a myriad of (often competing) ways. Just as there are demonstrated variations of culture and history across time and space (a point now well established in the main of cultural anthropology), so too do we see variations in people's understandings of education and of the significance of schooling. I have been using the banana grove as a point of entry for understanding the importance of schooling for people living on Mount Kilimanjaro. The banana grove has particular salience on Mount Kilimanjaro, though as I have been showing, its meaning is variable across groups and generations.

For now, my focus on schooling, inheritance, and banana groves in these pages serves as a way of responding to the riddle I started out with in this chapter, the riddle posed earlier by Mr. Uroki: What is the significance of banana beer and meat? It is also a commentary on the connections graduation speakers made between schooling and inheritance.

Mr. Uroki's riddle was typical of a style I came to learn and appreciate as a conventional instructional form. Although it was presented in an abrasive voice that was the antithesis of what I was culturally used to, it was in fact a teaching technique that many on the mountain thought shaped young neophytes. It was a pedagogic style that put students on edge with the hopes of inspiring them to learn, and it was a method I was later to see used in classes and during other educational activities (Chapter 5).

But the style of the riddle was only part of its mystery. Also at issue was its symbolic meaning. For Mr. Uroki had not intended that I reply, as I foolishly did at Samueli and Monica's wedding, that the items he showed me were, in the literal sense, meat, bananas, and beer. I suspect he wanted me to answer metaphorically if, indeed, at all.

Given a second chance, and in light of what I have recounted in this chapter, I might now respond to Mr. Uroki's question by first deferring more than I did to his expertise. I would do this as a way of better fulfilling the expected duty of guests—which I was—and of juniors: that they listen more than they speak. If Mr. Uroki continued to instruct me to answer, I might make explicit the material and symbolic connections I have described between the *kihamba* and secondary schooling. I might even say that "banana beer is the lineage wealth; like schooling today, it facilitates connections with other people." I might also say that "meat is the cowskin of the lineage; like a graduation certificate, it can never be lent or sold." In so doing, I would attempt to employ the parsimony and allusion so characteristic of Chagga discourse. I would attempt to reflect the cultural tendency I observed to speak of "tradition" in terms of male capacities to control activities associated with the land—though I would leave open the possibility, as others did, that girls and women could be extended inheritance rights, by referring to schooling as an inheritance. And I would as well admit the very real possibility (referring again to the adage about "strangers" introduced in Chapter 1) that no answer, however elaborate, concise, or cryptic, would satisfy Mr. Uroki unless he were willing to extend to a stranger the momentary privilege of inclusion in the community.

3

"Should We Drink Banana Beer or Coca-Cola?"

REDEFINING THE SIGNS OF TRADITIONALISM

ANOTHER teacher, Jocelyn Mtei, one of the few female teachers who taught for a time at Mkufi Secondary School, countered Mr. Uroki's trilogy. "How can he tell you banana beer, land, and meat are important when it's really the hearth (*jiko*) that makes the lineage?"[1] And a Form 3 schoolgirl responded to my question, "what do people mean by 'Chagga tradition'?" with the following: "female circumcision and initiation lessons are our traditional beliefs and practices—you know, the rituals that our grandmothers and mothers did—and also the things we learn about in history books." In conversations with women and girls, I heard less talk about banana groves and more about kitchens. I heard less mention of the "bones of men buried on the lineage land" and more about women's special skills as expert banana beer brewers and their particular knack for bearing children—a "process more painful than male circumcision," Stellah's mother told me repeatedly. And I heard less about the knowledge of *songwairiti* (in Kimachame, male elders) than the knowledge of female initiation teachers. "Mr. Uroki is telling you about what *old* men do, but he's not mentioning those who are young and school-educated," noted Jocelyn Mtei, adding that "men and women have different ideas about tradition, and so do educated and uneducated people."

In this chapter, I will continue one of the threads I introduced in Chapter 2—on the ways official education policies, especially Education for

Self-Reliance, establish categories of tradition and modernity. My focus here, home economics, provides an interesting counterpart to agricultural science. Home economics lessons present a model of motherhood and family that portrays the mother-child relationship as the core of the African family. It focuses on the measured pace of family planning and the importance of personal hygiene. Classes examine "basic needs"—food, clothing, and shelter—and teach students how to cook, clothe, and care for infants, young children, and aging parents. And yet there are many aspects of Chagga domesticity that home economics lessons do not address, including the nuanced, relational, and culturally informed conceptions people have of themselves as persons negotiating the ins and outs of the patriline, marriage practices, and inheritance rights. The home economics syllabus may indeed have introduced novel conceptions of an educated, domestically oriented person, as a rich literature on colonial domesticity has illustrated (Comaroff and Comaroff 1992; Gaitskell 1988; Hansen 1992; Hunt 1992). Yet as Collier, Rosaldo, and Yanagisako note in general about the emergence of the modern family (1997:76), complex state-governed social forms (including applied sciences activities and curricula) provide the institutional space people need to rethink and reconfigure lineal relationships in new familial terms. The home economics syllabus portrays the family not as an extended group of genealogically related people who interact daily and share material resources but as a parent-child domestic unit whose function is to nurture and grow a future citizenry. I examine how the home economics syllabus organizationally links the nuclear family to the state in the first part of this chapter. In the second section, I discuss ways in which many Chagga conceptualize ideas about domesticity. I do so by looking at how motherhood and family are contrasted with female circumcision and initiation. The irony of the home economics program is that in seeking to produce a certain kind of wife and mother—a "stay-at-home-and-raise-the-children" woman—it contributes to a multiplicity of visions about what is "best for women to do." Among these visions is a preference for leaving the home and setting up female-headed households.

HOW THE HOME ECONOMICS SYLLABUS CONNECTS WOMEN TO THE STATE

Students often receive home economics instruction at ad hoc times throughout the year.[2] At Mkufi Secondary School, for instance, as at other schools in Machame where there are no full-time home economics teachers, students study home economics whenever there is a teacher in the area available to teach. Preferably this teacher is herself a woman who can advise adolescent girls about menstruation, birth control, and childbearing. Although technically the Ministry of Education and Culture has specified that these days both boys and girls ought to learn home economics, school-teachers and administrators in Machame continue to associate home economics with the sexual and domestic education of girls, and many assume that these lessons ought to be taught by women.

In the following four sections, I illustrate ways home economics lessons link young women to the wider services of the state, and I provide a picture of what students are supposed to learn in the course of studying housecraft, mothercraft, nutrition, and dressmaking.

General Housecraft, the Maternal Unit, and the State

According to the syllabus, which was published in 1977 and is in use at most secondary schools in Tanzania, Form 1 students ought to begin by studying General Housecraft (Ministry of National Education 1977). Included under this broad topic are lessons on manners and grooming, on the value of soap and water as cleaning agents, on stain and stain removal, on types of disinfectants and their use, on the family wash, on the daily cleaning of a house, on budgeting, and on public health services. Two themes pervade General Housecraft: punctuality and personal hygiene. Lesson One, "Good Manners," is about the importance of displaying honesty and obedience, and is followed by a lesson on "Good Grooming"—a series of discussions about hygiene and attire that focus on the body management of adolescent girls. Both topics relate general housecraft to the development of girls' moral characters, and imply that girls' attire and manners are indications of their personal worth: by being on time, following instructions, and always appearing neat and clean, girls will embody the social values commensurate with their schooling.

Each subtopic under the rubric General Housecraft focuses on a particular part of the feminine body or on a particular task for which women are responsible, and presents its lesson as a matter of personal choice—a matter about which students must make informed decisions for themselves. For instance, the syllabus suggests that teachers present the "choice and use of hair oils," "types and choice of hair styles to suit individuals," "types and choice of shoes," and "choice and care of sanitary items." To the extent that girls have choice in their futures, and to the extent they choose the best course, educated girls, as leaders, are the ideal, the personal embodiments of fitness and health who then go on to instruct household members and become models for the rest of society. The feminine ideal that runs throughout the home economics syllabus, but which is never fully realized in practice, is most pronounced in lessons on sanitation and disinfectants. Sanitation is addressed under several subheadings: "menstruation—how and why it happens," and later, in lessons on "disinfectants and their use" and "dangers of house refuse to health." Schoolgirls are to learn about sanitary ways to dispose of their menstrual blood and how to disinfect the clothes and bed linens of patients suffering from infectious disease. Caring first for themselves, by cleaning all parts of their bodies and disposing of bodily secretions discreetly, future mothers are, it would seem, thus properly fit for attending to the needs and desires of their families. They clean up after the sick and infirm and are charged with the responsibility of maintaining the hygiene of others. Concern about health management and disease begins with them and extends to the wider society.

This focus on the female body in the home economics syllabus reveals an important connection between women and social reproduction, an assumption that is apparent not only in the home economics syllabus, but in official discourse about development and education generally (Meekers 1994; Ministry of Education and Culture 1995a). Schoolgirls' bodies are key components in health care programs seeking to control population growth and the spread of disease through family planning (Bradley 1995; Ministry of Education and Culture 1995a). The syllabus identifies and conceptually locates the female body within a social continuum that extends from individual to family to society. As a group, women are constructed as reproducers of the domestic household and, by extension, of the state. Take, for instance, the way home economics lessons extrapolate from girls' personal hygiene to the organization of household compounds, and from household compounds to the network of public health clinics that are administered by the state. In Form 2, after students have supposedly learned about good grooming and manners in Form 1, they are now supposed to learn how to clean a house and supplement family income. Lessons make clear that care should be taken to keep pit latrines at a safe remove from household water supplies, and to move large furniture and window dressings in order to wash and repaint the house at regular intervals. Thus houses of secondary school graduates ought to show signs of girls' secondary schooling, including painted walls and window dressings, and an orderliness to interior decorating that is more or less standard in design from one school graduate's house to the next. Moreover, these housing structures and domestic dwellings are connected to the social services offered by the state and, these days, by nongovernmental organizations (although the latter are not mentioned in the syllabus). The final lesson on General Housecraft offered to Form 2 students instructs students to meet the Public Health Officer and learn about "Maternal Clinics" and "Safe Food Measures" that are available and promoted in their areas. Girls are encouraged to play a part in collaboration with clinic officials by, in particular, registering vital statistics such as births and deaths with public services.

This progression from personal hygiene to girls' and women's participation in the public health services illustrates my point that home economics education seeks to integrate household economies with national- and in some cases international-level administrative structures. Households, as presented in the syllabus, are management systems linked to a bureaucratic system; their healthy organization is dependent on their integration with larger public and private health care sectors. Even though school curricula and self-reliance activities arguably integrate boys into the market economy to a greater extent than girls (Asayehgn 1979; House-Midamba 1990; King and Hill 1993), General Housecraft teaches girls about the importance of managing household money. Students are supposed to learn about simple bookkeeping, about how to allocate money for expenses, and about the advantages and disadvantages of buying on credit versus paying cash. Home economics ostensibly teaches students to be thrifty and informed consumers, and it develops in girls a discerning eye for selecting soaps, toothpastes, toothbrushes, stain removers, and the like. Lesson Six for Form 1 students, for instance, which is about "stain and stain removal," ideally instills in students awareness that hygiene can be managed through commercial products. Soaps and laundry bleaches, first promoted commercially on a wide scale by Europeans in Africa (Burke 1996), are today commodities marketed primarily for women and often sold by them as well.

But home economics lessons make it clear that girls' incomes will only "supplement family income" and not make them "self-reliant." Visits to local shops and markets that are suggested at the end of Form 1 will apparently teach girls how to be frugal with husbands' salaries, not to go out and make money or to provide their own sources of family income. Careful budgeting and bookkeeping of husbands' money will ensure that funds for buying medicines and cleansers will be available, but women's labor is not described as providing any portion of the family funds. Their job, instead, is to manage money carefully.

Cookery and Nutrition

Two points are noteworthy about lessons on Cookery and Nutrition. The first is that knowledge about cooking is presented in terms of lists and groups. Everything is categorized. Students are supposed to learn, for instance, how to classify different kinds of spices, different kinds of nutrients and beverages, even different kinds of cakes. They are supposed to distinguish one kind of pastry from another, to differentiate "legumes" from "nuts," and to select and prepare different "choice[s] and cut[s] of meat" so that they properly "complement" a meal. This way of ordering foods and spices runs counter to what most people do in practice: foods are generally described as sweet or bitter, filling for the stomach, or "something merely to chew on"—not categorized as the syllabus does in terms of carbohydrates, proteins, fats and oils, vitamins and minerals (Ministry of National Education 1977:72).

The second point is that lessons on cookery are often incommensurate with students' practical lives. There is a general disjuncture between the abstractions of cookery and students' living situations. Lessons on "Kitchen Hygiene," for instance, refer to equipment and food processing techniques that few in Tanzania own or have access to. Most Chagga families do not have stoves or refrigerators, and very few would be able to implement the suggestion that they select appropriate "convenience foods" for picnics (tinned meats or processed cereals) or that they use chemical or deep-freezing methods to preserve large quantities of preprepared meats. Yet about a quarter of the lessons are devoted to understanding how to perform such tasks in the kitchen. In Form 1 students study how to use egg beaters, cake tins, and roasting pans. They are supposed to learn the "most practical ways" of storing perishable foods: drying, bottling, canning, deep freezing, smoking, frying, and chemical methods. Some of these methods, for instance smoking and drying, are possible for some students to do, but most methods are not.

Similarly, many people living on Mount Kilimanjaro are not familiar with "Convenience Foods" and "Vegetarian Cookery" (two topics that are supposed to be addressed in Form 2). Unless people are served hot food that has been thoroughly cooked—preferably with meat—many people will often say that they have not eaten, or that what they have been served "is not food"—as did a person who complained when I served him meatless spaghetti with tomato sauce. But still the syllabus describes "points to remember when planning packed meals" and "points to consider when preparing meals for vegetarians." In Forms 3 and 4, students ideally learn about the kinds of foods to pack (precooked foods that will not spoil in the sun and can be eaten at room temperature) and about substituting protein sources for people who do not eat meat. Rarely, however, do Chagga have an opportunity to implement these lessons. Except for the occasional European vegetarian or Hindu-person who may visit, and except for the occasional times people travel on buses for all-day journeys and need to pack a meal, few would choose to eat preprepared food or food without meat. Of course there are some Hindu groups in Moshi who are vegetarian. And I do know one Chagga man who is avidly vegetarian. But the social dynamics on the mountain are such that few Hindu would eat at Chagga tables, and vice versa, and few Chagga are able to sustain vegetarian diets, given the ritual and social significance of roasted meat.

Instead it appears that instruction on vegetarianism, like instruction on packing convenience meals, or on the ways to use and clean electric stoves and mixers, is an exercise in exploring the ways other people live, not most people on Mount Kilimanjaro. It is a good way for thinking about possible ways of preparing food, but not for actually doing it. So too, instruction on how to select expensive soaps, detergents, toothpastes, and stain removers that most Tanzanians cannot afford is an exercise in exploring the different ways people attend to health and hygiene. These topics seem to be as much about imagining future and different cultural possibilities as learning about and living in the present.

Mothercraft

Form 2 classes on Mothercraft begin with a lesson on "The Adolescent"—a lesson that describes secondary school-aged girls who are preparing to marry and have a family. The emphasis on adolescent girls as future mothers here constructs a "teenage" category, not one that is "plugged into" the popular youth culture I will describe in Chapter 7, but a social group associated with a stage in life that is full of "psychological and social problems" (Ministry of National Education 1977:35). As a developmental category, adolescence is understood in Western psychodevelopmental terms as a physical, emotional, and psychological stage of transition from childhood to adulthood (Feldman and Elliott 1990). In some branches of educational psychology, it is associated with the reemergence of suppressed sexuality and ego-identity (Erikson 1950:306–325; Freud 1937; Harter 1990). Some elements of Western psychodevelopmental traditions are evident in the home economics section on mothercraft and childbearing, such as when the syllabus instructs that girls are to avoid the "temptations facing an adolescent with improper behaviour." Teachers are directed to give "practical examples of good and bad family life" and to make students fully aware of the "hardships faced by unmarried mothers." The conflation of lessons about biological reproduction with lessons about morality results in a complex assembly of cultural assumptions that are thickly encoded in a few short lessons. Girls are supposed to learn about "good family life" and about the "responsibilities of each member of the family." They are also supposed to learn how "sexually transmitted diseases" threaten unmarried or adulterous mothers.

Immediately following lessons on "The Adolescent," girls study lessons on "The Expectant Mother" and "The Coming Baby." In both of these, girls are supposed to learn the signs of pregnancy and the dangers of childbearing, and they are supposed to be able to describe and prepare menus for pregnant women and newborn infants. The syllabus states specific rules for expectant and nursing women, and it notes that when the infant matures, immunizations, foods, exercise, and lessons should be administered at appropriate times. Lessons on "Baby's Daily Routine" reflect the micro-management of time in the developmental process. Future mothers are told to schedule activities on given days, including bathing, eating, sleeping, and playing with the child. On a longer time frame, they are told to schedule regular medical visits to the baby clinic and to plan visits to a hospital that provides maternal/child health care in their region.

Underlying lessons on mothercraft is a cultural assumption about the universal linear trajectory of human growth and development and about the role of the mother in guiding the child through early stages of life. In orientation, this model resembles that of G. Stanley Hall (1904) and early developmental psychologists. Mothercraft lessons, like the rest of the home economics curriculum, derive in part from a psychological model introduced in the early twentieth century by German missionaries and, later, British colonials. But they also derive from American Evangelical efforts, through the Augustana Lutheran Church, to impose fixed structure in the mid-twentieth century on the social development of students by labeling them "adolescents." As with the cookery and nutrition component, this model of mothercraft is not always commensurate with students' lives. Growth and change are generally understood on the mountain as being processual, even ambiguous. Married people are sometimes called "children" or "youth," and youth sometimes extends into chronological adulthood. In other words, the linear framework of the syllabus does not always match up with what people value and do. Responsibility for instructing young women about sexual reproduction is generally turned over to grandmothers and aunts, and only occasionally do mothers comfortably talk with their daughters about marriage, pregnancy, and the biology and sociality of sex. Nonetheless, the syllabus proceeds as if open communication between mother and child were the most natural of social relations to cultivate and as if a unilinear trajectory of human development were the most self-evident mode of socialization.

Dressmaking and Textiles

More broadly, then, the syllabus illustrates the developmental trajectory of the person from infancy to childhood, to adolescence, and eventually to parenthood.[3] It is within this process of social development that every family member has his or her proper "role" and must be appropriately dressed to mark off the different stages of social life. In Forms 1 and 2, in lessons on Dressmaking and Textiles, girls are supposed to learn how to make "suitable styles to fit individual figures," and they are told they must learn how to design various styles that are appropriate for different occasions (Ministry of National Education 1977:159). Each pupil is instructed to collect "pictures of good and bad dress designs, styles, colour combinations, etc." and to "practice in planning personal and family wardrobes," taking into consideration "the African way of life" (p. 159).

The centrality of dressmaking within the home economics syllabus stems in part from the power of the adorned and dressed body to signify modernity and identify "the educated" in society.[4] Women are responsible for managing the social presentation of self by designing garments that suit various social roles. Men are to wear overalls and heavyweight work clothes that sometimes, the syllabus notes, must be patched and darned. Suits are in order for men and older boys, particularly on Sundays and for formal occasions. Children are to wear loose-fitting jumpers that allow freedom of movement and the chance to explore; their own proper development and early childhood education depend on their physical freedom, unencumbered by poorly fitting clothes. Primary and secondary students are supposed to wear standard-issue uniforms that, although not handmade, must be repaired and kept ironed. The syllabus instructs on washing and starching. And although the majority of lessons focus on making and decorating women's clothing (suggesting, as it were, that women are the most adorned social group), a key theme throughout the syllabus is that students ought to make things that are useful—things that they will actually wear. Students in Form 1, for instance, are supposed to learn how to make aprons and to draft slip and undergarment patterns. Aprons hearken back to lessons about cookery and nutrition, and slips and undergarments recall earlier lessons on sexuality. In Form 2, students progress to more complicated projects and are taught about drafting and making blouses with "darts," "French seams," and "trimmings." Their final lesson suggests that students experiment with "commercial patterns"—not that they necessarily buy patterns premade, but that they study the way professionals design dresses so that they might easily reproduce commercial styles.

A secondary aim of Dressmaking and Textiles is to occupy girls during their leisure time. Embroidery and knitting are two popular pastimes; many houses are decorated with doilies that cover chairs and tables. These doilies are called *vitambaa* in Kiswahili, and many households have several sets. Students in Forms 3 and 4 are supposed to learn how to make embroidered curtains and room dividers. The idea that sewing and knitting should occupy girls' leisure time implies that work and leisure are conceptually distinct.[5] It also suggests that girls must be doing something even when resting. The idea that "idle hands make for the devil's work" seems to underlie curricular emphasis on sewing and knitting. Adolescent girls, full of "psychological and social problems," may be kept occupied—and out of trouble—through sewing.

INTERLUDE: ON USING THE SYLLABUS TO RECONFIGURE MARRIAGE AND REPRODUCTION

I have focused here on the content of the home economics syllabus to point to places where it does not quite make sense. Taken at face value, much of what is included in the official curriculum has little bearing on students' lives. In many cases the technology is not available, or else lessons rest on ideas foreign to Chagga students. Gaps between curriculum and practice raise questions about the significance of the lessons. In certain regards, home economics is a "theoretical" in the classic sense. It is a set of facts students must memorize in order to pass exams, and in this sense, home economics has become precisely what early policy-makers warned *against*: the memorization of abstract facts and values that have little relevance or application to most students' lives. In "Education for Self-Reliance," for instance, Julius K. Nyerere stated that the "object of teaching must be the provision of knowledge, skills and attitudes which will serve the student when he or she lives and works in a developing and changing socialist state" (1967:282). It must "not be aimed at university entrance" (p.282) but should prepare students to contribute to the economic development of the villages and communities in which they live. A primary focus of "Education for Self-Reliance" has been to teach vocational skills and in the process, although not a focus, to develop a class system of manual workers. Home economics, technical subjects, and especially farming are key components— even today, when the socialist rhetoric of previous policies has been replaced with the language of privatization and markets. Yet, ironically, lessons about cookery, nutrition, and other domestic subjects, while on the surface appearing to be practical, in fact appear to translate only minimally into students' lives. They do not fulfill most students' basic needs, nor do they lead in most cases to paid employment. Moreover, the home economics syllabus is unevenly implemented. Many teachers stress different components, and in many cases omit much of the program. At Mkufi Secondary School, as I mentioned, very little of the home economics syllabus was taught at all, in contrast to another secondary school on the mountain (like Mkufi, a Lutheran-sponsored coeducational day school), where the syllabus was followed very carefully.

In light of the fact that home economics lessons are unevenly implemented and often irrelevant, it is apposite to ask, following Serpell (1993) and others (Gaitskell 1988; Hansen 1997; Hunt 1992), why home economics lessons are even taught at all. Mothers surely know what to do with newborns, regardless of what the syllabus says. Chagga women after all have been caring for infants for many years. And certainly they know how to clothe their families. As with lessons on Cookery and Nutrition, some of the "practicals" suggested in Dressmaking and Mothercraft are in fact not possible at all for many in Tanzania, and yet these lessons are taught to stu-

dents as something they need—something they must have before graduation. Students are introduced to sewing machine parts and types, even
though most schools and families do not have access to machines, and
teachers are instructed to take students to hospitals, even though many
people in Tanzania live far from medical facilities.

One answer is that home economics is a state project to refashion gender
roles; that it is an ideological state apparatus in the Althusserian sense that
"ejects" children "into production" (Althusser 1971:155). This answer
reflects an official Tanzanian ideology—that schools prepare students for
future participation in the state economy. Even though it implicates schools
in the production and reproduction of classed society—an implication that
Nyerere's policies sought to avoid but contributed to nonetheless—this
answer captures some of the political philosophy that Nyerere was trying
to develop through education. Nyerere wanted to make schools practical
entities: to get students to do "real life" activities. Mothercraft, sewing, and
the like were activities Nyerere felt well suited girls. Yet looking at the gender roles embedded in curriculum does not tell us why, in places such as
Machame on Mount Kilimanjaro, people agree to have the lessons taught in
the first place. Nor does it tell us why many would go out of their way to
find home economics teachers—as Mkufi administrators clearly did. Understanding that the syllabus is designed to prepare students for the world of
work and domestic relations explains in functional terms that the school is
designed to perform a particular operation. But it does not tell us how these
lessons transpire on the ground or how students accept and/or creatively
rework them. To understand this, we need to understand local ideas about
social progress and status change and how the school is viewed as instrumental in moving people from one social condition to another. When we do
this, we see that home economics lessons more generally are part of an
emerging, new, domestic imaginary, part of students' lessons in learning
about social class—not necessarily about what they have today, but about
what they might achieve. The syllabus does not insist that every student
needs to learn how to make cold-cut sandwiches or fruit pies, yet it clearly
implies that revising the domestic sphere is one step toward attaining
"modernity."

Moreover, the ministry's assertion that home economics "socially trans-
forms" is in keeping with a basic anthropology. Anthropologists have long
remarked that marriage is a fundamental process of social reproduction. It

not only enables the direct transmission of social value from one generation to the next, but creates as well the potential for transformation in the social system at large (John Comaroff 1980a:33). It brings together sometimes very different social groups and rearranges them structurally. Marriage promises—or threatens, depending on one's view—to challenge normative ideas of social organization.[6] It cuts across many institutional domains—legal, domestic, religious, and political—and sets social standards for cohabitation and sexual reproduction, involving a whole complex of social relations.

No wonder, then, that girls' domestic education should figure so centrally in the applied sciences in Tanzanian schooling. Establishing control over the terms of marriage and reproduction is one way that the state might be able to control the future. By positioning students within a system of economic production, by shaping them materially and ideologically, home economics classes, in conjunction with others, can help sketch a social map. They create a niche for school graduates to fill, yet put limits on the degree of social change that is possible. No wonder, too, that teachers and administrators at Mkufi Secondary School should have been so bent on finding a domestic science teacher. With female sexuality metonymically indexing the wider body politic (especially in Africa, where the female body in many cases stands for nationhood, even the entire continent, cf. Grosz-Ngaté 1997), home economics is an important course for channeling, and potentially redirecting, social change. Specifically, it is a state-directed mechanism for refashioning the lineage along nuclear family lines.

To get some sense of the ways people refer to home economics to signal a new form of "modern" femininity, I turn next to the ways I heard women discuss categories of femininity in connection with home economics and schooling. I argue that two categories of womanhood circulate in popular discourse that parallel oppositional categories implied in the home economics syllabus: "women of the house" and "big sisters of the city" conform with the culturally and historically constructed polar ends of tradition and modernity. After introducing briefly how people compare and contrast these forms, I discuss how these two categories are differently reflected in contrasting models of marriage. I then extend this comparison to a discussion of female circumcision and initiation, where I examine how schoolgirls contrast their views with elders'.

CITY SISTERS AND STAY-AT-HOME MOTHERS:
OPPOSITIONS ASSOCIATED WITH SCHOOLING

One of the very first things I was told about women *per se* was this from a church official: "Uneducated women brew banana beer [*mbege*], but school-educated women drink Coca-Cola." Driving down the mountain in the official's sports utility vehicle, we passed several women carrying buckets of *mbege* on their heads, walking to the local market where they sold the brew to individual shop owners and middlemen. Among the women was the official's neighbor, who, he explained, was not school-educated. "If she had gone even a year to primary school," he clarified, "she would have learned that drinking banana beer is dangerous," that "it is not nutritious," and that "it gives you dysentery." But since she had been "schooled in the traditional lessons of female initiation," as he put it, domestic science lessons about health and hygiene were "beyond her grasp." The church leader implied that schooling transformed backward, beer-brewing women into self-aware nutritionists, and that school-educated women were more informed about "things up to date" than these women who brewed banana beer. As we drove into the church parking lot, he added that school-educated girls sanitize their tradition. As he put it, they were able to "take their grandparents' ways" and "clean them up" with domestic science lessons.

This series of distinctions—between women who brew banana beer and those who don't, between women who have been ritually initiated and those who go to school—reproduces a set of oppositions embedded in the applied sciences curriculum: school-educated women versus mothers and wives; urban-oriented women versus the rurally bound. The curriculum does not directly impose these oppositions, but popular discourse frequently points to the school as the source of their making. Stellah's mother, for instance, evoked a dichotomy between modern-schooled and traditionally educated women when she laughed at my request that she explain the stages of banana beer brewing to me. She responded: "The work of Stellah's mother is to make banana beer, but *your* work is to teach in school. Didn't you learn from your home economics that brewing banana beer is dirty?" Stellah's mother, like many other women in the village, spent a lot of time huddled in her smoke-filled kitchen, cooking over a fire, shouting orders to children: "Run and get some sugar!" "Stay out of the kitchen!" "Go and see what the baby is doing!" Occasionally she would entertain my questions from the dark enclosure of her wattle-and-daub kitchen. However, more frequently she would put aside what she was doing, wipe her hands on her clothes, and come out to talk in the courtyard. She, like her sister-in-law and several neighbors, described herself as *mama wa nyumbani*, a mother of the house who had little income other than what she received from her husband. "Me, I'm only a *mama wa nyumbani*, a stay-at-home mother," she would say, qualifying her answers to questions that she thought were "*ya kisasa*"—contemporary. She often commented that schooled women her age would "laugh" at the way she cooked over a fire, noting that the gas stoves some women owned made cooking "a luxury."[7]

This self-identification as a "stay-at-home mother" introduces an important point, namely, that people self-identify in terms of, and attribute the formation of social groups to, the presence or absence of school education. Categories of schooling provide an anchoring rationale for defining and explaining personal and generational differences. Schooling is viewed as an inseparable factor in differentiating self from other, younger from older generations; it marks the difference between individuals' and generations' orientations to household life and urban living.

Mama Stellah, like many of her neighbors, compared and contrasted herself with *madada wa mjini*—big sisters of the city. By Mama Stellah's definition, *madada wa mjini* either had salaried jobs in Moshi or were thought likely to find them. They had attended one or two years of secondary school and in some cases had even graduated. Theirs was the world of fast cars and VCRs, of disco dancing and Coca-Cola. To Mama Stellah, many students in the first graduating class at Mkufi were "big sisters of the city." They were urban-oriented, fashion-conscious, and impatient with the ways of their mothers.

As differentiating markers, categories do not capture the profiles of everyone in the community; indeed, they are more heuristic devices for representing character types than for pointing to any one individually. And as a body of work in critical and feminist studies of education has illustrated, social identities are multiple and constantly shifting (Davies 1989; McRobbie 1994; Walkerdine 1990).[8] Never, for instance, did I hear students say they were working hard to become "big city sisters." Instead, students applied the label unevenly to themselves and others in certain contexts. Like "stay-at-home mothers," they used the label abstractly, to generalize rather than identify. Yet *mama wa nyumbani* and *madada wa mjini*, in the Weberian sense of ideal types, are objectifications of oppositions that are accompanied by beliefs about all sorts of differences in social interactions, ranging from the most mundane to the highly ritualized. That the school should figure so prominently in the articulation of these opposites is in keeping with what some theorists have identified about the institution of schooling: that it asserts the possibility that everyone can and should have some kind of identity (Anderson 1983:16; Stephens 1995; Wexler 1992). I only add to this that schools assert these possibilities in such a way that emerges from schools' interactions with local beliefs, processes, and categories.

By way of illustrating how schooling enters into discussions about traditional/modern differences, I would like to describe two models of marriage that correspond to the categories *mama wa nyumbani* and *madada wa mjini*. The two models of marriage correspond to competing ideas about education. One depicts and defines daughters and girls as members of the patriline; the other presents young women in terms of schooling and self-sufficiency. According to the first view, which itself has many variations, marriage complements the "growing" of persons on the banana grove and the succession of fathers and children through men (discussed in the previous chapter). Marriage, like inheritance, constitutes a particular social mechanism by which patrilineages are created and reproduced. Unlike inheritance, which involves the transfer of wealth in vertical, intergenerational directions within a single lineage, Chagga marriage unfolds through a series of ritualized exchanges that link different patrilines. The various ways women and men conceptualize these exchanges correspond with a multiplicity of ways they envision gendered relations.[9] Marriage, for instance, might be seen as a one-time event involving the relocation of a woman to a man's house, or it might involve long, elaborate negotiations between male elders of the prospective bride's and groom's lineages.

From a "modern" approach, marriage that unfolds through a series of exchanges is frequently termed "traditional" and stands in contrast to what many secondary school girls and graduates say they would prefer: a church-directed wedding in which bride and groom exchange vows in the presence of their families and friends. What I found in speaking with schoolgirls at Mkufi Secondary School and with several of Stellah's friends was that marriage provided students—particularly girls—with a metaphor for redefining themselves as members of independent families. In some cases, schooling provided a way out: "I do not want to marry," said Alilya, a secondary school graduate working in a dress shop in Moshi Town. "Why should I? I am educated." The ambiguity of marriage makes it possible for some school-educated girls to say that they are substituting "education" for "husbands."

SAMUELI'S AND MONICA'S WEDDING

In part, "traditional" conceptualizations of marriage are revealed by the adage discussed in Chapter 1: "A person who lives in a foreign place should not question the things she sees, but upon returning to her natal household, may comment all she wants." (*Kite kikamfika masaleni nnlyo kikomaa* [Kimachame]; *Mtu muoga akiwa sehemu geni haongei, lakini akifika kwao ndio anaanza kupiga kelele* [Kiswahili].) This adage, as mentioned, when told to young women, reminds them that they must speak positively in the presence of husbands' kin. Women are "strangers"—in a more charitable interpretation, "guests"—and as such must speak with caution and deference. Implicit in the saying is the idea that marriage is a process of social adjustment, a process in which, at least initially, loyalties are divided for women between natal and marital households. Such an adjustment is not always agreeable to school-educated young women, many of whom see their schooling as moving them beyond tradition.

In Machame, the most ritualized and elaborated of marriages involved a multistage process, beginning with the "taking of *mbege*" (*kuleta pombe ya posa*) from the groom's patriline to the bride's, and involving the birth of a male (*mrisi* in Kimachame) who would inherit a banana grove. Monica and Samueli, at whose wedding I was "tested" by Mr. Uroki (in the previous chapter), married in a way that many described to me as traditional and representative of Chagga custom. The marriage consisted of several steps: three or four gifts of *mbege* (banana beer); the relocation of the woman to the man's house; and the birth of a *mrisi* (Kimachame), a son to inherit the grove. I recount this so-called traditional model here not only because I find it absolutely fascinating that marriage should be so variably conceived cross-culturally, but because it contrasts with a "more modern" model as people describe it today. Toward the end of this section, I will contrast this highly formalized process with a less ritualized model described to me by some students. And I will discuss how some schoolgirls couch their ideas of marriage in terms that pit the "tradition" of beer against the "modernity" of Coca-Cola.

In the course of living near Babu Munissi's grove, I frequently encountered a nearby neighbor, Samueli. Samueli was a hospital staff worker who wanted to marry his neighbor, Monica Mushi. I had come to know Monica as a friend through Stellah and so was invited to participate in the marriage process—a series of banana beer gifts (prestations) to Monica's patrikin by Samueli and his fathers and uncles. The prestations culminated in Monica's moving to Samueli's newly built house on his lineage lands. The first beer prestation, "the beer for those who live in the woman's father's compound"[10] was presented without prior warning to Monica's patrikin. Kinspeople of the prospective groom, Samueli, along with a special messenger—here, Samueli's best friend—visited Monica's fathers and uncles to ascertain her kins' general interest in allowing her to marry. The special messenger clutched a sprig of dracaena that he had cut from a nearby hedge, and several of the men carried fifteen or twenty tins of banana beer that they intended to drink that afternoon with Monica's father. With these gifts they demonstrated the seriousness of their mission, Samueli said, for Chagga swear their deepest intents with gifts of dracaena. Samueli's friend did not come out right away and say, "My best friend wants to marry your daughter." To do so would frame the union in terms of a relationship between two individuals, not in terms of ritualized exchanges initiated between lineages. Instead, he stated indirectly, alluding to the banana grove, "I know someone who would like the child of one of your banana trees" (*Kwiifo ndu aketereva kyaana kya nginda mbe* [Kimachame]) and "I know someone who would like to suck your milk" (*Kwiifo ndu aketereva ionga ivee mbe* [Kimachame]).[11] Such allusions evoked a range of meanings, according to Monica and Samueli. For speaking in terms of the banana grove indicated that this request was extremely urgent. "Taking the child of a banana tree" was a potentially offensive request that could elicit ill will and evoke the accusation that the special messenger was a thief (*mwizi*).[12]

Following this, the messenger indirectly indicated which "milk" his friend wanted "to suck," which "child" of the "banana trees" Samueli would like to take. Monica's father then tasted a bit of the *mbege* that Samueli's representative offered him and wondered aloud if the banana beer was actually poisoned.[13] "Do you think I will vomit?" Monica's father asked Monica, looking for some assurance that she would not call off the marriage and make her father give back—or "vomit"—the bridewealth. A father's acceptance of this first banana beer gift is still no guarantee that his lineage is willing to enter into a relationship. Concern about vomiting, an inversion of the health and sociality banana beer is supposed to signify, suggests that the prospective bride's father is reluctant to accept—or to "swallow," as people put it—the guest's request. It also suggests that the recipient is reluctant, in a broader sense, to part with his daughter who has been "cultivated" and who represents the efforts of the patriline to "grow" persons of social value.

The second banana beer gift is typically designated for the women of the prospective bride's natal family. Whereas the first banana beer gift is given to the bride's father, uncles, and brothers, the second—"the banana beer for unwrapping the headrings"[14]—is drunk primarily by mothers, sisters, and aunts. Prior to drinking it, Monica's mothers and sisters untied the *ngagha* (headrings brought by Samueli's party, made out of dried banana leaves and used to balance jugs of beer on women's heads). The women untied the rings to make sure they had been woven tightly and properly. Like the men who tested the first banana beer for signs of poison and deceit, women checked the headrings to determine if there had been any irregularity—for instance, if a knot had been mistied or if the *ngagha* had been woven in two different directions. If there had been, women could have rejected the banana beer and, with heightened drama, called off the negotiations. But because no irregularities were detected in this case, the marriage negotiations proceeded, and the third banana beer—this one for the brothers of Samueli who now joined the men and women of the bride's side—was presented a few days later. "Banana beer for one's male relatives,"[15] the name of the third prestation, was drunk primarily by the male relatives from both sides of the negotiation. The inclusiveness of this penultimate prestation represents the larger commitment of both lineages to enter into a longer-term process, and the absence in some cases of either the suitor or the woman at the gift-ceremony reflects the extent to which marriage is a relationship between lineages, not between individuals.

The final beer, which marked the end of Monica's residence at her father's house, was known as "beer for everyone."[16] Beer was brought for all the neighbors, and this was the largest celebration of them all. For Monica and Samueli, as for many today, this fourth beer corresponded with a church ceremony (or, for a growing minority in Machame, a ceremony in a mosque). In the past this prestation, like those before it, was accompanied by a ritual slaughtering. Portions of meat were reserved for ancestors and a little bit of beer was poured on the ground.[17]

The process of these four banana beer prestations and the act of drinking and eating together represents one end of the continuum of what typically constitutes "traditional marriage" in Machame. At the other end of the conjugal spectrum are casual unions that are not formalized with banana beer. Even though marriage is an extended, multistep process, people in Machame also say that having sexual relations with another person may mean that they "are married." I was surprised, for instance, to hear a Chagga safari driver whom I had come to know say that he had married several women in the various towns we passed. He said he wanted "to marry" (*kuoa*) yet another woman whom we met at a roadside restaurant. At the same time he was married to these women, he was also married to a woman in Arusha; with her he had produced a number of children, one of whom he recognized as his *mrisi* (in Kimachame, male heir).

Such quick and, to me at first, seemingly casual relationships seemed to contradict what people told me about marriage—namely, that it was a formal and extended process. Yet these alliances, including marriages described to me by several secondary school girls, constituted marriage too. For "to marry" could be loosely used to describe either lineage—approved conjugal ties or casual liaisons. The slipperiness of marriage was what made it possible for some schoolgirls to say that education was their husbands. This point was driven home when I observed, about a year and a half after Monica's and Samueli's marriage, several secondary school students and a recent graduate deliberating about whether or not they should "be married" or apply to college. The first model they described, and that I first presented here, was identified by students as "traditional."

I was visiting Stellah's home during the Christmas holiday and stayed up late chatting with her and a couple of friends. The topic of conversation was how to avoid "getting married" by the "hungry" young men who were wandering the village. According to Angela, one of Stellah's closest friends who graduated the year before from Kuzuri Secondary School, Christmas was considered to be an especially dangerous time when unwitting girls could get married and get pregnant. Angela said that her cousin had been married the previous year. "One of the village youth came to her house late at night and took her home with him. He just stole her, just like that; first she was there, then she was gone." Since that fateful evening, Angela's cousin had borne this man a child. Now she was known as this man's *nka* (wife in Kimachame) and as *mama* (mother in Kimachame) of her child.

Now, at this Christmas holiday, Angela was confronted with staying inside with friends or going out and letting one of the village youth claim her and "marry" her. She had, Angela reasoned, completed her secondary schooling and was only halfheartedly considering going on to college. She was socially and chronologically old enough to marry, but not sure that she in fact wanted to.

Angela used the occasion to reflect on the kind of wedding that she envisioned for herself.

> What I want is a man to love me, to bring me flowers, not this nonsense of beer. And he should bring it to me directly, not go through my brothers or father or uncles. Then when we have agreed to get married, he should ask my father if it is okay, but this should just be a formality. We really wouldn't care what my father or uncles would say. . . . That is the way it really ought to be, because after all, I am educated. I'm not like those women in Dodoma [a city in central Tanzania where, according to stereotyped views in Machame, people are unschooled, ignorant, and backward]. There, girls' fathers accept hundreds of cattle in exchange for some boys to marry them. I'm educated and my husband will be too. He'll know that banana beer and cattle are foolish.

The picture Angela presented is very different from that of Monica and Samueli. It presents marriage in terms of a romantic model that approximates what others have described of romance in the United States (cf. Holland and Eisenhart 1990; Radway 1984). It suggests that schoolgirls take their own level of schooling into consideration when they think about their future unions (cf. Oppong 1981; Hollos 1998). In Angela's model, marriage unfolds not as a process predetermined by "tradition" but in accordance with the social standing of the woman and, as Angela also alluded, of the man. Schooling presents the possibility for moving people on to new, upwardly mobile social positions. It holds the potential for appropriating outside influences—for learning about "European ways"—and by doing so, strengthening the patriline and augmenting what is already valuable—to provide "everything that can benefit a child in life" as the graduation speaker quoted in the previous chapter put it.

Angela continued:

> The day itself will be really beautiful. Julius will play the organ. I'll be wearing a white wedding dress, my husband a tuxedo. My uncle has a video camera, and he'll tape the entire event. Aikande can be the

3. The flower girl and, to her left, the ring bearer at a wedding Angela described as one she would like to have when she gets married.

flower girl and Shirumisha can carry the ring. Then, when the ceremony is over, we'll go to Nairobi for a honeymoon. Isn't that what Mama Betty and Mzee Ndanshau did? Sure it is.

In a context where marriage is thought to move Chagga girls to higher social status—where marriage and childbirth are often seen as extremely desirable outcomes of a female gendered social role—it makes considerable sense that girls should seek to augment marriage by combining it with schooling. Getting married in a formal way ("in church" as Angela imagined it, where guests drank "Coca-Cola and not banana beer") signified a "modern, educated" Chagga femininity. A fully elaborated ceremony in church reflected graduates' material and educational social standing. Such a ceremony did not include the "traditional" trappings of banana beer, headrings (*ngagha*) or cryptic references to the "children of banana trees." Nor did it involve being quietly wooed in the night and relocated in the morning to a man's natal household. A church-style wedding, as envisioned by Angela and her friends, conspicuously materialized the effects of school education. It made their education visible and socially powerful in forms of the wedding dress, bridal party, and elaborate music and floral arrangements.

Angela's views about "traditional marriage" fed into her understanding of Education for Self-Reliance. "I have gone to school to become self-reliant," she asserted. "That means I don't need any husband to house or take care of me." In contrast to Nyerere's image of the African family, in which the family was a microcosm of the state, Angela's and other students' images of families were microcosms of a private workforce. Well-educated families would be nuclear, not extended, and would consist of an equal partnership; husband and wife would share in child-rearing and both would be employed beyond the home. In some scenarios, a woman could even set up a household and have children without marrying or living with a man. "Education is my husband," was one phrase bandied about, the main meaning of which oscillated between, on the one hand, forswearing marriage entirely, and, on the other, recognizing that even within a marital union, a woman's education would make her independent. Schooling could provide what men traditionally had a claim to: an income, a house, a social network, even the economic financing to educate and raise children. And although this ideal was not always realized, it pointed to a possibility that women could through schooling gain independence—including social and economic independence through education.

FANTA, or "Foolish Africans Never Take Alcohol"

Yet one person's meat is another's poison, and in contrast to Angela's ideal of marriage, Angela's mother offered another one. The context of the following conversation was a wedding ceremony at which the bride and groom had decided to "go modern." The groom was an organist in the local Lutheran Church and in keeping with the church doctrine, had forsworn alcoholic beverages, including the locally brewed banana beer. Wedding guests were served Coke and Coca-Cola products—Sprite, Krest (club soda), and lemon-and-orange flavored Fanta—yet this was a decidedly unacceptable selection to some, and it prompted a minor revolt:

> MAMA ANGELA: Look at these silly drinks we are given. This bridal couple thinks our tradition is dirty.
>
> AMY: Please explain to me, Mama Angela.
>
> MAMA ANGELA: Well, to begin with, look. This big sister [i.e., the bride] has even had a wedding ring imported from London. We never even had gold rings! Why do schoolgirls think they need them? And then, the bride and groom are afraid to drink *mbege*. They think it's poi-

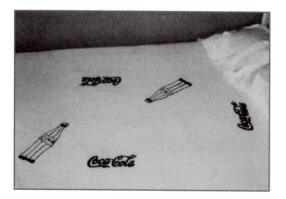

4. Bedsheets of a secondary school graduate who said she preferred to drink Coca-Cola over banana beer at church weddings.

soned! They don't even want to *hold* a calabash of beer. They won't even do it to show respect.

Look! See what I mean? [pointing to two young women] They actually like this Fanta and Coke! They learn in home economics that drinking *mbege* is bad, that it makes their stomachs gurgle with amoebas and pollution.[18]

At this point, Mama Angela's brother-in-law stepped in, adding that he could use a good calabash of banana beer and pointing out a standing joke that "FANTA" was an acronym for "*Foolish Africans Never Take Alcohol.*" He and his age-mates decided to go down the road to a bar and get some beer. They set up a small barrel containing banana beer near the church yet technically not on church property. From the reception, they invited all whom they suspected were "thirsty" to "come for a soda" (as they euphemistically called the brew). For a time, the banana grove was alive with old men and women sneaking in and out to get a drink, and I later was told that "even the bride and groom came to the barrel" though close friends of the couple denied this.

At this very same wedding where banana beer drinkers revolted, the kitchen staff were getting into a spat over similar issues. Stellah and her mother were preparing a special rice dish (*pilau*) and the classic Chagga *mishare tya nyama*, a starchy, thick dish of boiled bananas and beef, which the bride and groom and their extended families were to eat.

STELLAH'S MOTHER: Look at you, my daughter. You can't even make *mishare tya nyama* properly. You have no education. How are you ever going to get a husband? Mashoo [the bride] will be disgraced if you add too many potatoes. What did they teach you at secondary school? How to make potatoes and rice like Europeans?

STELLAH: But mother, potatoes are as good as bananas. Why don't we add some more of them?

STELLAH'S MOTHER: This is a wedding. We need bananas.

The bride and groom, along with their guests, eventually ate the potato-laden *mishare tya nyama*, though the groom's mother commented not only that there was not enough meat, but that the potatoes were mushy and rather grainy. The wedding reception proceeded well into the evening and was generally well attended. Yet the atmosphere among the roughly three hundred people was divided and rather testy. Again and again I heard grumbling among the elders, many of whom bemoaned the state of children "these days" and said that schooling was "ruining" their children and grandchildren—turning them into "little Europeans."

Many of the guests, including Stellah's mother, spoke about ritual initiation as a counterpart to the vocational sciences, "What our daughters need to learn these days is *mbyaa tya waniini*—lessons about growing up—like we learned in initiation! Instead, they get this nonsense in school—a couple of lessons on home economics!"

Although not everyone saw *mbyaa tya waniini* [Kimachame] and domestic science as mutually exclusive, home economics and initiation—like "big sisters of the city" and "stay-at-home mothers"—were often mentioned as opposites. After hearing snippets about *mbyaa tya waniini* here and there, and recognizing that many people, like Mama Angela and Stellah's mother, saw *mbyaa tya waniini* and domestic science as competing models—I decided to inquire about these ritual initiation lessons directly. I had read historical accounts of initiation in older ethnographies (see the following chapter, and Dundas 1924; Gutmann 1932; Marealle 1965; Raum 1940) and recognized that because *mbyaa tya waniini* had to do with initiation, its contents might be secret. But I was not so much interested in learning *what* initiates learned as understanding how people contrasted *mbyaa tya waniini* with home economics.[19]

FEMALE CIRCUMCISION AND INITIATION

In the final weeks of my longest research stay, I fine-tuned my eyes and ears to girls' initiation. I did not broach the subject earlier—unless it was raised by others in conversation—simply because the topic was sensitive to women who recognized that the Lutheran Church and Tanzanian government condemned it, and that the international community from which I had come had politicized the practice. Many people were hesitant to discuss circumcision or its ritual antecedent, initiation, with a foreign researcher. But by fourteen months, women apparently felt comfortable enough to inform me that a group of girls were undergoing the rites and that Stellah and I could observe a part of them.

On several occasions we spoke with an old woman whom Stellah and I nicknamed Bibi Muro. Bibi Muro described herself as a specialist in "cutting." She had recently circumcised a half-dozen girls and sent them off to heal at a neighbor woman's house. Before we visited the girls, we spoke with Bibi Muro about initiation and learned that in her opinion, and in other old people's views, schoolgirls' refusal to be initiated constituted a "break with Chagga custom." Stellah led the conversation:[20]

STELLAH: From what I understand, you said women are initiated just because it's a norm. But, isn't a girl better off nowadays if she isn't initiated?

BIBI MURO: Nowadays some of them have refused completely. They are refusing to be initiated.

STELLAH: Did you say they are refusing?

BIBI: Yes. Some of them, they even have children of their own.

STELLAH: I see.

BIBI: Yes, they are refusing to be initiated, and you must be initiated to be a full adult. Your mother is initiated and your father too. But some of the girls these days, they are refusing.

STELLAH: I even refused myself, grandmother.

BIBI: What!?

STELLAH: I refused to be initiated.

BIBI: It is true, it is true, some have refused.

STELLAH: Grandmother, why are people initiated?

BIBI: It's a custom.

STELLAH: Custom?

BIBI: Yes.

STELLAH: Custom? That's all?

BIBI: Yes.

STELLAH: I cannot believe this. Again, I have heard people say that girls have to be initiated so they don't fool around with men.

BIBI: Right.

STELLAH: Is that true?

BIBI: Yes, but people have refused.

As Stellah put it, it was mainly older women who believed that uncircumcised girls were "socially immature" and more apt to "fool around with men." Bibi Muro later commented that uncircumcised girls were jeopardizing Chagga culture. She put the message idiomatically, saying that girls were "uprooting the banana grove," and that the last thing the community needed at the moment were more teachers counseling schoolgirls to reject tradition. The problem with rejecting tradition, and with schoolgirls' refusing to be circumcised, Bibi Muro contended, was that girls were becoming more sexually active—unnaturally so, in her view. They were contributing to increased rates of HIV infection and were killing themselves, their children, and their husbands. Her argument was that clitorectomy, which preceded initiation, curtailed women's sexuality. This, in turn, reduced rates of HIV infection and kept society reproducing in a normative manner. But now, with neither religious leaders nor teachers advising girls to undergo initiation, girls' sexual "appetites" (*utamu*, as people put it in Kiswahili) were out of control, and school-educated girls were putting society at risk. They were making daily life "rotten" to the core. *Maisha yameoza*—life has rotted, Bibi Muro said.

Interesting here is that Bibi Muro saw domestic science as failing to deal with contemporary problems. From her point of view, the school introduced novel ideas about girls' bodies and sexuality and it violated what she saw as natural relationships established between men and women through initiation. According to Bibi Muro and others like her, Chagga tradition had its own logical basis; girls and boys were circumcised and initiated for a reason, and the ritual itself had a functional purpose. In a sense, Bibi Muro invoked the logic of the home economics syllabus to beat it at its own game. By arguing that ritual has a goal and that previous generations were unaffected by HIV, she called into question the very efficacy of an educational system that claims to improve and raise the standards of living through, among other things, domestic science.

Many schoolgirls rejected Bibi Muro's view. Stellah, for instance, thought Bibi Muro failed to understand the basics of empirical science. Shared razors and knives used during ritual circumcision were more dangerous, Stellah said, than remaining uninitiated. "Domestic science lessons tell you that sharing razors is out-and-out risky," she said. "How can Bibi Muro say that circumcision is safe when many of these girls share razors and don't use antiseptics?" Bibi Muro, in contrast, referred to "custom" and to the lessons circumcised girls learned during initiation: "Why is it we didn't have problems like AIDS around when everyone was getting circumcised?" She didn't want us to answer but replied herself, "Circumcised girls don't fornicate."

Several teachers at Mkufi Secondary School shared Bibi Muro's views— particularly her views about lascivious young women, if not always her views about circumcision. However, many of them, and many people generally, held several views simultaneously, and many people, including girls who were circumcised, changed their arguments depending on the situation. At least half a dozen schoolgirls in the community were convinced circumcision and initiation would "keep them clean" and yet they also wanted to capitalize on the knowledge that home economics could teach them about mothercraft. The girls whom we observed and interviewed at the initiation rite were primary school students, planning to enter Standard VII. All of them agreed that circumcision in general reduced the rate of HIV infections and that in order to "preserve our culture," as several put it, they had to do what their grandparents had done. Some of the initiands had boyfriends who had begun the marriage process of taking *mbege* to women's male relatives. Others had no foreseeable marriage plans but banked on the hopes that this ritual would trigger courting. No matter their plans, all six of the girls saw the ritual as integral to their cultural identity. As one initiand put it, "I have to learn what my mothers and grandmothers did; otherwise I will lose my culture and will become no different from you Americans."

The notion that domestic science moved schoolgirls from a Chagga to an American world resonated with the concerns Mama Angela and Mama Stellah voiced about school-educated girls interested in "foreign ways." It also dovetailed with what the chair of the Mkufi School Board implied when he asked if I would fill in as domestic science teacher: that lessons associated with the home economics syllabus are Western cultural signifiers. They are

viewed as foreign imports, although not necessarily (in his view) of a culturally erosive kind. The subtle balance between oppositional views that
home economics was culturally contaminating, on the one hand, and that
it could "benefit a child in life" on the other, provided grist for the mills of
social debate. In a context where social mobility and movement were recognized by many as part of Chagga sociality (see next chapter), the
question of "what's the value of initiation" was answered by some people
as "nothing, it keeps young women in the same place." Yet others contended that female initiation was a key component of Chagga identity. It
represented an essential element of "Chagganess" that was not to be lost to
school education.

In the end, the initiands whom Stellah and I observed had decided to
undergo initiation. Although their reasons for wanting to learn *mbyaa tya
waniini* were not the same as their ritual instructor's (in contrast to Bibi
Muro, they did not believe that circumcision would prevent HIV infection),
they nonetheless embraced the belief that undergoing initiation was central
to their tradition.

The ritual itself was conducted during the Christmas holiday—a period
of little activity in both the farming and school calendars, and a time of the
year when the abundant harvest could sustain girls' secluded feasting. The
days of their lessons had been announced in advance by the leader who was
initiating them, and the girls were informed that they should plan to spend
the month recuperating from their recent circumcision, "fattening" themselves by drinking *mlaso* (a soup of blood, milk, and fat), eating liver and
lungs ("women's meats"), and learning *mbyaa tya waniini*—lessons that
would prepare them for marriage and child care. The girls, who ranged in
age from fourteen to eighteen years, were recuperating from their cuts in
the enclosure of their leader's house, and were listening to and learning a
series of dances and songs about sexual reproduction. Unlike girls whose
families hoped to send their daughters to secondary school, these girls performed some of their initiation dances openly, in the highly visible space of
their female leader's courtyard. Not all lessons were performed in the open,
for the "secrets of womanhood" (*siri za wanawake*) were taught only to
initiands in the house. But the girls were quite accommodating to us and
indeed wanted their photos taken.

The public display of girls' initiation contrasted with the secret initiation
rituals that some girls at Mkufi Secondary School had undergone the year

5. Female initiands with their teacher, on the right.

before. Secondary school students mentioned to me that at least three of their peers had been initiated, but that because the school condemned these rites, they could not speak openly about it. None of the initiands whom Stellah and I observed was planning to attend Mkufi. Indeed, Mkufi teachers and students told me that these girls would never qualify for Mkufi Secondary School. Not only had they had broken the law (as mentioned, it is illegal to circumcise girls in Tanzania), but they came from families who could not afford to pay private secondary school fees.[21]

Nonetheless, three of the six girls had hopes of going on to a different school, not Mkufi, and in conversations with their parents, I learned that despite parents' overriding contention that their schooling was wrong in condemning girls' initiation, parents drew many parallels between the school and the ritual ceremony. Both initiation and secondary schooling were portrayed as transforming rites ("They make our children grow up," said one parent). Schooling and initiation involved teachers (*walimu*) and students (*wanafunzi*). Parents even drew a parallel between initiands' attire and school uniforms. Each girl undergoing the rite wore a green dress similar to the dresses girls wore at Machame Girls' Secondary School. The cotton dress—short-sleeved, knee-length—was made specifically for this occasion. As one parent put it, these initiands' dresses were their domestic science attire; wearing them, they looked like the secondary schoolgirls who were working on home economics chores around the school.[22] Green dresses were—and are—a part of every boarding school girls' wardrobe. In a sense they are the "housedresses" that boarding girls wear when working around the school—when cleaning their dormitories, assisting in the kitchen, working in the garden, washing their clothes. They are also the dresses secondary schoolgirls wear when exercising in the village market area and jogging down the main tarmac road. At the end of the school week, students at a school near where I lived typically jogged through the local market, dressed in their green uniforms and chanting loudly about how strong, fit, and healthy they were. My neighbors near the girls' school, particularly younger men, would stop their work to watch the girls, noting with both shock and pleasure that "their dresses are so short you can see their thighs!" Indeed, the dresses were cut to reveal more of the body than the regular school uniform would allow. The above-the-knee cut and the fact that students did not have to wear socks when jogging suggests that these girls are sexually maturing, that they are preparing to become sexually active, possibly to marry, and yet are not quite ready for full adulthood. Initiates' ritual instructor supervised them in public, and school students' teachers accompanied students on jogs throughout the village.

The public display of girls' physical fitness—and as some interpreted it, of their sexuality—was analogous to initiands' final celebration of their rites in the village market. On the last day of seclusion, initiands left their teacher's hut, stepping first over a banana bast that had been laid at the doorstep (symbolic of their reentry into Chagga social life), and then running together to the market, singing about their strength and vitality. Bibi Muro's daughter, an adult woman with several children, referred to this final ceremony as initiates' "graduation." Like every school student, she told us in an interview, "these initiates graduate to better things; they return to either their fathers' or husbands' households and eventually have the higher social status of *mfu*," a married woman who has received a clitorectomy.

When I returned three years later to conduct follow-up work, I had the opportunity to meet with two of these six girls again, and they filled me in on what had transpired and how their aspirations had shifted. None of the six had attended or been admitted to secondary school, even though three had aspired to such. Two of the three who had been engaged to marry each had had two children; the other had had several miscarriages. One of the others was living with her parents; the other two had been recently married. The young women, to my surprise, all described themselves as *mama wa nyumbani*, noting with a combination of pride and disappointment that theirs was the life of the home and of taking chare of extended family members' children. The one unmarried young woman was brewing *mbege* and selling it to middlemen in the markets twice weekly. One of the married women with children was cultivating tomatoes and beans for local market sale, and both of the recently married women were keeping livestock and selling milk to a village dairy cooperative. Stellah, who in the interim had worked for other foreign researchers and a travel agent, had moved for a time to a house in town. In contrast to the initiated women whom we had observed three years before, she appeared to be the embodiment of a "big sister of the city." She had moved from her natal household, independently and without getting married, to a house and salaried position.

I'll return in a few pages to this discussion of the differences objectified in the categories *madada wa mjini* and *mama wa nyumbani*. For now, having introduced the general dichotomy and the competing frameworks of womanhood associated with the oppositions, I'd like to extend this discussion in the following chapter by focusing on the ways people refer to initiation to express their views about societal and generational transformations. Short of observing initiation rites from beginning to end, I decided to look at older ethnographies and to listen carefully to the way people spoke about the history and practice of initiation. I found that many of the activities people described to me in the 1990s bore a striking resemblance to colonial accounts—not surprising, since colonial reconstructions have entered popular discourse through, among all things, formal schooling. Gutmann's portrayal of Chagga culture (e.g., 1926; 1932) dovetailed with his writings on African education (e.g., 1935a; 1935b), and Raum (1940), who worked with Chagga teachers-in-training to collect information about life on the mountain, framed his research as "a call for the reform of colonial educational policy" (S. F. Moore 1996a:ix). I discuss colonial accounts in the first portion of the following chapter before I examine the plans three "city sisters" have for implementing their school education.

4

"EDUCATION IS MY HUSBAND"

GENERATIONAL TRANSFORMATIONS

AS PART of the unstructured discussion time at the end of our household interviews, Lameck and I would engage people in conversations. Because we had already set the stage with questions about formal schooling ("how many years of schooling have you had? how many years for your children and grandchildren?"), conversations usually continued to focus on the subject of education. In many cases, older people who had been born in the 1910s, twenties, and thirties contrasted their schooling with what they had learned during ritual initiation. One woman, Mama Lucy, whom Lameck described as a stay-at-home mother (*mama wa nyumbani*), said that everything she knew today she had learned during initiation. Her conversation sounded the themes of what many older women were to say during interviews: that even though they had had little schooling, their mothers and grandmothers had taught them specific lessons.

I found it interesting that Mama Lucy and others spoke of ritual initiation in terms of "lessons." For judging from what I had read in earlier ethnographies and had gathered through some of my other interviews, initiation had not been about taking tests or about sitting young people down and teaching them what they needed to know; instead, it had been a matter of subjecting young people to grueling feats that tested their moral characters.

Certainly schooling, in the sense that it organizes practical preferences through the mastery and embodiment of social schemes (cf. Bourdieu

1977), does the same: it tests students' moral characters by subjecting them to grueling feats. However, if Chagga initiation rites were anything like the initiation practices of other groups in the area, then initiation, to a greater extent than schooling, probably reinforced what initiands already knew. Audrey Richards's (1956) account of Bemba female initiation in eastern Zambia, for instance, portrayed female initiation as a rite of passage that effected ontological transformations. Female initiation was "danced" or performed to make girls grow into adulthood, and initiation instructors were teachers to the extent that they helped foster in children the transition to productive adulthood (p. 125). Similarly, Victor Turner's (1967) account of Ndembu male initiation emphasized that initiands already knew much of what they were being told, and that the ritual itself was more about effecting "changes in being" than about teaching them specific lessons. Jean LaFontaine's (1978) description of Gisu female initiation likewise emphasized the self-validating effects of ritual. She has shown that the ritual process was itself more important than the information: "What is significant [about initiation]," LaFontaine writes, "is not *what* the secret is, but that there *are* secrets" (p. 424).[1]

I too had heard some people talk about initiation as a ritual process. Some people's comments suggested that initiation did not so much teach novel facts as buttress social precepts, often by challenging initiands with allegoric riddles, figurative exploits, and cryptic questions. For instance, when Lameck asked one man "What did you learn during initiation?" the man said that initiation was not like schooling; there had been no specific lessons, and initiands had simply danced the entire time. And yet, here and in other conversations, people described initiation as a fixed body of information. Some said that they had "read schoolbooks" during the ritual; that they had taken, and for the most part passed, their "tests;" and some people even said that they had gone through "graduation ceremonies" and collected "diplomas."

Why? I wondered. Why were some people talking about ritual initiation much the way they were talking about schooling? Why were they calling their ritual instructors "schoolteachers" (*walimu*—the Kiswahili word for teachers) and their dances and songs "school lessons" (*mafundisho*—the Kiswahili word for school instructions)? I could not imagine, based on some older ethnographies, that "education" and "learning," as a package together, were seen as discrete processes and practices in this area prior to European rescriptings. And I could not believe that some of these oldest people would have called their initiation rituals "graduation ceremonies." Graduation ceremonies had only recently been popularized. Primary school graduates, and now secondary, too, had ceremonies in their honor, but during the time when older people had been initiated, graduation ceremonies would have been less familiar events.

There were reasons, of course, and I could think of two, one of which had to do with the kind of questions I was asking. By introducing myself as an anthropologist studying schooling, people returned to me some of the categories I extended.[2] I asked them first about levels of schooling; they then continued by talking about teachers, lessons, and instruction, even when the conversation had shifted from schools to other subjects. But there were also other factors, I surmised, judging from what people said, independent of my questions. In the course of observing and overhearing everyday interactions, I noticed that schooling and initiation were regularly contrasted; people often spoke about the two in the same breath.

In the following section of this chapter, I examine the ways people compare and contrast schooling and initiation. Doing so requires first demonstrating how objectifications of schooling and initiation have come to enter the level of discourse through some people's readings of colonial ethnographies. I then discuss how colonial visions are incorporated into arguments about city sisters. In the last three sections, I describe three school-educated women and examine their family situations. The point of the final vignettes is to illustrate how some people attribute new marriage preferences to new school opportunities.

THE LEGACY OF COLONIAL ETHNOGRAPHIES IN CONTEMPORARY FORMULATIONS OF "EDUCATION"

A bit of digging reveals a simple answer to my question: why do people sometimes talk about initiation as a form of schooling? Integral to a particular genre of colonial ethnographies are comparisons between schooling and "African tradition" (see S. F. Moore 1996a). Missionary and ethnographer Bruno Gutmann, for instance, played a prominent role in identifying and reconstructing initiation as a form of schooling. A university-trained anthropologist, Gutmann sought to modify—or as he put it, to "preserve"—Chagga culture by integrating it into the organization and structure of colonial schools. Gutmann correctly anticipated and played a major role in developing schools as transformational institutions. While setting up a new mission station in 1906 in Lower Machame, he reflected on the value of schooling for retaining the "natural, organic" qualities of African life. These thoughts, later articulated in an essay on the problems of social organization in Africa, reveal how Gutmann combined missionary philosophy with his vision of African pedagogy. "The only African school deserving of its name," Gutmann wrote,

> would be one in which the ideal would be to try to instruct the pupils in the structure of the folk-group down to its foundation and teach them to appreciate its value, recognizing its importance in two ways: by allowing the *structural connexions of the pupils them-selves to continue to exist in the school*, and basing the activity of the school world on these; and by gathering *the community, represented by the group-leaders, round the school as a co-directing council*, thus bringing the school more and more into organic connexion with the people as a whole. (1928:514; abridged translation of original; emphasis added)

Gutmann studied Chagga rites of passage, including marriage and ritual initiation, and he catalogued his findings in a three-volume series entitled *Tribal Teachings of the Chagga*. Gutmann's scholarship has been appropri-ately described as "a major work" in the field of ethnology (Felix Krueger, in Gutmann 1932), yet less often acknowledged is the indirect role he played in the reification and reconstruction of Chagga tradition. *Tribal Teachings of the Chagga* provided a source book for colonial missionaries; European educators incorporated its findings into the African system of formal education.

Another anthropologist, O. F. Raum, went even further in linking initia-tion with colonial schooling. Raum's ideal, like Bruno Gutmann's, was to provide a blueprint for colonial educators. Raum was the son of a Lutheran missionary who wrote a doctoral dissertation entitled *Chaga Childhood*. The work, building on Gutmann's, was a picture of what children "learned" in a pristine situation—before Europeans arrived and began to change things. Like Gutmann, Raum was interested in understanding the basic dynamics and principles of a social system, such that the work he produced provides a neat (if not overdetermined) packaging of what he thought amounted to "Chagga lessons."

Raum devoted a substantial part of his book to rituals of puberty and the formal instruction that accompanied them (1940:285–380). Although he did not have as specific a vision as Gutmann about an African Christian community, he did, like Gutmann, advocate that colonial educators base educational policy on "Africans' traditions."

> All those who are responsible for education in Africa, whether missionaries or government officials, should study the native educational system in its widest sense in order to assess what place there is in that system for the "alien" contribution of European schools. (Raum 1940:vii)

Embracing the challenge, the headmaster of a colonial government school, A.T. Lacey, wrote this about the inclusion of "tradition" in schooling:

> The internal organization of the school has been based on the principles of tribal rule and authority. Outside the classroom this holds good in every activity of the day's round.
>
> The boys are divided under [four] "tribes" which are more strictly geographical or administrative districts. . . . This division does not coincide exactly with the actual tribal divisions but it provides an extremely workable basis, and in the majority of cases a boy finds himself amongst boys of his real tribe. . . . (U. K. Public Records Office 1925:51, cited in Kerner 1988:81–82)

Colonial ethnographies that compared initiation and schooling had a profound effect on African education. Some Chagga even regarded them as repositories for a vanishing tradition. Two conversations I had in the course of conducting field research illustrate this point. One conversation was with a very old woman, Bibi Eshimuni, who said that Bruno Gutmann had taught and baptized her. Her words, and the comments of a former colonial civil servant, whom I will introduce in a moment, helped me see more clearly how colonial visions have been partly incorporated into popular discourse.

Bibi Eshimuni was one of the oldest people I met; she was the great-grandmother of the Mbasa children, whom I introduced in Chapter 1. Very frail, she could barely whisper into my tape recorder. One day, in the presence of one of her great-granddaughters, Bibi Eshimuni spoke about the "lessons I had learned as a young child":

> First of all, all the girls were getting circumcised and initiated in those days. Not just a couple of girls in the village like today. You had

to go through it so you would know how to open yourself up [*kuji-fungua*, in Kiswahili, "to give birth"]. There were a lot of special things to learn, like how to take care of your husband and parents-in-law. How to cook good food. How to get pregnant. How to go through labor. These weren't easy things to do because you had to do them in a special way. The lessons were written on the *mregho* [Kimachame]—that was the name of our schoolbook. . . .

When we were finished we all passed out of our school and went through a graduation ceremony in the market. The girls all danced and crossed over a banana bast before they went running through the market. From then on, we were graduates. We could go on and get married. . . .

There were a lot of things initiation told us, everything about sexual life, domestic life, and the type of food to eat, the type of relationship to have with all of the people surrounding you, even neighbors.

Bibi Eshimuni salted her picture heavily with school images of books, students, and graduation ceremonies, perhaps emphasizing for her great-granddaughter the ways in which initiation paralleled today's schooling. She also mentioned that Bruno Gutmann had written a book about Chagga initiation, and that although she had never read the book, she *had* read the Bible that Gutmann had given her.

The connections Bibi Eshimuni made between schooling and initiation were socially pervasive.

Mr. Ngowi, for instance, described initiation as a "little classroom." The excerpt below, from lengthy interview during which Mr. Ngowi spoke nearly uninterrupted, illustrates how initiation is objectified as "information people needed to know."

After the teachers sing, the initiands listen, and then they reply and then listen some more. Sometimes initiands do not understand the words teachers use, and so the teachers try to interpret it for the students. "What I have said is this," the teacher says, and tells the students until they have understood. Because students have to reply that they have understood. So, and the students sit there listening.

Then they, the students, try to interpret to their teacher what the song he has sung means. But the initiands had to recite. Why, I don't know. They couldn't just paraphrase the lesson or explain it in an offhand way. The student had to repeat exactly what the teacher said. It's very laborious. It's torturous, very very laborious. Because you had to memorize. Like a little classroom. And that means one had to memorize all these things. It was *information that people absolutely needed to know.* . . .

When you're initiated and getting prepared for marriage it means you're becoming an adult, and it means *you have to know all our customs and traditions* to enable you to manage a home. You see, within our society, you have to know things to the grass root. *Our customary laws* about domestic life, family relations, clan relations. You have to know them before you are married to qualify. You have to be coached on how to, you know, manage life with your wife and things like that.[3] [emphasis added]

Mr. Ngowi had worked as a cultural adviser in the British colonial system. As a colonial employee, it had been his job to broker what the British, who employed him, saw as two different cultures: the African and the European. Mr. Ngowi's position epitomized the idea of British Indirect Rule: that traditional practices could be codified as "customary laws" and that these laws could provide the basis for European administration (cf. S. F. Moore 1986). It also attests to the extent to which early ethnographers had succeeded in matching schooling with initiation, for Mr. Ngowi, as this next excerpt suggests, derived much of his own knowledge about culture from Raum and Gutmann.

These days we depend upon the books now written about African marriages. That now becomes our stick [i.e., our *mregho*]. . . . In addition to Gutmann's books, I have another by Raum, a huge book, *Chaga Childhood*. It has got this.

He referred to a picture of a *mregho* stick that Raum reproduced in his ethnography (Illustration 6). Earlier, he had surmised that *mregho* carvings "sometimes resemble Greek writing. . . . If you look at Hebrew writing, even Russian writing, some of the alphabets are almost like this. This thing, if it were properly written, then we would have a Koran or Bible. Yes, we can equate it to a Koran or Bible."

The *mregho* stick, which Bibi Eshimuni had also identified as initiands' "schoolbook," was a four-foot wooden pole etched with patterns that corresponded to what Raum translates as initiation "teachings" (*ngyifundo* in

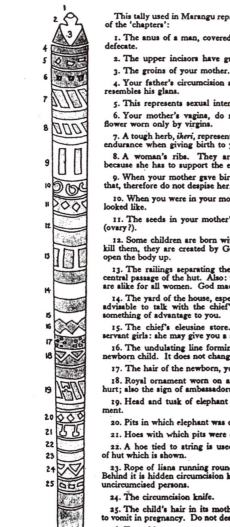

This tally used in Marangu represents in combination several of the 'chapters':

1. The anus of a man, covered over with skin: he does not defecate.

2. The upper incisors have grown first, kill such a child.

3. The groins of your mother.

4. Your father's circumcision scar; from this downwards it resembles his glans.

5. This represents sexual intercourse.

6. Your mother's vagina, do not look at it. Also a red flower worn only by virgins.

7. A tough herb, *ikeri*, represents virginity and your mother's endurance when giving birth to you: never despise her.

8. A woman's ribs. They are more bent than a man's because she has to support the embryo. Do not despise her.

9. When your mother gave birth to you she split open like that, therefore do not despise her.

10. When you were in your mother's womb this is what you looked like.

11. The seeds in your mother's body look like these spots (ovary?).

12. Some children are born without lower orifices. Do not kill them, they are created by God. Call a medicine-man to open the body up.

13. The railings separating the animal's quarters from the central passage of the hut. Also: the female sex organs. They are alike for all women. God made them.

14. The yard of the house, especially the chief's court. It is advisable to talk with the chief's watchman, he may know something of advantage to you.

15. The chief's eleusine store. Look out for one of his servant girls: she may give you a sign to warn you of dangers.

16. The undulating line forming the edge of the hair of a newborn child. It does not change, it runs in the family.

17. The hair of the newborn, you were born with it.

18. Royal ornament worn on arm. Its bearer is not to be hurt; also the sign of ambassadors.

19. Head and tusk of elephant used in making royal ornament.

20. Pits in which elephant was caught.

21. Hoes with which pits were dug.

22. A hoe tied to string is used in describing circular site of hut which is shown.

23. Rope of liana running round the inside of wall of hut. Behind it is hidden circumcision knife lest it be discovered by uncircumcised persons.

24. The circumcision knife.

25. The child's hair in its mother's womb, causing mother to vomit in pregnancy. Do not despise her.

26. Top of hut.

6. A *mregho* (tally) stick as it appears in Raum's ethnography, *Chaga Childhood* (Raum 1940:327).

Kimachame; on *mregho*, see also Kerner 1995). According to Raum, *mregho* inscriptions conveyed a moral code. Boys and girls each had their own version of *mregho* corresponding to different gender roles and reproduction.

Made of *mringonu* wood (botanical name *alangium chinense;* Steele 1966:185), it had come from a tree that Mr. Ngowi said provided medicinal powers. One of the functions of the stick, Mr. Ngowi and Bibi Eshimuni both conveyed, had been to help women through childbirth and to teach men how to build new homes. The reason it was sometimes called a "firebrand," Mr. Ngowi said, was because male sticks were used to light new fires.

It struck me as intriguing that Mr. Ngowi's and Bibi Eshimuni's accounts should both have made reference to colonial ethnographies (compare with Dundas 1924:207–227; Gutmann 1935c; Raum 1940:285–380). However, in light of Raum's and Gutmann's interest in teaching "culture" through colonial education, it is not surprising that a register of functionality should today pervade some older people's explanations. Bibi Eshimuni and Mr. Ngowi had both attended school during colonial times—Bibi Eshimuni only off and on, Mr. Ngowi through Standard VIII.[4] It is impossible to say how Raum's and Gutmann's works were specifically incorporated into schooling, or how extensive and influential they have been in reestablishing initiation as "tradition" today. However, the connection Bibi Eshimuni makes between schooling and initiation, and that Mr. Ngowi makes between his own and Raum's analyses, indicates a degree of translation. What schooling "has," initiation "lacks" (a "scientific approach to the study of reading and writing," Mr. Ngowi said). Vice versa, too: what initiation had, schooling lacked—in Bibi Eshimuni's words, "respect for elders and tradition."

And so it would seem that a reified portrayal of tradition enters conventional discourse through historical sources and processes. Indeed, as I have illustrated briefly in this section on initiation and schooling, process and history are key to understanding how schooling is viewed today (see again S. F. Moore 1996a). To understand why people contrast big sisters with stay-at-home mothers, or schooling with initiation, we need to know that "tradition" has been framed, historically, as something pedagogic.

Having established, then, that recollections of traditional initiation are themselves historically constructed, often through the objectifying qualities of colonial ethnographies and schooling, I would like to return to the larger theme I am developing on gender and generational transformations. I would like to continue by discussing the differences between *madada wa mjini* (city sisters) and *mama wa nyumbani* (stay-at-home mothers), particularly as they emerge through the words and lives of three young women who had gone to school.

ESHIMUNI'S SUCCESS: AN EXAMPLE OF SOCIAL AUTONOMY WITHIN LIMITS

To borrow Marjorie Mbilinyi's phrase (1972), city sisters might be thought of as "new Tanzanian women." Many are young, still in their childbearing years and either newly married or single. Many prefer to traffic in the terms of *ya kisasa* (Kiswahili)—literally "of right now"—rather than the terms of *kibushi*—"of the bush." Mbilinyi uses the phrase "new Tanzanian women" to refer to an emerging cadre of female wage earners in the early 1970s, when an expanding cash economy brought more women into the ranks of paid employment. These women organized and lobbied for political representation and equal rights. Today, "new Tanzanian women" question patrilineal authority and scrutinize women's place within the national political economy. Young, cosmopolitan women make independent decisions, earn incomes of their own, disregard male elders and brothers, and look increasingly to magazines and international personalities for advice and ideas.

City sisters—a category that connotes many ideals and does not necessarily describe any one Tanzanian woman—balk at the demands of extended kin and school authorities. They instead pursue lifestyles that education and independent income can afford. Many, for instance, aspire to build their own houses and to have children without going through marriage processes. Instead of obtaining land from their husbands' fathers, some strive to acquire land independently. And instead of passing their husbands' wealth to their male sons, some plan to distribute their own wealth to each of their children, male and female. Although young women who hold such a view appear not to be in the majority,[5] the fact that some female school students and graduates use education to argue for new family models suggests they also see the effects of schooling as extending to many aspects of social life. By way of illustrating how some young women connect their own social autonomy with state-sponsored education, I would like to examine the visions and life courses of three young women who describe themselves as "city sisters."

Consider, for instance, Eshimuni's situation, which illustrates how school-educated women sometimes use the cultural logic of schooling to argue *against* rituals of circumcision and initiation and *for* new family models. Eshimuni once made the comment that "I don't need any man to buy dresses for me. Education is my husband!" Four of us sat eating dinner one day, talking about marriage and schooling and Eshimuni's situation. "Education is my husband," she repeated, in response to a Chagga man's suggestion that she get married soon, "before it is too late." "You are almost too old to have children!" protested this man, who himself was recently married at the age of 35. But Eshimuni, a 27-year-old university graduate and a full-time college teacher, assured him that she would never marry yet she would (if she could) have children.

During our dinner conversation, Eshimuni went on to say that she did not value cattle, banana beer (*mbege*), or the banana grove—some of the salient cultural signs of Chagga identity that constitute the media of marriage exchange. She did not want any hypothetical husband to give her the comforts of a "modern" life—commodities like a car, a cassette player, a TV, a VCR. Instead, she wanted to earn these material luxuries by herself, by buying them with money she earned as a college teacher. Indeed, she noted that "educated men don't like gatekeepers these days; they don't like women who sit around at home, waiting for them to bring home nice things." What they preferred, she said, were self-reliant women who "went out, earned money, and bought these things themselves." To Eshimuni, this translated into the possibility that women, in some cases (like one she envisioned for herself), did not even have to marry: education could be their husbands. If men wanted women to be self-reliant, she reasoned, why shouldn't women take this possibility all the way? Why shouldn't they do entirely without men and let education "be" their husbands?

At first glance, this piece of conversation appears to touch upon cross-cultural feminist themes. Eshimuni's remark might have been made (albeit slightly differently) by a woman in the United States, or in Sweden, Indonesia, Japan, or England, concerned about starting, managing, and maintaining a professional career. Eshimuni herself was feeling the tension between retaining her autonomy and conforming to social expectations. On the one hand she loudly voiced the sentiment that with schooling, she did not need to have a husband, yet on the other she worried that she would go on in life without ever having a child to be her heir. She wanted her brothers to marry, sure enough, though she did not think their marriage needed to depend on hers.[6] "What's the point of that?" Eshimuni asked at the dinner. "My brothers should do what they want without me, just like I should go on in my life without them."

But her resoundingly feminist theme had cultural variation. I came to view Eshimuni's concern for an heir as an innovation. It played upon a prominent patrilineal social concept: that inheritance should ideally be reckoned through the male line (see Chapter 2). Sometimes Eshimuni, like other school-educated women, spoke passionately about the need to have male heirs—*mrisi* in Kimachame; *mrithi* in Kiswahili—but unlike her forebears, she tended to speak of her future children as *nonpatrilineal* heirs; that is, as children of a maternal and not paternal line. When Eshimuni said she wanted an heir, she sometimes spoke as though this child would be solely hers—not placed within the descending ranks of the child's father's patriline. Yet at other times she spoke of her offspring as a child descended through its own father's lineage. For despite her bold statement that "education is my husband," Eshimuni also recognized that it was important to maintain some form of patrilineal inheritance; such after all was the way she reckoned her own kin connections, when she was not speaking of herself in terms of education.

As it happened, Eshimuni married a man named George Makia about one year after this conversation. George was the son of a village neighbor; he had been studying engineering in India. George returned after nearly eight years' absence to look for work in Tanzania (he found it pretty quickly with a British multinational company in East Africa). Four months later, Eshimuni and he were married—a church wedding with beer prestations preceding the ceremony. Teachers at the all-girls school near where I lived who knew both George and Eshimuni said that they were perfectly matched. Eshimuni's female friends said that, in terms of status, George could reasonably "handle" Eshimuni. They said that even though Eshimuni was highly educated (she had attended primary and secondary schools), George was even *more* highly trained; his Ph.D. in engineering located him in a socially and economically more privileged position. And even though Eshimuni had already moved out of her parents' house and was now teaching full-time at a teacher preparatory college, George was poised to work in an urban center and to travel internationally. As such, he would be able to provide for Eshimuni in ways that she could not equally reciprocate.

On Mount Kilimanjaro, as elsewhere in sub-Saharan Africa (see, for examples, Bledsoe 1990; Hollos 1998; Oppong 1981), marriage strategies reveal that a rigorous gender ideology and a hierarchy of schooling are conceptually intertwined. People often maintain that marriage partners must match one another in terms of education. By this, they typically mean that grooms' school levels should equal or exceed that of brides. The number of years spent in school is sometimes interpreted to represent the kind of husband or wife a person may turn out to be. A highly educated woman may become, after marriage, socially dominant to her uneducated husband, and a more highly educated man may desire in a wife a less well-educated woman whom he can command. Men and women sometimes calculate before marriage the degree to which their future partner's schooling will translate into their own autonomy. If a man were to marry a more highly educated woman than he, he might expect that she would become hard to control. If a woman were to marry a man more highly educated than she, she might anticipate that she'd remain his subordinate.

The matrix of reasoning that intertwines gender and schooling embeds moral judgments about different kinds of social persons. Highly educated women, although independent, are sometimes judged as being immoral or dangerous. Eshimuni herself sometimes reasoned this way, as when she determined that city sisters were sometimes threatening.

> City sisters turn into bar maids. They run these guest houses and carry guns in their dresses. [She laughed, knowing this was an exaggeration.] City sisters have a lot of fun, but where do they eventually go? Ping, ping [she makes the sound of bullets, more laughter]. *Chota maji, chota maji.* ["Carry water, carry water," she says in Kiswahili, referring to the menial and unending task of hauling water that we'd observed a female guest house owner doing that very morning.] City sisters don't really live well. Not even these city sisters who run their own businesses. Being a big city sister is fun, but it's dangerous.

In this and other conversations—as when Eshimuni noted that city sisters are involved in relationships with men she called sugar daddies[7]— Eshimuni seemed to be arguing that social independence was not all it was made out to be, at least not for women. In order to have some social security, she said, women had to marry. Although marriage still did not necessarily mean that they had to give in entirely on their autonomy, it meant some minimal commitment to working within the patrilineal system that reckoned descent through the male line. Eshimuni pointed to a prominent woman Member of Parliament (MP), who, although married, still had great economic and social independence. The MP, wife of a college professor, had had children but was now living independently in Dar es Salaam. Eshimuni put it this way:

> Mama Zubeda [a pseudonym] is a big MP. People say she couldn't become an MP until she married and became a *mama*. She had to take care of that first. She had to have kids, so she just did.

It's important to note that Eshimuni worked within a patrilineal framework of marriage and inheritance to argue an innovation:

> George is a good person to marry because he'll be away most of the time. I'll get to know my sisters- and brothers-in-law well and they can help take care of my little children. That's the way it works, you know; they'll have to do that. They'll be the caretakers of my husband's kids. Then I'll have my freedom.

In this brief statement, Eshimuni called up a normative ideal that patrilineal kin and affines are responsible for the social welfare of husbands' children. With a husband, she could call upon these relatives, she reasoned; without one, she'd have to ask her mother or her brothers' wives. The latter were not likely to care for her children with the same quality and concern that they'd care for their own. For as an unmarried woman, Eshimuni could be seen as an affront to the system these conventionally married sisters-in-law perpetuated. *They* would be working to reproduce the normative patrilineal family, *she* to take advantage of its technicalities in order to get ahead herself.

Within this patrilineal framework, schooling was a way to challenge male-privileged gender hierarchy. Eshimuni posited that the scenario she was imagining would be possible because she was educated. In other words, Eshimuni anticipated that she would be distinguised from her sisters- and brothers-in-law because, unlike them, she had attended secondary school and was herself a college teacher. Typically, a newly incorporated female affine has lower status than lineage men and women or than senior women who have already "married in." However, Eshimuni was, in effect, calculating that her school-educated status would place her ahead of other family members and that, because of her schooling, she would be able to command a disproportionate share of the family's resources. This social projection reflects a careful calculation of gender against education: it illustrates a fascinating cultural process by which people sometimes translate the value of schooling into social reproduction.

Several months on the heels of Eshimuni's and George's wedding, Eshimuni bore a son, then moved to Dar es Salaam with George and their child. Stellah Mbasa, who visited Eshimuni approximately two years later, described Eshimuni as a city sister. "She looks terrific and has her hair all curled. She really looks like something out of a fashion magazine," Stellah commented. Stellah's depiction of Eshimuni as a city sister struck me as being rather ironic, for Eshimuni had recently declared she was moving *beyond* this rank as a married woman. And yet to Stellah Mbasa, Eshimuni was the personification of a cosmopolitan woman. Stellah reported that Eshimuni effectively lived alone with her child most of the year—George, now gainfully employed, traveled and lived much of the time in Botswana. Eshimuni was teaching English and had recently bought herself a cow and car. Her child was being cared by a "housegirl"—the daughter of one of George's unmarried sisters—and was attending preschool part of each week, even learning English at this early stage. Eshimuni continued to travel from Dar es Salaam to Machame as she pleased, and in 1999, the last I heard from her, she was running a small tourist kiosk that traded with British and American companies.

As I mentioned at the beginning of this section, "city sister" connotes many ideals and does not necessarily describe any one Tanzanian woman. City sisters and house mothers, taken as character types, represent two cultural loci in the picture of possible education outcomes. Like "modernity" and "tradition," they are the symbolic opposite of one another and define one another mutually—each in terms of what the other is *not*. City sisters have advanced levels of schooling. They've studied home economics and know about the "proper ways" to make a salad and serve tea. They know how to sew a dress and bottle-feed a child—at least in theory. But they do not know how to thatch a roof or curse with a cooking pot, nor can they properly "handle a firebrand" to "stoke the ashes"—at least not according to older, circumcised women, who view these qualities as essential. For city sisters have not been initiated, nor have they been taught the secrets of *mbyaa tya waniini*—of female initiation.

Certainly Eshimuni derived some of her standing from being George

Makia's wife, though she was hardly the house mother that she said her own mother was. In many ways, Eshimuni was autonomous, and indeed she had gained some social independence by getting married. Her earlier words, that "education is my husband," returned to describe her married situation rather fittingly. When I reminded Eshimuni just days after her church wedding ceremony that I had once heard her argue that she'd never marry—that she'd never need to because, as she had once put it, "education is my husband"—Eshimuni came back with a discerning reply. "But education *is* my husband. Don't you see? My schooling made it possible for me to marry George, and now I don't need him anymore." Her self-assessment echoed what her friends had said about the calculus of marriage. Eshimuni's schooling demanded that she marry an even more highly educated person, and, once married, the highly educated person, by the nature of his work, would provide her with social autonomy. Once the church wedding was closed and cleaned up, however, the calculus about social standing and schooling went through another formulation. The operative principle was no longer that George was highly educated enough to be able to provide for Eshimuni adequately, nor conversely, that Eshimuni was less well schooled than George and therefore suitable as his partner. Now what was at issue were the ways social differentials associated with schooling could be played out against lineage gender hierarchies. Eshimuni could go on her way rather independently, playing her educated status off against less well educated in-laws; and George, now with wife and a son, could, himself, travel and work internationally.

EMI SHOO: AN EXAMPLE OF FALLING SHORT OF AN IDEAL

Emi's story reflects another way in which gender hierarchies intertwine with schooling and female autonomy. As a recent Form 4 graduate, Emi looked up to people like Eshimuni for a model she hoped to achieve. When I first met Emi in 1992, she was working as a receptionist in a maize-grinding mill where I received weekly phone calls from my family in the United States. Emi announced at our first meeting that she wanted me to teach her English on weekends. She was interested in learning colloquial English and in chatting informally, as was made apparent when she occasionally intercepted and answered my long-distance phone calls. By her pronunciation, "Emi" and "Amy" were phonetically the same, and one day, when she

7. A secondary school graduate employed full time as an office worker. The woman has one child and lives with her parents. Like Emi, she said she aspired to build a house with her earnings and to remain unwed.

answered the phone with a "Hi! This is Amy," she declared that she could take the call on my behalf. That assertion, which struck us both as funny, cemented a relationship that lasted the next several months.

Compared to Eshimuni's family, Emi's was not economically well off yet neither were they poor, as was Neema's family, whom I'll introduce in a moment. They owned two cows and had recently upgraded their house by putting in cement floors and replacing the banana thatch roof with tin. Emi's father was a farmer and part-time carpenter; her mother described herself as a *mama wa nyumbani*. Emi had grown up in a modest four-room house on a one-acre plot. Her parents had encouraged her to attend primary and secondary school, and indeed, they had great expectations for both their sons and daughter. I very soon learned that Emi herself aspired to become a primary school teacher. She said that she not only loved teaching children but also wanted to teach them the "benefits of English."

With clarity and vision, Emi outlined her plans: to go back to school, become a teacher, and then live and work in an urban center. "If I stay in the village, I'll get married very young," she said. "I'll become another *mama wa nyumbani*. That's what my mother is and my grandmother and all of these other grandmothers in the village. I don't want that." Instead, she wanted to follow some of her former classmates out of the village and into urban centers: "Dorrine is in Arusha these days, Joicie is in Nairobi, and Susan in Dar es Salaam," she said of former classmates. "There's nothing in the village for me to do anymore. I don't even have any friends there to talk with."

Emi's ideals about English and mobility evidence widely held views about social advancement. English was one of the most prominent signs of a person's level of education: whereas Kiswahili was the official national language and the language of instruction of the majority of students in primary schools, English was used in secondary institutions and universities. English was the language of autonomy and independence, of international travel and cosmopolitanism. Kiswahili, in contrast, was seen as the language of the nation and the language that kept people in the backwaters of tradition.

Briefly conveyed, Emi said that schooling had created in her a "desire" *(hamu)* for independence, yet the exact parameters of what she wanted to get out of schooling, she implied, had never been fully delineated for her by teachers. Emi wanted to have children, she said, but not necessarily to get married. Two of her former classmates were building houses in Boma Ng'ombe, a rapidly expanding district administrative community located at the southwest base of Mount Kilimanjaro. According to Emi, these women were planning to raise children on their own, without a father. "A lot of my friends want to have a house and one or two children, but not necessarily a husband. That's what I want too," she said, maintaining that the benefits of raising children without marrying would outweigh the costs of having a husband.

When I asked what was the appeal of becoming so independent, Emi explained in terms of schooling and marriage. She maintained that educated women could avoid "men [who] beat wives," and they could raise *mrithi* (heirs) of their own.

> EMI: I'm educated. I can't go back to the village and take up the hoe again [i.e, go back to the village to farm]. I want to find a man who will give me some money, maybe father a child, but I don't want him to marry me.
>
> AMY: Why not?
>
> EMI: Married men beat their wives. They just come and hit you then take your money. Then what do you have?

Wife-beating was a common reason many young women gave for postponing—or even avoiding—marriage.[8] Even Lameck admitted that some husbands beat wives and demanded that their wives turn over income earned independently. Although I did not hear or see direct evidence of this, the fact that it was invoked as a real possibility—even that it was seen as being within the conventionally defined rights of husbands over wives—was deeply disturbing to Emi, as well as to me. Primary school children whom I once observed playing in their yard mimicked the social roles they associated with men and women: the child playing the father verbally and physically assaulted his wife, the child playing the wife deferred to male authority. And secondary school students at the all-girls school near where I lived put on a skit that depicted similar roles: the plot revolved around a drunken husband who stole money that his wife was saving for their daughters' schooling.

Emi said that if she avoided marriage, she'd have more control over the money she earned on her own. She'd be able to save money for her children's school fees without ever worrying that her husband would commandeer her savings, and she'd be able to put a little bit aside over time in order to keep adding on to and improving the house. Emi envisioned that she'd even be able to travel to and from Dar es Salaam and Moshi on her own, without the verbal permission of a husband who, she said, "would be jealous if I traveled more than he did."

At times, Emi anticipated that such independence would present some hidden problems, such as: What would she do when her children were small? How would she support them *and* earn an independent income? Where would the social support come for her children, she wondered. From her own kin? From the absent father's?

But more often she characterized such independence in terms of self-reliance. Whereas the phrase "education for self-reliance" had been used in earlier national policies to signal the government's intent that secondary schooling should produce self-sufficient school graduates (cf. Nyerere 1967), Emi used the idea to mean that she would be independent of men and husbands. Like Eshimuni, she calculated that her schooling could be converted into a special kind of social capital: she hoped that her schooling would enable her to start a lineage of her own.

Several secondary school girls and recent graduates shared Emi's general vision about never marrying and yet still having children, though most of them said they would do this *after* they had completed secondary school. Neema Mushi, whom I describe below, entertained this possibility; and in my return visit in 1996, I noticed many more were articulating this as desired reality.

It is important to note, however, that this ideal of autonomy is not something easily—or even eventually—achieved. There are in fact many reasons for avoiding it, not least the possibility of being stranded with house and child and no source of steady income. In the event of absent father/husband, the plan can rapidly backfire, and the desire to avoid or postpone marriage is nowhere near a universal ideal. At Mkufi Secondary School (and in others for that matter), many schoolgirls spoke openly about future marriage. More often than not, schoolgirls admitted that, realistically, they would return home and "take up the hoe." In one group discussion I had with seven Form 4 girls, six said that they fully expected to—although they hoped that they would not—get married soon after graduation, have children, and continue to live in a rural area. Most parents whom I interviewed spoke about marriage as a part of their daughters' futures. Although many also portrayed themselves as a group as being more open than parents in other regions of the country, the majority of parents nonetheless put marriage ahead of employment for their daughters (cf. Cooksey, Malekela, and Lugalla 1993).

Gender ideologies and practices are not always easily overturned by money or formal schooling. In the matter of marriage, as with so many other decisions, it's hard to know how students and parents choose in the end among the options they perceive. When I asked Sabatina, an assistant Lutheran pastor in the area, how widespread she thought the ideal of avoiding marriage was among young educated women, she confirmed my suspicion by noting that there was no way to know definitively. Not only did people hold different views—and sometimes contradictory views concurrently—they also held shifting and ambiguous conceptualizations of marriage (see Chapter 3). Yet Sabatina noted that, "more so these days than when I was in school," older schoolgirls and recent female graduates subscribed to the idea of social autonomy. She described a group of students in her parish and said that a handful of the girls wanted to break from fathers and husbands. In Sabatina's words, these women were "young feminists" who "wanted what every woman would naturally want: independence." But Sabatina also noted, as though reminding herself that the extreme independence women sometimes enjoyed was fragile, that women who were seen as being "too independent" were sometimes labeled—wrongly so, in her view—as prostitutes.[9] One businesswoman she knew in the Moshi market had recently used legal means to reclaim custody of her son, but because this businesswoman was not officially married, her son was not legally hers. Sabatina described the situation as "unfortunate," for in the process the woman had been accused of selling sex and of sexually entrapping her son's genitor. Emi's situation was, so far, less complicated. Emi simply wanted to save some money, go back to school, get a teaching job, then build a house and have a child. At least that was the most common plan of several competing ones that Emi presented to me.

Toward the end of my stay, I visited the maize mill and learned that Emi was no longer working there. She had become pregnant and was living with her parents, back in rural Machame. I was surprised, not only because I never expected her to get pregnant before going back to school, but because she had returned to her parents instead of breaking away. I thought: Why doesn't Emi put her vision into effect, or at least one variation of it? Why doesn't she ask the man who impregnated her to partly support her financially? Or, why doesn't she marry him, claim child support, then go on living more or less independently?

Perhaps I should not have even asked these questions or been so surprised that Emi had moved back home. More than one anthropologist—more than one "stranger in a foreign land"—has misjudged human desires and motivation. Emi's situation was common enough. Indeed, I had only recently learned that a secondary school student at Mkufi Secondary School was dropping out of school because she was pregnant, and pregnant schoolgirls were not allowed to continue at school. Yet I was nonetheless surprised, largely because I had thought Emi would surely go ahead with her plans. Little did I know that Emi thought she was in fact beginning them; she later told me that at the time she thought she would still eventually get a teaching certificate and live and work in Moshi. For the moment, however, it looked quite the opposite; indeed, there was no way of knowing how the situation would turn out. The majority of others I saw in Emi's position—that is, those who wanted more schooling and yet found themselves pregnant—usually called off schooling and went home. Although the law technically allowed pregnant and parenting students to continue, most secondary school teachers disapproved, and students in these situations usually quit.

At the time, Emi's female peers who knew about Emi's situation didn't think she was being unreasonable in deciding to move back home. Quite the opposite—it was what many of her close friends said she *had* to do. "Where's she going to go?" they asked rhetorically. "The child's father's not going to marry Emi, and Emi can't live on her own right now." Yet just weeks before I had heard Emi herself argue that:

> Education for self-reliance means that everyone has to carry their own load (*kila mtu abebe mizigo yake*).[10] If I work hard and save my

money, and put myself through nursing school, I can carry my own load. I can get out of my parents' house and maybe build my own. I can become self-reliant.

Perhaps her words were more ideal than a plan. Perhaps I got too caught up in her vision. But on the face of it, Emi's ideal here was one variation on the argument the state promoted in official policy: one reading of state discourse on education was that the goal of schooling was to create self-reliant citizens, and self-reliance meant social and economic autonomy. By 1996, when I returned for follow-up work, I saw that Emi was neither living independent of her parents nor continuing with further schooling. Although she still held the ideal of building a house, she did not now think it realistic. Nor did she, in 1996, still have plans to become a certified teacher.

For at least thirty years, official educational policies have been crafted on the belief that a populace schooled in industrial and technical training—as well as in the "scientific" techniques of modern farming—could lead the region into the twenty-first century and contribute to overall national development. Such a philosophy has been tempered in recent years with a strong dose of advice from external funding agencies—most notably the International Monetary Fund (IMF) and World Bank (see Samoff 1993; Stein 1992; Tripp 1997; World Bank 1988, 1991)—and emphasis on using education for economic development is not limited to Tanzania. It is also practiced in Latin America and other African countries—indeed, the world over (see Carnoy and Samoff 1990; Knight and Sabot 1990; Levinson, forthcoming; Luykx 1999; Psacharopoulos and Loxley 1985).

What is interesting about Tanzania, however, is that official policy has been reworked to many ends. Not only has the national government been revising the meaning of "self-reliance" (the emphasis now is on market forces rather than socialism to move the nation toward economic development); so, too, have *individuals* toyed with the meaning of self-reliance. The "self" in question no longer refers to national advancement but to individual gain. Consider, for instance, how Emi's main ideal—to gain greater independence—subtly transformed the language of self-reliance. Emi cast her ideas in terms of greater autonomy and spoke about using education for economic development (*maendeleo*). While Emi was sometimes critical of the turn government was then taking toward privatization, she drew upon the repertoire of images so prominent in official rhetoric. In particular, she played upon the ambiguity of "the self" in education. At times, Emi reasoned that the "self" referred not to the collectivity of the state or to the well-being of fellow citizens, but to the self-interests of the atomistic subject and the needs of individual students—in her case, to her*self*. Emi her*self* wanted to build a house, have a child, whom she could call her *mrithi* (heir), then continue to work, without any support from her child's genitor. I ultimately learned that Emi's interpretation of the "self" in self-reliance, like many people's, was multilayered, ambiguous, and often shifting. There was some built-in ambiguity to the "self" in "self-reliance," and Emi, like many others, played upon it.

Short of attaining a teaching certificate, Emi confounded the official theory that predicted school graduates would economically benefit their country. Prior to getting pregnant and going back home to live, she was the personification of a school-educated citizen. She was clever and studious, had drive and vision, and, as a recent secondary school graduate, wanted to contribute to her own and to national development by teaching. And yet in the end she returned home and raised a child with neither employment nor much extended family support. Emi's was the future not discussed in most class sessions and never mentioned in the home economics—or any other—syllabus. Emi went on to become what the school negatively modeled—a school graduate who lived at home.

If, as a body of educational literature implies, families' educational strategies are aimed at maximizing children's chances for upward mobility and at reproducing dominant cultural values of taste, moral reasoning, and economic strategies,[11] then Emi was an ideal representative of a liberal social model for academic success. Her family supported her through secondary school, and she was poised within her family and community in ways that many around her were not. And yet, ironically, Emi's story mixes up both state ideals of education for self-reliance and liberal academic notions.[12] Instead of putting her plan into practice, instead of matriculating to the next stage of the system and then going on to become professionally employed, Emi returned to the village to have a baby and, eventually, to farm. The retrograde direction of her trajectory raises an important question: What more is behind educational success and mobility than hard work, state plans, personal vision, and supportive families? What else influenced Emi's life course—or indeed, did she hold contradictory plans simultaneously?

I never caught up with the father of Emi's child, though Emi later told me

he had become a medical doctor. The professional vision he had held for himself had, unlike Emi's, been realized some five years later, and Emi's
pregnancy did not appear to derail him in the way it seemed to change Emi's
plans. Nor in general did male school graduates to the same extent as female
seem to break from the anticipated school-to-work trajectory. By 1996, more
boys than girls who graduated from Mkufi in 1993 were gainfully employed
(albeit many with seasonal jobs: coffee picking, agricultural sales, and working within the tourist industry). Out of a group of twenty-five female
graduates, all except five continued to live and farm at home. Indeed, it was
not uncommon for Lameck and me to encounter female secondary school
graduates in the course of conducting household interviews. Whereas most
of their brothers had moved to relatives' houses in urban centers—in Dar es
Salaam, Arusha, or sometimes Nairobi—most of these girls were taking care
of parents, grandparents, and younger siblings.

In the face of such seemingly unequal outcomes, and with so many
female school graduates returning home, the ideal of becoming a city sister
seems short-lived and in some cases quite illusory. At least this appears so
for the short term; it is quite possible these "stay-at-home women" go on to
continue schooling in later years, a phenomenon Johnson-Kuhn (1999) has
found in rural Cameroon. However for the short term, pregnant girls more
often than not return home. One wonders: Why? It would be simple enough
to say that biology sets males and females on different life courses, and that
future family and employment ideals are determined differently for young
women and men. To some extent this is certainly so. For no matter how
global and encompassing state or liberal academic theories of educational
advancement may be, the direct school-to-work trajectory embedded in theories of equal opportunity and advancement is sometimes interrupted and
put on hold by those who choose to have babies. (Or, indeed, by those who
have babies without choice.)

However, the realities of students' decisions and biologies don't give us a
complete picture of Emi's—and many others'—situation. Nor do they tell
us how decisions are made in the context of marriage strategies and inheritance rights. One of the reasons Emi's suitor refused eventually to support
the child or to have anything to do with Emi in the way of the child or marriage, Emi's brother said, was because Emi was (like Eshimuni) *too*
educated. As a school graduate, she was seen by men in general as potentially *too* independent and not likely to heed her husband's—or any male

supporter's—calls. Indeed, such was Emi's own self-assessment: she was too educated to live with a pugnacious husband; nor did she even want to be married to a man who, though he may appear to be calm, could lay claim to her hard-earned money.

Several months after the child was born, Emi changed her mind from wanting to live singly to wanting to marry her child's genitor. But in her child's genitor's views—as conveyed by a schoolmate of the genitor—Emi was "too educated to marry." She "knew too much," was "too strong willed" and on top of this, had a touch of the "blood of Palestinians" (*damu ya Mapalestina*) that I mentioned in Chapter 2—a feature seen by many men in the area as maritally damaging for Chagga women.

In other words, with reference to my question—what else, other than egalitarian state discourses and liberal ideals of self-advancement, influenced Emi's life course?—one answer is that culture intersected and overlapped with—indeed, helped to define—state discourses of education.

People's understandings about family and the home, and gendered roles within them, find expression in the school curriculum and emerge through debate about "what school education is." In cases where highly achieving women are perceived as becoming too self-reliant in the wage-paying world, women's personal goals are susceptible to being criticized for threatening to undo conventional gender roles. Such women are potentially subject to scrutiny for unraveling *new* conventional domestic roles embedded in the curriculum. Even though vocational syllabi officially treat men and women equally, the gendered components of home economics versus agricultural science reproduce some old—and set up many new—inequalities.

This is a point often acknowledged in critical educational research on Tanzania (e.g., Maliyamkono 1980; Mbilinyi 1973; Omari 1991)—that inequalities are embedded in liberal academic models of educational achievement and economic advancement (cf. Hurtig 1998). But within a body of work that subscribes to what Levinson and Holland have called "the Western schooling paradigm in global context" (1996:17), this point is often minimized. Scholars who have discussed the globalization and standardization of society through mass schooling (cf. Inkeles 1998; Meyer et. al. 1992) have tended to view school-educated persons and their values as caricatures of Western beliefs and social systems (e.g., Fuller 1991). Such a paradigm misses the mark of seeing schooling as both a product of and a contributing factor to people's understandings and definitions of moder-

nity. School-educated women who are labeled city sisters and who sometimes seek to change prescribed social roles—to redefine femininity by
reinterpreting the goals of education—are potentially scrutinized for not
abiding by "rational" or "modern" state discourses of education. Emi's own
brothers said they understood her child's genitor's reasons for not marrying or supporting Emi. Said the oldest, Ibrahim:

> IBRAHIM: Chagga women have a reputation for being stubborn and suc-
> cessful. When they're educated, they're even harder to boss around,
> that's why nobody wants to marry them. I'd rather marry a woman
> from Dodoma than someone from Mount Kilimanjaro. I mean, not
> really, but in some ways it wouldn't be a bad thing [chuckling].
>
> AMY: What about the guy who got Emi pregnant? Should he marry her?
>
> IBRAHIM: No, he shouldn't. [Ibrahim pauses.] The only problem is here,
> this is my sister.

So-called modern views, sometimes called city sisters', come back to haunt
some of these school-educated women, as when, in Emi's situation as well
as Eshimuni's case above, these women eventually *want* to marry but are
deemed "too educated" and "wrongheaded." School-educated women are
seen as successful, as being informed and highly insightful (the positive
side of the same coin that calls them, as Ibrahim did, "stubborn" and "hard
to boss around"). However they are also seen as potential and even likely
failures who unintentionally—some say deservedly—slip back into the
grips of what people view stereotypically as "tradition." Like Neema
Mushi, my final case focus, they try so hard that their plans appear to some
people (though not all) to be inevitably foiled.

NEEMA MUSHI, WHO LEFT SCHOOL

Everyone with whom I spoke regarded Neema's situation as unfortunate.
Neema said herself that she did not know she was pregnant until it was too
late and too risky to have an abortion. Unlike some other schoolgirls who
conceived unintentionally (see Stambach, forthcoming), she was not able to
raise money through friends to have a safe but costly (and technically illegal) abortion. Nor did she want to go to a local woman for medicines
(*madawa*) to make her miscarry. Indeed, Neema said that schooling had
taught her that locally procured abortions were dangerous, and although

she felt she would have trusted taking local medicines earlier in her term, she did not want to risk infertility by aborting in the second half of her pregnancy.

Neema was a student in a Form 2 class I regularly visited. I saw her almost every day, yet did not know her as well as Emi or Eshimuni. Neema's peers and teachers described Neema as *mhuni*—promiscuous and socially deviant—and noted that her quiet classroom style masked a prankish, almost roguish character. Indeed, Neema was one of a core of four Form 2 girls whom several teachers facetiously labeled big city sisters (*madada ya mjini*). Whereas in the cases of Emi and Eshimuni, "city sisters" signaled an element of respect for high-achieving, upwardly mobile, and self-motivated young educated women, the moniker here was disparagingly used to indicate what teachers thought Neema would likely never become: independent.

Neema and a group of others in her class often hid in the brush to escape classes and work detail. Their rejection of school authority and teachers' commands earned her and these few classmates a poor reputation. The problem was not that Neema and friends challenged their teachers' intellectual authority—although that too would have drawn teachers' complaints. Rather, it was that Neema and friends derived some of their power from material possessions their teachers could not afford. Several in this group donned the latest fashions, wore their hair in expensive styles, and peppered their conversations with Kiswahili and English slang. Neema often came to school with expensive sweaters and stockings, fingernail polish, and hair ornaments, and several teachers interpreted Neema's and the other schoolgirls' fashions as a threat to teachers' social position of authority.

Neema also described herself as a city sister, though to her this label was socially empowering. She wanted to do what Emi herself had described—build a house in a new area and have a child without living with a husband. All of this was to take place, as she said in conversation, after she had graduated and had been earning a respectable salary.

Neema's mother was a single parent of four children who had sent Neema to live and work for wealthy, distant relatives. In exchange for Neema's labor, these relatives paid Neema's secondary school fees. As Sally Falk Moore notes (1986:86), in the past some Chagga sent their children to relatives living in other compounds, and children were lent as depositors for debt. Third-born children were considered especially suitable, as indeed were any children beyond the first two. Debt incurred by families "lending" girls was returned to the creditor in the form of bridewealth; when the girl married, the lending family paid bridewealth earned from the suitor's lineage to the guardians. Neema's situation was not exactly this, for the arrangement in which she was involved was not tied to marriage but to schooling. In fact, her arrangement, like those of other girls "lent" these days, put the burden of debt on the family who had "adopted" her; they— that is, the extended relatives with whom she was now residing—were deriving the benefits of her domestic labor.

The power dynamics of child fosterage are highly unequal. Neema felt she was to an extent at the mercy of her employers/relatives for financial assistance. In the context of this relationship, she began accepting money and gifts from a man. Some speculated that it was from one of the young men who lived in the household where Neema lived and worked, and as such, one of her relatives. As with other schoolgirls who accepted gifts from wealthier men, Neema later found that this man expected sexual favors. Neema obliged him during times of the month she felt were safe, and inserted a rag into her vagina or "drank strong medicines" (as she put it) to prevent conception and regulate her menstrual cycle. Such methods, as Raum notes, have been used by Chagga women for many generations (Raum, 1940:67), although according to the Tanzanian Demographic Health Survey (1993:35), Neema's choice of birth control is considered unreliable by well over 90 percent of the women interviewed in 1991 and 1992.

When Neema found she was pregnant, she dropped out of school (she would have eventually been expelled, people said), left her place of employment, and returned to her natal home. As in many cases involving schoolgirl pregnancy, the genitor of Neema's pregnancy was never named. In our conversations, Neema considered that it was possible that her neighbors and peers would eventually forget or downplay her pregnancy and that she would marry or have children in the future in a more socially accepted way. However, she recognized that should people believe that the male genitor was a relative of hers, the immediate response of the community would be that her actions had been shameful and that she had violated normative ideas about exogamy.

In any event, many people saw Neema's fate as fitting her "crime," which was, in the eyes of Bibi Muro, who knew her, showing off and acting uppity (kuringa). Bibi Muro maintained that city sisters these days were setting themselves up—and the country as a whole—for failure. Their wanton ways she saw as sure to backfire because, after all, city sisters had not been properly initiated. They had not undergone the necessary rite that would "correctly" and definitively socialize them into Chagga adulthood.

Sadly, Neema, when I saw her last, had not yet put in place the city sister model to which she, like some other students, had aspired. Her schooling had not yet provided the means that she had idealized and envisioned. Important to note, however, is that Neema saw schooling as the source and means to a city sister end. Schooling, as she saw it, was the institutional means to transforming her life beyond that of her own mother, whom she referred to as a *mama wa nyumbani*. Such an end was, indeed, what curriculum and policy suggested: the transformation of old social relations into new ones that moved students off ancestral land. But the future embedded in official school discourse was not Neema's particular ideal—nor was it her reality.

SCHOOLING AS A FACTOR IN IMAGINING NEW POSSIBILITIES

An interesting point about all three girls' life trajectories is the way schooling figures as a factor in imagining new possibilities. Eshimuni, Emi, and Neema pull the lessons of their education together, though in ways never detailed in any syllabus. It is not the content of lessons that empowers the three to think of themselves, in various ways at different times, as city sisters, but the symbolic wealth and cultural capital that schooling provides as a discursive, symbolic system.

In this regard, city sisters—or as I introduced them, paraphrasing Mbilinyi (1972), New Tanzanian Women—take on the appearance of embodying the values of the curriculum—modernization, commoditization, global orientation—even though, as I have described, they often reject the authority of the curriculum to define them. Some women's plans not to marry circumvent established channels of inheritance. They reconfigure the shape of Chagga families and also change typical gender relations and women's roles within households. Men are "traditionally" in control of the formal channels of social reproduction, but in a context in which women decide their futures and arbitrate their own inheritance, the control of reproduction slips from men to women, at least in some hoped-for cases such as Eshimuni's. In Emi's and Neema's cases, where marriage was not an alternative, the control of reproduction remains more in the hands of these young women's fathers. Yet even here, having had a secondary school education endows these single mothers with a degree of authority not granted "traditional mothers." Secondary school students—whether they graduate or merely attend for a few years—come to represent a new Tanzanian woman versed in the language of home economics and other aspects of "modern" mothercraft.

To many people living on the mountain this is unacceptable, and women like Eshimuni, Emi, and Neema are chastised for undoing tradition. Nonetheless, this particular view (called "modern" by many Tanzanians) is growing in certain circles, and understanding it is critical to understanding the manner in which people attribute transformations in culture and society to the lessons and routines of schooling.

Having examined in this chapter and the previous three some of the arguments people make about schooling, I turn in the remaining pages of this book to look specifically at classrooms and students. So far, I have shown little of what actually goes on between teachers and students in schools. I have done this intentionally, to emphasize that an important component, if not a necessary starting point, for anthropological works about education is the cultural context and meaning of "education" in its broadest sense. As Philippe Bourgois notes (1996:251) "perhaps the greatest weakness of education ethnographies . . . remains their arbitrary focus on a single institution—the school—and worse yet, the classroom within the school." Bourgois goes to the other extreme—scarcely looking at what schools themselves are all about—but his words are well taken and have guided my decision to look at marriage, inheritance, and kinship first. On Mount Kilimanjaro, the lineage and banana grove are key organizational institutions that structure Chagga social life. Marriage, inheritance, and initiation all figure into debates about the effects—good and bad—of formal schooling. Schooling, in turn, is viewed as inseparable from the internalized relations conditioned through nonschool practices; years spent at home versus in the school mark social status differences and individuals' and generations' different orientations to household life and urban living.

The point of these first four chapters, then, has been to illustrate how some people on Mount Kilimanjaro self-identify and attribute the formation of social groups and categories such as stay-at-home mothers and "city sisters" to the presence or absence of school education. Categories of schooling and of nonschool institutions provide an anchoring rationale for defining differences. Colonial ethnographies, no less than schools themselves, all in conjunction with local cultural and historical processes, have played a role in producing the traditional/modern dichotomy. The following chapters extend this insight by exploring several areas where new gender roles are forged: in classrooms, during extracurricular activities (particularly students' popular culture), and through teachers' supervision.

5

"Boys, Preserve Your Bullets; Girls, Lock Your Boxes"

GENDERED MESSAGES IN CLASSES AND THE CURRICULUM

ARLY in my stay I had the opportunity to travel with two college instructors to several secondary schools. In the course of five whirlwind days we visited seven schools, sat in on more than a dozen classes, met with teachers and administrators, and observed the general organization and physical conditions of the schools. The trip gave me an opportunity to get an overall picture of classrooms and teaching styles, and to identify common themes in several institutions that were to become points of investigation through my work—in particular, the interrelationship of school and society, and gender and age-related transformations.

The schools varied tremendously in construction and overall maintenance, from well-tended school grounds and painted buildings (Illustration 8) to half-built frames with dirt floors and bare cement-block walls (Illustration 9). Classrooms typically faced inward toward a central compound that served as a gathering site for morning and late-afternoon assemblies, and student areas were usually set apart from the quiet repose and shaded areas of teachers' offices and administrative buildings. In most cases, the designs of schools allowed for students to move progressively "up" as they matriculated through the system, either toward the highest physical point on the school grounds or toward the teachers' offices.

Unlike the college instructors whom I accompanied on these rounds, I was not interested in evaluating students' comprehension or teachers'

8. *above* This long-established secondary school has recently received a fresh coat of paint.

9. *right* One of the many secondary schools under construction on Mount Kilimanjaro. Visible to the left are student-made cement blocks. To the right is an unfinished building in which classes are being held.

skills. Rather I wanted to get some general sense of the organization and flow of what went on in secondary schools, with the general aim of understanding how students and teachers shaped gendered and age-graded social roles. I wanted to observe how teachers and students interacted with one another, moving as it were "with-then-apart" (Goffman 1977:316) in an intricate choreography through space and time. I kept an eye out for the ways in which age and gender were structured into and out of the rhythms and movements of classroom activities, and I made it a point to note how students framed their responses and questions to teachers, and vice versa.

I found that many classes followed a typical pattern regardless of the school or form level, producing with great efficacy particular relations of authority and hierarchy through the ritualizing effects of call/response and repetition. It was difficult sometimes to know when and where gender and age were relevant, for gender, like age, as Barrie Thorne eloquently puts it, "waxes and wanes in the organization and symbolism of group life" (1997:64). Its salience comes and goes in the course of classroom interactions, and gender is often neutralized or challenged by other teaching practices.[1] But a number of interactions and early observations tipped me off that gender and age were operative social categories. As with a body of research on gender in U.S. schools, I found that students in Tanzania are separated first by age, especially according to their school years, and then by gender in ways that frequently corresponded to but did not fully mirror male/female categories of sex.[2] I found this a simple but remarkable starting point for thinking about education comparatively.

In what follows, I provide illustrations from three of the more than one hundred classes I observed at twenty-seven different secondary schools.[3] I have selected the vignettes for the ways they illustrate characteristic aspects of teacher-student social interactions, particularly around age and gender. Although readers may be interested in seeing how and what information is taught to students in the course of instruction, this is not my main focus here. Instead, I am interested in continuing to explore school-society interconnections and in looking at how people evaluate schools and society in terms of one other. Thus readers are reminded in advance that curricular content, interesting as it is, is not the center of my attention. More to the point is how age and gender are expressed through teachers' lessons.

In focusing on schools, I found that even though the spatial layout of classes gave the visual impression that gender and age were salient features of classroom life, teachers' and students' interactions, at least on the surface, rendered those categories at first meaningless. I did not detect from most of my early observations that gender and age were socially significant; gender and age were rarely mentioned or articulated by teachers, and students—male and female—participated in teacher-directed exercises in roughly proportionate numbers. But then, after a few weeks observing and listening, I began to see how gender/age were socially embedded. The remarkable aspects of gendered and age-related interactions in schools were the ways they related to actors' understandings of the wider world—not only to the market economy, which was just opening up in Tanzania at the time, but also to the *kihamba* (banana grove) regime and social relations threaded through and embedded in it.

GENDER ASYMMETRIES IN GEOGRAPHY AND ENGLISH CLASSES

One of the very first classes I attended—Form 1 Geography at Kilimo Secondary School—began in the way I observed many others, with students seated and separated, girls on one side and boys on the other.

Younger students sat in front; older students, toward the back. Of the forty-five pupils, roughly 60 percent were girls—a percentage that mirrored what I observed on the average in Kilimanjaro Region.[4] The teacher, Mr. Ulotu, was no more than twenty-five years old, and students' ages varied from fourteen to twenty-one.

As in other schools, the lesson at Kilimo Secondary opened with the teacher announcing the "topic for the day." He read from his handwritten notebook, and then copied his notes on the blackboard. The following vignette is excerpted from my observations and illustrates a common pattern of teacher-student interaction.

A VIGNETTE

The subject is geography; the topic is equatorial zones. The class begins when the teacher and two observers enter the room. The observers include a Tanzanian college professor (a woman in her late twenties who has come to evaluate his teaching) and me. The teacher appears to be in his mid-twenties. The students—Form I students—stand to greet the adults. They recite in unison, "Good morning, Sir and Madams." "Good morning," their teacher answers. "Sit down." After general introductions, the observers sit in the back, the teacher pulls out his notes, and the class proceeds. In large block letters on the board the teacher writes:

SUBJECT: GEOGRAPHY
TOPIC: EQUATORIAL ZONES, 0° to 15° LATITUDE

The students copy these words into their notebooks. The teacher turns to the class.

"Who can give me a definition of 'equatorial zone'?"

No one replies, and after a long moment of silence (perhaps as long as 15 seconds), the teacher repeats his question and waits. Finally, after more silence, he chooses a student, a boy sitting to his left in the front. "Aluseta," the teacher calls, and Aluseta stands up to answer. The response is inaudible to most of the class, and perhaps it is just as well. The teacher declares it "Wrong!" and students chortle at Aluseta's attempt. The teacher asks his question again. A student raises her hand, and the teacher calls on a girl whose name is "Verynice."

"Where there are rain forests," she says in a hurry.

"Yes, what else?" asks the teacher.

With no other volunteers forthcoming, the teacher reads his definition from his notes. "The equatorial zone is the region of the world 0° and 5° latitude [sic] where certain kinds of plants and animals live." The students copy his definition word for word in their notebooks while the teacher writes it on the board.

The class continues in what seems again from my perspective a disjointedly slow and painful pace. The teacher pastes up a map and asks students to come to the front of the room to point out areas that fall within the equatorial zone. Four students do so, two boys and two girls, while the class looks quietly on. The teacher then asks students to point out the rain-forested areas: Amazonia, Ghana, and parts of Uganda are the desired answers to the exercise. Again, three students (here all girls) identify these, and the teacher writes the names of these countries on the board. Again, students copy into their notebooks what the teacher has written.

A third question is posed (the class was already twenty minutes into its scheduled forty-minute session): "Who can name some animals found in these areas?"—that is, again, in the equatorial zone as it is identified by the teacher on the map. The question is repeated several times, more slowly each time, until a few students raise their hands. Monkeys, snakes, crocodiles, birds, and baboons are eventually listed and copied into notebooks. Three students, all girls again, suggest lions, elephants, and hyenas (interestingly, these are animals which live on the plains below Mount Kilimanjaro and with which many students are familiar),[5] but the teacher says these answers are incorrect; he writes these on the board with a big "X" struck through them.

The lesson ends fifteen minutes later—five minutes before the scheduled end and just a few moments after the teacher has reread his notes on the subject and reiterated what was written on the board. As the notebooks of lists and definitions close one by one, the two visiting teachers and I leave the classroom full of quiet students.

No doubt the evaluator's and my presence affected the tone and direction of the class. No doubt, too, the approach to the subject was related to the teacher's interests and experience. But in the course of observing many classes, I came to recognize that the method of delivery and note taking and the call/response interaction of teacher and students were standard dynamics of many classes—not only in classes that were being evaluated.[6] Presentation styles did not vary much between teachers-in-training and those who were fully certified. Any subject, not just geography, could be initiated with a definition. "What is a noun?" "Who can define 'literature'?" "What is 'biology'?" And even though students did not always listen—some doodled, others daydreamed—teachers appeared from their narrative style to operate on the basis of absolute authority (cf. Maurice Bloch 1993). The process of listing and copying notes from the blackboard was repeated again and again. As the teacher spoke, students wrote in their notebooks, or "copied," as they put it. Both feet on the floor, facing forward, most used a ballpoint pen—a "Bic," colloquially. Notebook pages were filled with writing, words extending to the very edges—top, side, and bottom. And most were written in neat, well-defined letters, I noted in looking through students' writings later. Teachers collected and evaluated students' *daftari*, as the notebooks are called in Kiswahili, not so much to check on students' interpretations or correct answers, but to make sure students were paying attention—that they were "catching" everything. The point of it, one teacher bluntly put it, was to keep students occupied during class.

At several junctures, the teacher stepped off his platform at the front of the room and walked up and down the aisles. To my surprise, many students physically cowered and looked down, apparently afraid. On one student's desk, the teacher dotted his chalk, leaving white marks on the upper corner. In another case, the teacher twisted his thumb on a boy's shoulder, rather mildly, and tapped him on the back. Although I did not see this particular teacher tweak students' ears or pull on their shirts and hair, as I saw some teachers do at other schools, I did notice what was to become a gendered pattern of students bodily pulling back in teachers' physical presence. With the exception of Verynice and another girl, whose eyes belied that she was not afraid, girls generally giggled and shied away, sometimes whimpering in response to prods and pinches. Boys more often, unlike Aluseta, mentioned above, spoke directly and with authority. Even when Mr. Ulotu grabbed them, they generally stood steadfast and silent to the end.

On the whole, however, students appeared uncomfortable being asked to respond and approach the board, and even when Mr. Ulotu encouraged participation, his words often silenced students with authoritative formality.

The teacher conducted the entire exercise as though following basic notes on how to teach. "Ask students questions; insist that they participate"— these were the apparent imperatives that motivated his performance.

Henrietta Moore observes that bodily praxis "is not simply about learning cultural rules by rote; it is about coming to an understanding of social distinctions through your body . . . and recognizing that your orientation in the world . . . will always be based on that incorporated knowledge" (1994:78). Students in Mr. Ulotu's class on the equatorial zone seemed to be learning not only about geography but also about negotiating the power/knowledge relation between teachers and students and surrounding their subject matter. Students were involved in learning how to manage their own physical and intellectual responses and how to comply—or at least *appear* to comply—with teachers' directions for the term of the class. This observation, that learning occurred through indirect participation not direct instruction (cf. Lave and Wenger 1991), prepared me to think of gender issues as being more than matters of numerical representation. It led me to look at the ways in which gender was embedded in and constituted through what people say and do, and it prompted me to think about how gender equity was figured in more than numerical terms.

In this particular geography class, where enrollment favored girls three-to-two, and where a girl held the comparatively high-status position of class monitor, girls participated in the classroom activity in roughly equal proportion—maybe even slightly more. The geography vignette indicated that girls were numerically more responsive and that they provided the answer the teacher wanted more often than boys, but in terms of boy-to-girl ratio, girls' contributions were approximately proportionate. I kept a rough account of how many times male and female teachers called on girls and boys respectively. At first I was surprised to see that the numbers were in every case roughly proportional to students' enrollments, and that on the surface male and female students' mode of response and interaction were basically the same. Girls, like boys, stood when answering (standing to answer is routine in Tanzanian classrooms), and all students generally abided by classroom rules and responded in ways that conformed with teachers' expectations—even if they did not always have the answer being solicited.[7]

I had entered the classroom expecting to see something different—some evidence in terms of enrollment numbers of the reproduction of gender inequalities that filled popular Western media stories about girls' schooling in sub-Saharan Africa.[8] At the very least, I expected to see fewer girls than boys enrolled in classes, and I anticipated that girls would sit quietly and patiently while boys jumped to answer most of the questions. But in terms of numbers, I was hard pressed to find evidence of gendered differences and inequalities. Both girls and boys remained generally quiet throughout, and both slowly and most times reluctantly responded to teacher's requests. To be sure, none of the girls openly volunteered; and except for the volunteered response of one boy, the teacher called upon the students. But even so, girls and boys seemed accustomed to complying—if not always immediately willing to comply—with their teacher's methods.

I saw this general pattern in other classes too, in the course of my tour to schools of all types. Although I came to recognize that this was not necessarily the case throughout all of sub-Saharan Africa, I thought it important to note and explain, particularly insofar as this picture of schooling challenged the blanket assertion that girls in Africa are unschooled, underrepresented, and poor.[9]

Several weeks after visiting Kilimo Secondary School and after completing my tour with the college evaluators, I was invited to observe an English class at Mkufi Secondary School. Mr. Uroki taught the class (I introduced Mr. Uroki in Chapter 1, and it was he who asked the Chagga riddle in Chapter 2). Mr. Uroki imparted his material in a deliberately challenging and cryptic way. He presented the lesson as a series of taunting questions. He tried to engage students by asking provocative questions and by goading them with comments—such as "educated girls these days are haughty" and "you boys must learn to lead!"

As in the geography class, I noticed immediately that girls and boys sat on separate sides of the classroom, though again I did not fully understand at first what this seating pattern might signify. Mr. Uroki's class began, as did the geography lesson just described, with students standing to greet the teacher—"Good afternoon, sir," and Mr. Uroki responding, "Good afternoon, sit down." Students then read, one by one, from a story printed in a textbook. The text, interesting in and of itself (it was from a workbook entitled *Moments*, produced by the American publishing house Macmillan & Co. in 1973), was similar to the one that follows:[10]

Better Never than Late

There once was a boy named Toby N. (Nothing, Nobody, Nonsense) Turvey. Toby was an orphan who traveled from town to town looking for people to be his parents. Unfortunately, nobody wanted Toby. People felt sorry for him, and would shake their heads with sadness when they saw him.

One evening in autumn, just as the cold winter was beginning to set in, Toby climbed up into an apple tree near the outskirts of a village and prepared to go to sleep. All of a sudden he noticed some lights in the village down below. The lights were in the shape of a circle, and the circle had twelve points on it. Toby didn't think much of this and fell asleep dreaming of parents.

The next day Toby awoke to the sound of seven loud strokes of a bell. [An accompanying illustration to the text shows that the town—called Meridian-on-the-Bay—is indeed round; at the center of Meridian-on-the-Bay is a church with a clock on its steeple.] Toby watched with fascination the activities of people in the town. By 8:00 A.M. the doors to the school and factory were shut fast and people were busy working. Those who arrived after 8 o'clock were locked out and left to wander idly about the village.

Toby was intrigued by what he saw and decided to go down and investigate. The first man he met in Meridian-on-the-Bay was the mayor of the town. The mayor carried a hefty book and wore a watch around his neck. [Another picture illustrates a large man with red cheeks, carrying a book and wearing a watch.]

"Who are you?" the mayor asked Toby, to which Toby replied with his name.

The mayor looked in his hefty book, which was called the *Tome of Time.* "I don't see your name here. This is the *Tome of Time* and the *Tome of Time* runs the town. You must be a stranger." Toby explained that he was an orphan and was looking for someone to adopt him.

The mayor rubbed his chin with pity and offered to help Toby. "Come back here at 5 o'clock, and I'll introduce you to our citizens. Be here promptly. Remember: 'Better never than late!'"

At the appointed time, all the villagers had gathered in the courtyard near the clock tower. The mayor introduced Toby N. Turvey and described him as a punctual young lad. "I asked him to return here at 5 o'clock, and he did so in good time." The mayor explained that Toby was looking for someone to be his parents. People murmured with sympathy for the boy and shook their heads in sadness.

No one responded for several minutes, but by 5:15, just as the clock struck quarter past the hour, an old man raised his voice. "I will adopt this fine young man, for clearly he is well behaved." Toby was then taken into Meridian-on-the-Bay, where he joined other boys of his age in school and where he has lived and worked to this day in the good company of the villagers.

From my initial reading, which was shaped by my recognition of the publisher as North American, Toby N. Turvey typified a particular American view of a self-motivated individual—a person who lives by the clock and personifies efficiency. The half-fairy-tale, half-real depiction of him looking for parents in this pastoral setting romanticized struggle, glorified perseverance, and rewarded punctuality. From students' perspectives, however, I could not imagine it would have what I thought was the publishers' intended significance. How were students supposed to interpret this story? What did it—and by extension, the English lesson—mean to students at Mkufi Secondary School?

When Mr. Uroki quizzed the students using questions he had written on the board, no one answered the questions correctly—at least not as Mr. Uroki had intended. Indeed, no one at first had anything to say, and it was only after a great deal of prodding and pulling and, literally, a quick pinch to a few of their arms and ears, that any student responded at all, and then answers were brief and quietly uttered. Students who responded stammered and cowered in the face of Mr. Uroki's questions, and several girls audibly whimpered at the callousness of his physical prompting.

"What was the most serious thing that disturbed Toby?" the teacher demanded. "What does 'N.' mean? Where did Toby live? Why did people shake their heads on meeting Toby?"

Facing silence, Mr. Uroki stepped off his platform and asked students belligerently, "What, nobody knows? Are you all fools? Who can answer my questions?" Pulling one girl up out of her chair by her shirt, he reiterated his first question, "What was the most serious thing that disturbed Toby?"

The girl gasped and responded, "I don't know, Teacher," though this admission of ignorance only further fueled Mr. Uroki. Dissatisfied and angered, he pushed her back into her chair and looked around for another student to question.

"Why was Toby disturbed?" he shouted at another, pulling at this schoolboy's ear and speaking so hard that spit flew into the student's face.

The student flinched and tried to ease away, but Mr. Uroki only tightened his grip. "What was Toby's problem? Why was Toby upset?" Like the first, this student said he did not know. "Are you all children?" the teacher asked vehemently, chastising students for being "lazy" and "dull." "Are you all asleep in this class? I will have to send you back to primary school, where you can take naps and sleep like children. You come here to secondary school and just waste my time. Why do I teach you? I am asking you: Listen! *What disturbed Toby?* "

I had the sense that Mr. Uroki was, in part, performing for my benefit. The energy with which he questioned students was at a slightly higher pitch than what I observed in other teachers during other classes, but his general approach and the force behind his voice were methods other teachers also employed. Eyeing me to see that I was paying attention, Mr. Uroki called on yet another student.

"Why was Toby disturbed?" Her response—"Because Toby was lost, Teacher"—prompted an exclamation, "Ah ha! Very good! And why was he lost?" Now she could not answer. "Why was he lost?" Mr. Uroki repeated, saying now that the girl who had just answered was a "high-minded girl" whose schooling had "gone to her head." He sat her down and turned to another student, pulling her to her feet with a tug on her sleeve.

"Because Toby couldn't find a home," this next student replied, looking at the ground, clearly anxious to sit down. But Mr. Uroki was not satisfied; he was not going to accept her answer just like that. "You are not thinking. You are wasting time. Why couldn't Toby find a home? What was his problem? Tell me, what?"

This standing student continued in her defense, "He did not have a home. His parents were lost, Teacher." And the exchange between this student and teacher continued with several more turns.

"His parents were not lost. You are not thinking. Where were they? *Where?* "

"Teacher, they weren't in the village. Toby was an orphan."

"Okay, that's okay. Toby, he was an orphan. Okay. Class, do you hear what she said? Mark it in your books."

"Toby was an orphan," the student said again.

"Okay. Mark it down!" And then, to the standing student, "Eh heh. Thank you. You may sit down. Thank you. You will do well on the exam."

The lesson continued much in this fashion for the next forty-five minutes. Students were asked, one by one, to answer questions the teacher had written on the board. The exercise reproduced, to some degree, Toby's own lesson on accountability:

1. How did Toby know there was a town below?
2. What shape was the town?
3. What made the town alive in the morning?
4. Why were the doors of the school and factory shut fast?
5. Why was the mayor wearing a watch?
6. Why was Toby asked if he was punctual?

At one point, Mr. Uroki launched into a lengthy lecture about how stupid school students were. The lecture, from my view, came out of the blue, but students appeared generally unfazed. Mr. Uroki said that the schoolboys were "dim-witted" and "dull," that they were too lackadaisical to get jobs outside the village. He described the girls as "big sisters of the city" who were trying to "wear their brothers' pants." His images of schoolgirls, in particular, resonated with what some older women and men were saying: that schoolgirls were becoming more and more like men and that they were threatening to destroy "natural" Chagga relations. "It's not so bad that you want to become educated," Mr. Uroki said to the girls who were all sitting to the left as he faced the students. "It's that you're ruining yourselves and society in the process. You cannot even answer simple questions. If you do not know how to answer simple questions, how are you going to raise your children?" he asked girls. "This schooling you're getting is not supposed to keep you ignorant. It's supposed to help us build our nation."[11]

The gender differences Mr. Uroki painted placed girls under greater scrutiny than boys. He called Chagga girls "Palestinians"; like city sisters, he thought they were unnaturally strong and aggressive. "You have the blood of Palestinian women," he joked, criticizing educated women's independence.[12] With girls, I noticed, he stood very close, shoulder to shoulder in more than one instance. "If you do not watch your ways, you will become so haughty and proud no one will want to marry you," he said, articulating again the implicit notion that marriage preferences, gender ideologies, and schooling are all intertwined. With boys, I noticed, Mr. Uroki more frequently stood face to face, challenging them to live up to his own social and male-gendered standard. "I have a job and am a local village leader. You must learn how to lead like me."

The entire lesson lasted longer than the scheduled forty minutes, and unlike the geography class described above, students continued working well into the next scheduled session, which in this case was lunch. Some got quite tired standing for so long, others had red marks on their arms and ears from the teacher's pinches and prods, and everyone, it seemed (except the teacher) was hungry and exhausted.

The idea that the teacher's rhetorical style was a carry-over from colonial times crossed my mind, but it was belied, in large part, by what I had read in older ethnographies. Gutmann, for instance, mentions that "deprivation" (1932:3) characterized Chagga male initiation, and Raum (1940) describes numerous instances in which humiliating tactics were used to imprint adult knowledge on initiands' bodies and minds. According to Raum, initiation lessons were staged between a preceptor and an interpreter, and initiands were supposed to unlock the deeper meanings of riddles posed to them.

One of the examples Raum describes prepared me to think about schoolteachers' methods in terms of the ways elders conveyed ritual knowledge. Describing one riddle in particular, Raum writes that ritual preceptors demanded of interpreters, in a dramatic and didactic style, as follows:

PRECEPTOR: You rash and inconsiderate fellow, you, who obtrude on the affairs of men, tell me where you were? Tell me at once! . . . Tell me, where did you pass through?

INTERPRETER: I tell you that I came on the road.

PRECEPTOR: Who was it [who] dug this road? Tell me!

INTERPRETER: *Ee*, elder of God, I tell you that he who dug this road is the chief!

PRECEPTOR: I told you, you would not be able to please me always. You are near being defeated. I shake my head at your answer. I refuse it. Tell me who it is?

INTERPRETER: My elder, teacher of God! . . . You are not satisfied? But the downfall of a man brings him to his knees; therefore I do not tire supplying you with answers. I tell you it was dug by the men.

PRECEPTOR: Do you imagine this is an answer to satisfy a wise elder? You might try to deceive a stupid person with it, but not me! Tell me the maker of the road!

INTERPRETER: Elder, what can I do for you, my elder? What will satisfy you? I have only one answer left now. I think it will suffice you. I tell you, elder, the maker of this road is the father of all things!

PRECEPTOR: Truly did you reply; truly I am satisfied! May you live long, and he who begot you, too! Indeed, you reached my brains [the seat of wisdom][13] with your answer. (Raum 1940:323–324)

The insulting and demanding style of the Mkufi teacher resembles the threatening style of the initiation preceptor, and the cryptic form of the English lesson sounds a lot like the riddle of initiation. In both cases, "wise elders" control the desired response and offer praises and blessings to the student who responded appropriately. "May you live long!" the preceptor says in the end, in response to the correct answer he has been given. "You will do well on the exam," the teacher predicts, acknowledging the student's efforts and rewarding her with a wish for good luck. Again, gendered and age-graded social relations established in the wider society are evoked. Adult males are thought by many to bless or bestow goodwill upon their juniors, and juniors—in schools and society, both male and female—look to male elders for assurance of success.[14]

Much as Maurice Bloch (1993) has illustrated in his study of Malagasy literacy and schooling in a rural area, teachers' voiced authority on Mount Kilimanjaro resonates with age and gender relations in the wider society. In nonschool settings on the mountain, male elders preponderate at formalized rituals;[15] when it comes to everyday interactions, they are also accorded the greatest respect and highest authority. Teachers' verbal assertions and physical prods recapitulate a broader valuation, one that is subtly male-gendered and based on an age hierarchy. For embedded in the discipline and fear that for some students characterize classroom lessons are messages about the ways social relations are, or ought to be, normatively structured patrilineally and vertically in terms of age. It is not until one looks at some signposts from the wider social world beyond classrooms that one begins to see the gendered relations embedded in classroom lessons.

With some understanding of teacher-student interactions in ritual pedagogy, I came to see that one of the reasons students so carefully listened to teachers was that teachers' authority was, at least in part, like adult elders': it was beyond question. Male elders (*wazee wazima*) embodied command over a symbolic system—a system that in turn placed male elders at the pinnacle of patrilineal authority. To be sure, many students regarded this system as "traditional" and "outdated," but teachers themselves capitalized upon it when they needed students to defer to adults' authority.

COMMENTARY ON THE GENDERED
CHARACTERISTICS OF TEACHING

Emerging from these vignettes and forthcoming in the third is the observation that the call-and-response repetition of teaching reinforces general values of patrilineality and male authority. Put another way around, the ways people talk about gender and act on it says a lot about the regulation of movement and value within society. Gender is not always clearly institutionalized but exerts itself through persuasive pedagogic action (cf. Bourdieu 1977:87–88). More than a category of individual identity and more than what men and women as separate groups say and do, gender differences and dynamics are also indicators of the way power and authority are woven into the social environment.[16]

Mr. Uroki's calling up of gender differences and asymmetries reinforces on Mount Kilimanjaro a patrilineal social system, even as schoolgirls' comments that "education is their husband" (Chapter 4) contribute to the creation and maintenance of *new* group boundaries and identities. Mr. Ulotu's rhetorical style of silencing students (illustrated in the lesson on geography described above) mirrors gendered patterns of male speech styles in extended families: according to older men and comparatively younger school students, only old men may speak when important news bears mentioning. Only men and oldest sons can whistle and sing on their own patrilineal compounds, and even though many schoolgirls claim that they have the right to whistle and take charge "these days," few ever, in my observations, took the initiative on father's compounds. This latter point is interesting, for it suggests that perhaps even those girls who proclaim that "education is their husband" are making assertions but not following through—not whistling, so to speak, even though they claim the right.[17]

Mr. Uroki's concern that educated schoolgirls will never marry because they have "too much schooling" is not, I believe, a reflection of his concern about girls' eventual spinsterhood. Instead, it reflects his general desire to see the patrilineal system reproduced through marriage. As I discussed in Chapters 2 and 3, many people view marriage as socially central. Without young women moving on to husbands' households, transacting bridewealth and banana beer, and bearing children, the larger social order within which Mr. Uroki was raised—and within which he was able to become a secondary school teacher—is shattered. It is culturally transformed in such a way that changes his and other men's—and women's—positions within it. As my discussion of Eshimuni, Emi, and Neema illustrated (Chapter 4), some young women are in favor of using schooling to defer marriage. But as Mr. Uroki's comments above suggest, some teachers are themselves wary of changes. Indeed, the majority of the all-male teaching staff at Mkufi Secondary School felt school-educated girls were big city sisters.

One way that teachers thought they could "improve" students' character was to provide regular religious instruction. The Ministry of Education and Culture permitted religion to be taught as a subject at both government and private schools, and most students received about two hours' instruction weekly. With initiation occurring less frequently these days and, if at all, on ritually smaller scales, teachers at Mkufi Secondary School contended that students were running around ungrounded in moral instruction. Religion classes, they said, could in effect substitute for the initiation lessons students lacked. At the very least, they could counterbalance the unscrupulous leanings some teachers identified with students' material culture.

One of the two college instructors whom I accompanied on rounds to secondary schools compared lessons in moral instruction to "lessons of the lineage." To her, moral instruction was real educational "beer"—the "meat," she said, of students' education. Lessons in geography, English, and the like, in contrast, were the "dried fish" (*samaki wakavu*), as she put it, of schooling. The instructor's culinary metaphors imaged key symbols that characterized to her the good and bad aspects of African society, and they spoke to the theme of gendered sexuality that was sometimes embedded in the lessons I observed on moral instruction.

The example I give next illustrates more clearly how gendered interactions and subject matter introduced at school occur in the context of broad social institutions that go beyond the immediate lessons and routines of school. The family, marriage, inheritance, and ritual initiation are some of the more salient factors in the following lesson.

MORAL EDUCATION: GENDERED LESSONS ON MARRIAGE AND SEXUALITY

Mahali Secondary School was a coeducational day school sponsored by the Lutheran Church. Like Mkufi Secondary School and four of the other seven secondary schools in Machame, it had been built during the era of rapid secondary school expansion between 1986 and 1992. Mahali was located approximately eight kilometers up the mountain from Mkufi Secondary School. The school compound was well tended, with gardens of flowers blossoming near classroom doors, and teachers who met me showed with pride the school vegetable garden, which they said was sure this year to yield ample crops.

As I did at the other secondary schools, I first spoke with the headmaster, who then directed me to various classes in session. The instructor in the first class I visited was a local religious leader. He was in charge of teaching students morality and ethics. He later told me that students of different religious identities—predominantly Muslim and Christian—participated.[18] Wearing blue jeans and projecting an air of youth, the pastor employed the conventional call-and-response form of teaching. His words suggested that schools could rescue students from the grips of what he painted as sexual immorality:

PASTOR: Now, we have said that we will complete the lesson that we had started on religion. Now let us all read.[19]

STUDENTS [speaking in chorus and reading the title of today's lecture from the blackboard]: *The Sanctity of the Life of the Youth.*

PASTOR: Now, how can a Muslim youth or a Christian youth be sanctified? John 1 2:14 says, "I have written for you young people because"—you have what? "Because you are strong and the word of God lives in you." Is that not so?

STUDENTS: Yes, it is so.

PASTOR: Okay. We have seen, we have learned that the relationship between a boy and a girl is good. Or when there is attraction, we say that is God's grace. Isn't it so?

STUDENTS: Yes.

PASTOR: And then I also said if that attraction is not there, it is possible that you have what?

STUDENTS: A problem.

PASTOR: Yes. If this relationship is not guarded, and if this desire that is in the human body is not properly guarded, it is very easy for this thing to obsess people, and that is why the world is beset with the problem.

That is why we have seen that whenever young people feel aroused, they have sex like animals. But what is required here?

STUDENTS: Control.

PASTOR: Self-control. But we said that young people have to control themselves in order to escape this problem. And what is this problem comparable to?

STUDENTS: To fire.

PASTOR: Relationships between boys and girls are not bad, okay? But this relationship ought to be based on whose word?

STUDENTS: On the word of God.

PASTOR: Be sure that your thoughts are pure whenever you have this kind of relationship. Don't light your fire any which way, carelessly. We will call that madness [kichaa]. The important thing is to control one's fire so it can be a positive force.

The subject of this lesson—sex—appeared to interest Mahali Secondary School students more than lessons on history and geography. In other classes I had observed at Mahali, I had seen students withdraw and try to hide, much as I had seen students do at Mkufi and Kilimo Secondary Schools. But here they were wide awake—alert and ready to acknowledge and answer their teacher's questions. Perhaps it was because this particular lesson was conducted in Kiswahili, not in English; or perhaps it was because these students found answers to real-life dilemmas in the messages the pastor gave them. Perhaps, too, the pastor, as religious leader, commanded greater moral authority than ordinary teachers. In any event, the students did not take notes, as they did in other classes, but instead focused their full attention on the pastor and participated as he instructed.

Listening to the pastor, I noticed that he framed his messages for "everybody," but that he broke his audience down into girls and boys at various junctures in his informal sermon. When he spoke of sex in terms of war he presented a male-gendered vision of reproduction.

Boys, you become wise when you are able to control your thoughts and make them pure. I am advising you that if things are that way, then you need to preserve—preserve your bullets in their case. When the time for war comes, your bullets will start working. That is my advice to you.[20]

"Preserving bullets in cases" was a euphemistic way of saying that boys should restrain their sexual energy (Popenoe, personal communication).[21] Here in the classroom, discussion of bullets set the stage for differentiating male from female sexuality.

When he spoke of marriage, the pastor used the Kiswahili verb (*kuoa*) that described men's active role in partnered relationships. "Now, it is easy for men to marry (*kuoa*). But can you marry without courting (*utaoa bila kufanya uchumba*)?" In conventional Kiswahili, women *are married*, designated by using the passive verb, *kuolewa*.[22] The active form, *kuoa*, is used habitually to designate a male social role in the marriage process. When the pastor spoke to the entire group, he used the active form, *kuoa*, suggesting that he projected a masculine identity onto students generally. But when he spoke to girls, he employed the passive version, marking his specific audience in feminine terms. The use of *kuolewa* here in the circumscribed space of the classroom reinforced the notion of male normativity. It highlighted the sociocultural tendency for people to speak of student culture as a male signifier, a tendency that I later saw reflected in students' descriptions of themselves and in popular culture (next chapter).

After drilling home the point that boys should "preserve their bullets," the pastor moved on to lecture girls. His message to them was that they should guard themselves from men and think twice about taking birth control pills.[23]

> I don't know whether these pills are meant to destroy or prevent pregnancy, but if you start swallowing pills, every time, they will give you problems. When you see somebody looking at you, you become self-conscious and start questioning yourself, "Why is he looking at me?" As a result, you will find that others have very big locks for their boxes. She has secured it so that another person does not peep and see what is inside. Secure your boxes well. Girls, you should lock your boxes.[24]

Like "preserving bullets," "big locks for boxes" is a sexual metaphor.[25] In the context of schooling, the metaphor refers to the trunks schoolgirls bring to boarding schools. The boxes themselves are kept locked under girls' beds; like girls' sexuality, they must be carefully guarded. Whereas boys themselves are in charge of "controlling bullets," girls are faced with controlling *themselves*, with securing their bodies so that others do not "see" inside.[26] The pastor advises girls to look around to see why boys are looking at them. The reason, he suggests, is the girls' own fault: by taking birth control pills and not barring offenders, girls, in essence, are inviting problems.

The pastor continued:[27]

PASTOR: And then there is something else. Let us all read.

STUDENTS: Drunkenness is dangerous [read in unison from the blackboard].

PASTOR: You know this fooling around with sex gets in the way of people's progress. You cannot get ahead at all! At all! Truly, you will drink, drink, drink, and later beer will kill you. Now you mix this sex and beer, where will progress come from? Drunkenness is—?

STUDENTS: Dangerous.

PASTOR: What?

STUDENTS: Dangerous.

PASTOR: Please read!

STUDENTS: Drunkenness is dangerous!

PASTOR: Sex and beer reduce wisdom. . . . The brain normally does not function. I have told you from the beginning that sex and drunkenness reduce wisdom. The ability to learn is gone. . . .

Through a series of allusions and comparisons between what "girls" and "boys" in good moral standing ought to do, the pastor here presents a set of normativizing injunctions about sex through the threat of drunkenness. Drunkenness at the time was a powerful idiom for talking about cultural loss and struggle between generations. The Lutheran Church was divided in arguing for and against the consumption of alcohol, including the culturally very loaded drink, *mbege*, with which people swore their closest secrets and sealed important social relations, including marriage. In imploring students not to drink alcohol, the pastor was pulling them into a well-known and socially contentious debate. Villagers, teachers, pastors, and parents were all aware of the controversies surrounding *mbege*, and people were of many minds about the church directive to abandon alcohol. Some saw it as an attack on Chagga custom—as a "European" influence that chipped away at Chagga culture. Others saw it as an expression of self-control and social and economic development. Abstemious Christians often promoted the latter argument, contending that prohibition was a step toward spiritual purity.

What was threatened by students' drunkenness, the pastor implied, was not only their brains or, by association, their abilities to learn—although these consequences would have been important to the student audience to whom he was speaking. Also at stake were the gendered relations that gave root to and helped grow the patrilineage. To any student looking beyond the immediate message that the pastor simply wanted them to stop drinking, his words would have been seen as a powerful criticism of students' lifestyles and self-determination. By, as he put it, having "sex like animals" and not controlling themselves in their most basic functions, he suggested indirectly that precocious school students threatened to abuse the opportunities they had been given. They threatened *not* to develop the nation through education but to undermine a whole complex of social relations. His words echoed those of Bibi Muro in Chapter 3, who said that school-educated girls were undoing the family, and they hearken back to the very opening quotes of this book, where parents and elders were seen to be disputing the relative worth of sending children—boys *and* girls—to school.

The extent to which young people in the past abstained from sex and beer is itself questionable. Historical sources indicate that beer was drunk by people of secondary school students' age, and that although premarital sex was in some cases punishable by death, having children before the entire bridewealth was transferred was also sanctioned in some situations (Raum 1940). What is important about the pastor's lessons is not their connection to, or departure from, recorded history, but the way his arguments against student sex and drunkenness are implicitly framed in terms of a sociomoral order. Drunkenness and sex are the source and symbol of a disrupted sociomoral order—an order that school-educated youth bear the burden of either reproducing or reconfiguring.

In short, the pastor's lesson on sexuality and morality condensed several cultural expressions of Chagga life—namely, the banana grove (on which beer-brewing bananas were grown), male-female interrelationships and their fulfillment through a socially recognized form of marriage, and the development of a local cultural community through the benefits and functions of school education. His lesson not only reflected male normative ideas of gender and authority; it also portrayed students *in general* as "male-gendered" and active, and girls as recipients of others' instigations. The pastor positioned himself as wise knower and students as uninformed recipients. In so doing, he challenged and nipped in the bud what he characterized as students' disregard of elders' authority.

Taken together with the geography and English lessons at Kilimo and Mkufi, this lesson on human sexuality and morality demonstrates that schools are not isolated social institutions where gendered identities and age-based relationships are newly formed, refined, and then passed down. Rather, schools are highly fluid cultural sites that are connected to other nonschool social institutions. Gender relations, I have argued in this chapter, are broadly embedded in relationships between and among men and women, in the social positions and teachers and students, in the content of lessons, and in the ways what is taught is differentially applied and directed to males and females. Even though schooling at times deals at the level of the student with what she or he learns and is expected to do, at another level schooling is a cultural system, a series of "institutionalized discourses and rituals" (Varenne and McDermott 1998:209). It expresses not just cultural notions about what girls and boys—"educated persons"—ought to do; more fundamentally, it helps reinforce and revise relationships of power and authority between men and women, between various social spaces and activities, and even between material and ideological differences between local and larger world systems.

In other words, each of the lessons presented here illustrates that schools are culturally contentious social spaces where gender and age are subtly woven into and out of nonschool life. Instead of constituting a kind of privileged space where gendered ideologies and sex-role stereotypes are defined, held up, and then passed on for students to learn, schools are places where gendered interactions compete with the values of a broader society.[28]

Classroom lessons, as these vignettes illustrate, are stultifying for many students, for teachers typically operate on the basis of their own prime authority. However, as I discuss in the following chapter, classroom lessons take up only a fraction of students' lives. Indeed, teachers are often absent from school or, if present, are otherwise occupied during classroom time (cf. Cooksey, Malekela, and Lugalla 1993). Students may be scheduled for forty hours a week in class—as they were at Mkufi Secondary School—but they are formally engaged in classroom activities with teachers for only about 25 percent of the time. (According to a three-week record I kept of a Form 3 class at one school, students averaged less than eight hours' instructional time each week.[29])

In light of the fact that classroom contact hours are typically irregular, the question arises: What do students do during the rest of their time? What are they doing outside of the classroom that so compelled some teachers to talk about students' need to exert self-restraint? What is student life and culture all about?

Having examined some of the characteristics of teaching—call-and-response exchanges led by teachers, not students, bodily coercion through teachers' verbal and physical prods, copying notes from the board, and identifying students' silence as an indication (to teachers) of their "stubborn and uppity" ways—I turn in the next chapter to student culture and to the ways schoolgirls and schoolboys express themselves.

6

"THINGS WITH SOCKS"

STUDENT LIFE AND POPULAR CULTURE

IN THE previous chapter, I focused on the dominant social order of classrooms and considered how gendered identities were defined and presented through selected lessons. In this last ethnographic chapter, I would like to return to issues of the ways gender and generation are symbolically structured into student-teacher relationships and look more specifically than I did in Chapter 5 at how some students challenge curricular and cultural constructs. This chapter begins with an illustration of one aspect of students' lives—controversies surrounding the school uniform—and then examines parallels between students' playfulness, on the one hand, and the ambiguity of students' positions as "youth," on the other. The second section looks further at the ways students integrate outside influences with local values by extending and appropriating the stylistic/symbolic discourses they associate with success and mobility, and at how they describe their experiences at school using idioms of kinship and adult male wisdom.

"SOCKS"

In classrooms, as I discussed in the previous chapter, gender remained highly contextualized. Girls and boys did the same basic activities and participated in numbers representative of girls' versus boys' enrollment. They copied notes, responded to teachers and carried their books, and read out loud. Different-sex groups might sit on opposite sides of classrooms and talk among themselves when the teacher's back was turned, and occasionally a lesson might touch upon gendered issues, at it did in the lesson on drunkenness and promiscuity. But overall, the space of the classroom was marked only indirectly in gendered ways. Even though there were gendered components to teachers' authority and teacher-student interactions, gender as an organizing dimension of student activity was minimized, neutralized, sometimes even ignored.

In contrast, the signs and symbols of student culture outside the classroom were saturated with images of gender and also images specific to age and social development. I saw this most clearly early in the school day, when students performed "cleanliness" chores around the school grounds.

Part of my routine at Mkufi was to circulate among groups of students before classes. Girls were supposed to collect water from the irrigation canal and tidy up chairs and desks, boys to collect firewood and remove stones from the main dirt entryway. These duties often fell to a dozen or so responsible students, while the remaining either loitered behind buildings or tarried in arriving. Initially I accompanied the teacher on duty, who disbanded groups of idle students, but eventually I circulated by myself and found that students—largely, I believe, because they knew I would not tell on them—would carry on their usual activities in my presence.

On most days, I encountered groups of students talking in low voices about other students. Sometimes their conversations turned toward teachers, whom students described variably from "very fine" to "terrible," but typically students talked about what they had done the previous evening or weekend. Upper-level boys had their regular spot just outside the window of their classroom. Lower-level boys congregated dangerously near the teachers' staff room, which, by virtue of their lower status, was the only semiprivate place for them to be. Form 1 and 2 girls sat at their desks, often huddling together to talk quietly, and upper-level girls socialized with the cook and hung out behind the kitchen building. If I did not find upper-level boys in their usual spot, I knew many were in the brush below; cigarette smoke would float from the area they had cleared, revealing their hiding place. And if I did not find Form 3 and 4 girls near the kitchen, I knew they were possibly making food runs to the upper-level boys—girls occasionally would beg bowls of porridge, complaining they had had no time to eat at home, and then they would sneak the porridge to boys.

One day in March, when I ventured down to the brush where students often hid, I encountered what to me was a strange sight. Just as teachers were aware, I also knew that students ran over the hill to get away, but I did not know that they had created something of a grotto amidst the scrub brush and rocky soil. Several girls sitting a distance from the boys—and in this configuration reproducing a typical social structure of gendered separation on their own—were pulling down their socks into doughnut shapes around their ankles. Some had brought a second pair—lace knee-highs that replaced their standard issue. When I moved to the coed group, I noticed that none of these girls was wearing any socks. One of the boys had removed his shoes and was wiggling his bare toes as he talked about a teacher, Mr. Mboro. I said nothing, not wanting to sound their alarm or act as though I were the teacher on duty. But I was intrigued to see that several of them put regular socks back on before going up for routine inspection.

Up on the hill, assembled in front of teachers, the two girls who were still bare-legged stood in the middle, careful to avoid eye contact with the teacher and two student prefects who inspected students' uniforms. I caught a glimpse of the two girls later that morning, still sockless as they sat in Mr. Mboro's math class. When they passed the staff room in the early afternoon, they shot sideways glances at the teachers' open door, seemingly skittish and still bare-legged. By the end of the day they had returned to official dress and stood at the edge of assembled students, wearing socks. All seemed well, and the routine procedures of drill and roll call proceeded without a glitch. But when I looked at other girls' legs, and those of two boys who stood toward the center of the student assembly, I was not surprised to see that several of them were sockless. *What was going on?* I wondered.

As many have noted, student rituals of resistance often constitute an acted metadiscourse on the tacit rules of the social order; they call into question the logic of school rules even as they operate unconventionally within them (e.g., MacLaren 1993; McFadden 1995; Willis 1977). At Mkufi, one of the most contentious signs of school authority was students' school uniform, particularly socks. Officially, students were supposed to wear white socks—girls, knee-high stockings that reached from their ankles to the hems of their red skirts; boys, white socks underneath black trousers. But many preferred to roll down their socks or even take them off. In some cases girls would exchange lace stockings (technically not allowed) with friends' solid standard issue. Boys would pull their trousers down over their shoes to disguise the fact that they were sockless. Most would then redress properly at the end of the day for evening inspection and dismissal. The whole process of removing and exchanging socks was something of a game—a game that, if not carefully played, could result in punishment from teachers.

Socks were controversial for a reason. Many people living throughout East Africa regard legs and thighs as one of the most sexualized parts of female bodies. Students generally know that "good girls" kept their legs covered and that "good boys" follow teachers' instructions. But they also know that grown-up adults do not wear knee-high socks or uniforms, at least not those among the professional cadre whom students hope to emulate. Knowing both sides of this argument, students sometimes conform to, other times flout, school rules regarding student dress. Girls and boys with sockless legs are imbuing their actions with sexualized and precocious meanings.

Moreover, Remmy Ongala ("Dr. Remmy"), a Tanzanian reggae singer, had produced a song called *Mambo kwa Soksi* ("Things with Socks") in 1989. Written in metaphoric language, "*Soksi*" revealed a conversation between two people about, among other things, the use of condoms as a means for preventing the spread of AIDS. The song conveyed the message that lovers needed to be careful, that they needed to wear condoms and limit the number of sexual partners they have, and that what was "normal" about sexual relations in the past was not necessarily so today.

Students picked up on the controversy and redirected the message of the song to comment on authority at school. The phrase "*mambo kwa soksi*" became a way of distinguishing those "in the know" from those outside. Some of the more salient lines from the song include:

Mambo kwa Soksi (Things with Socks)[1]
By Dr. Remmy Ongala

. . . UKIMWI ni hatari, jamaa, eh, jamaa, eh.
(AIDS is dangerous, people, oh, people, oh.)
Naogopa mambo,
(I'm afraid of things,)
mambo, mambo,
(things, things,)

kwa soksi!
(with socks!)

jamani mambo
(hey, people, things)

kwa soksi!
(with socks!)

mambo ya sasa
(modern things)

kwa soksi! . . .
(with socks! . . . .)

. . . *Sasa kuna timu gani unavaa soksi?*
(Now, which team wears socks?)

Timu ya baba.
(Father's team.)

Ah! Inacheza na timu gani?
(Ah! What team does it play with?)

Wanacheza na timu ya mama.
(They play with mother's team.)

Sasa timu ya baba wacheze na soksi.
(Now, father's team plays with socks.)

*Ah. Timu ya mama wanacheza
pekupeku.* . . .
(Ah. Mother's team plays barefoot. . . .)

. . . *Na ukiingiza goli nani ataandika?*
(And if you score a goal,
who will keep score?)

Hiyo siri yenu.
(That's your secret.)

(Oh!)

Eh!
(Yeah!)

*Na uwanja gani wanacheza
huo mpira wa pekupeku?*
(And on which playing field do
they play this barefoot game?)

Uwanja wa fundi seremala. . . .
(The carpenter's playing field
[i.e., a bed]. . . .)

Despite what appeared to some Tanzanians at the time as its socially responsible message, "*Soksi*" was officially banned by the government and could not legally be played on Radio Tanzania (a government-run station) or sold in any shop. In an effort to ensure that he would be allowed to continue performing nationally, vocalist and songwriter Dr. Remmy declined to play "*Mambo kwa Soksi*" publicly or to record it on any professional label. But the song found an audience among Tanzanians who regarded themselves as informed, progressive, and somewhat radical. People would quote parts of it while drinking at a bar or would recount the scene of two teams—one "jerseyed," one "barefoot"—playing soccer on "the carpenter's playing field." And people would flood to buy tickets to concerts in Dar es Salaam, where Remmy performed when he was in the country.

Not everyone approved of Remmy's music, however. Some said that Remmy was out of touch with the majority of Tanzanians who never use condoms, that he was singing about "socks" just to generate controversy and make money, and that he was "corrupting the youth" with ideas about sex and promiscuity. This view was prevalent among teachers and village authorities, including leaders in the Lutheran Church who, although less critical than Catholic leaders, found the song too suggestive for school-aged youth. At a school assembly devoted to discussing AIDS and its social ramifications, one Lutheran pastor conceded that the song had some educative merit, but he, like the Catholic nun who was leading the program, insisted the song was fundamentally immoral. The nun and the pastor advised students to "stay clear of Dr. Remmy."

Despite (or more likely because of) the controversy, the song captured the attention of secondary school students, many of whom knew parts of the song by heart and referred to it indirectly in their everyday speech. Students, girls and boys, would often greet one another with the question, "*vipi, mambo?*" ("hey, [what's the] thing?"meaning, "What's going on?") to which the appropriate response was "*kwa soksi,*" "with socks." This exchange—in its short form, "*Mambo?*" "*Kwa soksi*"—repeated the title of the song itself and distinguished those "in the know" from those outside. It separated teachers from students, old from young, cosmopolitan (*ya kisasa*) from rural (*shamba*) students and blurred the boundary between school-educated "girls" and "boys" for reasons that require further explanation.

AMBIGUOUS TERMS AND CATEGORIES: SORTING ADOLESCENTS FROM ADULTS AND CHILDREN

Students had a lot to say "with" and "about" socks, but in ordinary contexts it was often difficult to tell whether students were talking about sexual awareness or the garment. In pulling down, taking off, and replacing their socks, students were combining the elements of expressive culture in new ways. They were modifying the uniform, playing the role of Lévi-Straussian *bricoleur*,[2] and replacing the puerile attire with the styles of power and school-educated culture. Remmy's message, clearly expressed in his text, was that condoms were essential; "if you stop wearing socks you'll die," he says, noting rather despairingly that the medicine for AIDS is a box with four sides—the coffin. In taking *off* "socks," students were neither abiding by the letter of Remmy's message—that people wear condoms—nor were they directly contradicting it. For even in rolling down and taking off socks, they drew attention to the literal item, and in so doing challenged the official school policy that students should remain sexually inactive—and, practically speaking, lack knowledge about condoms—until they graduate and marry.

Students' highly contextual references to "socks" fueled the debate that school-educated girls were becoming more like men. Schoolgirls took off socks to flirt with teachers, or so some teachers at Mkufi maintained, and several schoolgirls themselves confirmed that their sockless legs were deliberately alluring. No one disputed that taking off socks provoked or piqued teachers' sexual interest. Yet the gendered dimensions of the provocation were often ambiguous, as when girls took off socks and called them "condoms." In doing so, were they suggesting that as lovers they would remove their male partners' condoms? Or that they were, as educated schoolgirls, likely to insist their partners use them? Girls' command over "socks" called into question the issue of who was in charge and who was the follower.[3] Teachers said they could not always tell if schoolgirls were flirting or making fun—or both. Some thought sockless girls were enticing teachers into a trap where teachers would eventually be censured. Others thought sockless girls were inviting comment, perhaps asking for answers on the next exam—for some teachers admitted that some of them had been known to leak tests to students in exchange for sexual favors.[4] In either event, girls' command of socks suggested to some teachers that girls were controlling what men would (or should) wear during sex, and that they were drawing an analogy between their legs and men's penises. It raised the rhetorical question for teachers: were schoolgirls trying to subvert adult male authority? Or were they merely flirting? Were they, indeed, doing both simultaneously? Or, more benignly, nothing of the sort?

Like other researchers who have studied student culture (see, for instance, Eckert 1989; Hansen 1998; McFadden 1995; Valentine, Skelton, and Chambers 1998; Walkerdine 1990; Willis 1977), I was struck by the ambiguity of students' messages and by students' constantly shifting connotations in manipulating the meanings embedded in popular culture. When schoolgirls took off their knee-high white socks, many said they did so simply because they were physically hot. The sun beats down in the late afternoon with stifling heat in January and February. And when some of them put on lace stockings they said it was because their solid socks had been lost or stolen by siblings at home. The ambiguity surrounding students' socks, like the obscurity of the song *"Mambo kwa Soksi,"* raised a nexus of interrelated questions within local discourse about the social status and positions of students, as "youth."

Youth, as a category, includes people of a wide age range in much of sub-Saharan Africa, from children to people in their late thirties. The category is open and fluid and has different meanings in different contexts. Like the indexical qualities of "education," "youth" evokes and connects the present and the past. International efforts, including an Austrian-sponsored project at the time in Machame, target youth as a primary category. Youth are perceived as a socially malleable group that can be controlled and transformed through education, through family planning programs, and, more subtly, through the media and popular culture. As with the meaning of socks, the status of students is unclear and context-dependent; students are neither adults (*watu wazima*) nor little children (*watoto wadogo*), but something in between. They make up an intermediary social category that lies between two extreme social states. And because they are the object of cultural instruction and reform, they often lie at the heart of cultural struggles over gender and age-based authority.

In part, the social category "youth" is defined through such lessons as "moral instruction" and through rules governing school participation stipulating students must be of an approximate age. But even these curricular and administrative definitions define the social category in negative terms, in terms of what youth are not: neither children nor adults, neither older than about twenty-five nor younger than fourteen—the youngest age at which students may enroll in secondary school.

It would seem that cultural conceptualizations of youth as a transitional time in the life course are reflected in the contradictory messages attached to student culture. Evidence of this ambiguity is clear when analyzing conventional uses of the term *kijana*, "youth." The Kiswahili term *kijana* is

used many different ways—sometimes approvingly, other times pejora-
tively—to refer to people between two idealized end points, childhood and
adulthood. The term also means different things depending on the speaker,
be it someone in his or her thirties, a teenager, or an officer of a government
agency. As explained to me by the Director of Youth at one of the Lutheran
churches, girls who have begun menstruating and boys who have been
recently circumcised are generally considered to be among the youngest of
the *kijana.* At the other end of the spectrum are people who are childless. So
students anywhere from Standard V or VI and older, as well as their same-
aged peers who do not attend school, are *kijana,* as are some of the lightly
graying bachelors and unattached women who attend church youth camps.
The director said that he was in charge of all the people his age or younger
(he was about thirty-five) who did not have children. He himself was in the
process of marrying and considered that he would remain a youth until his
first child was born. He was also supervising a cadre of *vijana* (the plural
form of *kijana*) who were part of the Lutheran-run "youth project." The
director's rather precise definition seemed to conform with the ways community leaders spoke about youth in other situations, but it was different
from the way school-aged students generally talked about themselves.

Most students themselves described youth as a stage corresponding
solely to the years they spent in school. Upper-division secondary students
anticipated that after they graduated they would become *watu wazima,*
full-grown and healthy adults. They would refer to their friends still in
school as *vijana* or "little siblings" (*wadogo wetu*). This was the way Stellah
Mbasa and her friends described their vision of the future to me. Several
young men and women who graduated with Stellah, for instance, said that
they were on their way to becoming *wazima* who issued commands to
juniors in the village, and that as graduates they no longer would have to be
treated like children by their domineering teachers. Graduation was a rite of
passage they were looking forward to. Even if they were not graduating *to*
a job or a *to* a higher class within the school system, they were at least graduating *from* the liminal stage of "youth."

The developmental period identified as adolescence (*ujana*) is institutionalized at several levels. The National Education Act (1978) is usually
interpreted to mean that students must remain single and childless until
they either graduate or drop out of school, and although the law does not

state explicitly that pregnant schoolgirls must leave school, many authorities invoke it to this end.

Adolescence is also alluded to in the charter for Mkufi Secondary School: community leaders in Ndala noted in their description of the school that youth in the area are "not fully grown up to cope with life on a self-reliance basis. They need a few more years in school to mature both mentally and physically" (Project Proposal 1989:2).

It would seem from these and other statements (for instance, Ministry of National Education 1977:135) that youth, in some situations, is associated with latent sexuality and with "temptations" that result in "improper behavior." It is a time of life that requires careful monitoring and close supervision by adults. Yet this notion is in play with another that sees *ujana* not as any neatly bracketed phase of life that comes to an end after school, but as a period of social transition that is regulated in other ways.

As another subset of people in Machame sees it, however, usually those who are less formally schooled than church leaders, secondary schooling extends youth too far; it keeps young women and men locked within a developmental category that dangerously exaggerates their puerility. Bibi Muro (Chapter 3) and others who advocated that Chagga girls undergo circumcision and initiation argued that secondary school-aged girls were unnaturally kept in a state of immaturity. They maintained that school rules about deferring marriage and motherhood, rules that scorned the "traditional" rites of puberty, were wrongly stifling girls' course of development. The dangers of this, their arguments went, were evident in what they saw as the collapse of the lineage. City sisters and *wazee wazima* (a student group that I will discuss in a moment) were the by-products of a school system that kept students locked in an extended state of youth.[5]

Together, these contrasting views contribute to a scenario in which secondary students are treated as youth at school but take on adult roles at home. At school, when students take off or roll down their socks, teachers say students are behaving like children—that students are "old enough" to be adults but socially immature in terms of their behavior. Many students, in contrast, maintain that removing their socks is adultlike. A group of schoolgirls pointed to their same-aged peers in the village who were not enrolled in school, and one noted, "they don't have to wear these ridiculous socks; why should we?" They also noted that *not* wearing socks was a sign of a "modern" school-educated status. Another in the group of girls maintained, "After we graduate, we're not going to have to wear white socks. Why should we have to do so now?" Putting on this part of the school uniform (or any part, some students felt) was seen by many upper-level students as a sign of childishness and immaturity; taking socks *off* was grown-up.

Some students followed up this line of argument with examples of the adult roles they were given outside school. Some said that at home, school-aged girls were responsible for helping to take care of younger siblings, school-aged boys for farming and tending banana groves. Many of those who were not enrolled in school were already married, male and female. They were treated as responsible adults and in some cases had already built houses and borne children. Perceived differences between school students and their same-aged independent peers fueled some students' complaints that while they played adult roles at home, at school they were treated like oversized children and disciplined and monitored constantly.

Separating the criteria for adult status in schools versus homes was also difficult for some teachers: what constituted an offense depended on how one viewed the social status of students. Were students young adults temporarily removed from their development outside school? Or were they older children who needed more time to mature mentally and physically and needed to be conditioned by school rules? Teachers' attitudes toward students ranged from those who treated students like adults to those who constantly denigrated them. A group of secondary schoolgirls and schoolboys said that Mr. Lyimo, the Mkufi biology teacher, treated students like adults: he never caned them (as did most other teachers) nor did he pay much attention to their socks, and Mr. Lyimo defended students against other teachers' criticisms. He reminded his colleagues that most teachers themselves had been married when they had been students' age; this to him was a reasonable reminder that students, although in teachers' charge, were socially mature and responsible.

Mr. Mboro did not agree, however, and he was at the other end of the teachers' spectrum. Mr. Mboro was especially notorious for holding students to the letter of the rules. One day grasping a schoolgirl's wrist as she pretended to shy away, his actions demonstrated in a few moments what schoolgirls had for months been telling me: that Mr. Mboro physically provoked and angered them. Mr. Mboro called his captive a "dull and bad student" for having replaced solid white socks with see-through lace stock-ings. The two were engaged in a mock form of discipline, in which the tone of their voices contradicted their words. Mr. Mboro told the student to "put on her socks," yet his teasing voice conveyed admiration and approval. He yanked on her arm in ways that made her flinch, yet she continued to match his flirtatious tone. Mr. Mboro interrogated the girl for about fifteen minutes, repeating again and again that she was *mhuni* (promiscuous, someone who does not follow social norms). The girl protested that she did not have her socks, that her younger sister had taken them, and that she would have to wait until the following day—either that or go home early now to get them. Yet her gleaming eyes and subtle smile suggested that she had removed the socks and put them in her desk, and that she could easily go back and put them on. In the end, the student did just this, and Mr. Mboro protested (too much, a few teachers said) that "these lascivious stu-dents are to blame for the failure of our school."

Added to this was the story secondary schoolgirls frequently told that Mr. Mboro enticed schoolgirls to his house, where he lured them with the ruse that a "letter awaited" and then demanded that they "cook him din-ner." Schoolgirls said that they themselves had mixed views about such relationships. On the one hand they maintained that such actions bettered some girls' chances for doing well—for Mr. Mboro would allegedly leak exams to students in advance of the day of the test. On the other hand, they saw teachers' sexual demands as abusive and, indeed, illegal. Those who observed the exchange between Mr. Mboro and the schoolgirl on this day later mentioned to me that he was setting the stage. One observer specu-lated that "he will probably tell her later that she should come home with him, saying that he let her off lightly at school by not beating her."

REFLECTIONS

Teachers offered a couple of explanations for the authoritarian behavior of some of their co-workers. One was that some teachers were simply abusive and mean-spirited—they had deranged senses of morality and were not fit to work in the teaching profession. More typically, however, teachers explained interactions such as that between Mr. Mboro and the schoolgirl in terms of a weak institutional social structure: the rules of the school were not adequately defined to help students successfully matriculate through it.

The problem, went their argument, was that schooling was open-ended and ritually nebulous. Unlike rites of passage (and in this context, teachers brought up "traditional initiation," noting that unlike schooling it concretely marked the transition from childhood to adulthood), matriculation within the school system was slow and poorly defined. Students, they maintained, were progressing through a system of unnaturally lengthy and grueling examinations and were experienceing frustration and confusion about the roles they were expected to play. As a consequence, teachers reasoned, students were not clear about their status relative to teachers (nor, one might add, were teachers to students); this was why students such as the schoolgirl above flouted dress codes and provoked their teachers. Teachers regarded co-workers who harshly disciplined students as generally compensating for a flaw in the institutional system; authoritarian teachers were not necessarily abusing power—but simply stepping in to clarify their roles as presiding teachers.

Margaret Mead, of course, popularized the view that clear institutional structures facilitated clear social transitions, when she described American adolescence as "the period in which idealism flower[s] and rebellion against authority [is] strong, a period during which difficulties and conflicts [are] absolutely inevitable" (Mead 1928:1), and when she later attributed the emergence of adolescent anomie in Oceania to the introduction of formal schooling (Mead 1970). Although Mead dismissed information that did not fit her model, and in so doing overstated the differences between Samoan and American cultures, her insight into connections between schooling and the emergence of an adolescent social category is useful to an extent for thinking about *kijana* social categories on Mount Kilimanjaro. For it would seem that some Mkufi teachers also attribute students' rebellious behavior and actions to ambiguities in the institutional structure of the school. Students are, by teachers' definition, junior to teachers and ought to be constantly monitored. Even though they are often not far apart in terms of chronological age, teachers often feel they must make sure that students know who is boss in the classroom.

The always contextual social structure of the school conspires to elevate the ambiguities surrounding student culture to problems and troubles "in students' heads" or to problems "with students' behavior." The "rebellion against authority" and the period of "difficulties and conflict" that Mead anticipated appear to have taken root in some Mkufi teachers' assessments—albeit in a different way from what Mead described of Oceania. One Mkufi teacher said of Form 3 students, for instance, that "these students are not quite right in their heads; they defy adult authority." And another said that schooling generally "raises so many doubts in students' minds; it introduces Western ideas that confuse and trouble our children." These and other comments—including a teacher's assertion that "students are overgrown children; they think they are all grown up physically, but they are really children wearing adult clothes"—capture the sentiment that students are in a transitional stage, struggling with conflicting pressures. On the one hand, students are supposed to conform to the standards and rules set out by school administrators; on the other, they are lured by material influences and prematurely attracted to adult lifeways.

Yet these comments also suggest that it is not the social structure of the school alone that configures adolescents and adolescent social categories. Teachers' emphasis on external pressures—particularly on "Western ideas" and "adult authority"—suggests that students' expressive culture draws upon themes of mobility and movement—gendered persons, things, ideas, knowledge, and symbols that come from far away and are closely watched. Perhaps a more dynamic way of looking at student culture than Mead's institutional explanation is to consider how youth categories and discourses mediate social class and embody oppositions that are hegemonic in the broader society. To put this in terms of student life on Mount Kilimanjaro, it is not the school's institutional structure alone that defines social ranking among student groups, but this structure in combination with students' own interchange of ideas that contributes to the social categories by which students operate. Students' categories—*wazee wazima* and the popular categories of stay-at-home mothers and city sisters, for instance—establish and reinforce a ranking system that sets up differences between school-educated students and nonschooled peers. Stay-at-home mothers are less socially valued by many students than city sisters whom some schoolgirls hope to become or emulate. *Wazee wazima*—a term for wise old men that I will explicate below—is likewise not embedded in age-ranked hierarchy of classes at schools but draws upon relations of hierarchy that play out in the wider world.

Thinking about youth culture in terms of local social values makes it possible to consider why student culture is not everywhere uniform despite outward similarities, and it begins to redress what McRobbie has identified as a problem with cultural analyses of education. "What get ignored" in work on youth culture, she writes (1994:180), "are the interactions between the various discourses [by which she means "the media"] and also between the young people and the wider social and institutional relations which they inhabit." My own emphasis here is on the ways students themselves draw on cultural meanings, such as those embedded in "socks" or *wazima*, and combine these meanings with conceptual patterns they observe and experience through material culture.

A number of studies on schooling in the United States and Europe have looked at the ways cultural categories and discourses mediate material culture and student groups. They are helpful for thinking about "the gendered nature of cultural flows across social and national boundaries"—including Dr. Remmy's song about socks—and the "ways in which such flows are mediated by local gender constructs and relations"—including Mkufi students' ideas about schooling and sexuality (Grosz-Ngaté 1997:8–9). Paul Willis's (1977) examination of working-class alienation in British high schools, for instance, focuses on the ways two groups, "lads" and "ear 'oles," symbolically express different orientations to school authority (and to the adult world in general). His work is important for illustrating (among other things) how the internal heterogeneity of youth culture relates to cultural differences in the adult world. Much of the literature on adolescent culture published since Willis's study has treated youth categories as culturally heterogeneous and as indicative of choices that adolescents see themselves confronting. Penelope Eckert's (1989) discussion of American adolescent categories, "jocks" and "burnouts," for instance, and Douglas Foley's (1990) analysis of Texan students' distinctions among *Vatos*, "town kids," and "kickers," illustrate how youth culture integrates the forces of neighborhood and family experience in ways that parallel class and ethnic differences. Along with many others,[6] they expand the notion that youth, as a social stage, is structured through the extended and nebulous rituals of schooling. They do so by showing how social differences develop *within* the social structure of schooling, and how the expressive forms of student culture contribute to the creation of social groups inside and outside schools. Willis notes of British "lads" (1977:17) that "opposition to [school] staff" is "made concrete" in "certain stylistic/symbolic discourses centering on the three great consumer goods supplied by capitalism . . . : clothes, cigarettes, and alcohol." Opposition is similarly expressed by some school-aged youth in Machame, where shop owners cater to youth in Ndala Village and where clothes, cigarettes, alcohol, and music are important stylistic expressions of student culture.

Yet as with British and American cases, there is something unique about what students do in Machame—on western Mount Kilimanjaro it is that they incorporate themselves into the increasingly commodified world using idioms of kinship and age hierarchy. There is a core, if nebulous, set of beliefs that people on the mountain identify as "Chagga." I have been referring to them in this work in connection with inheritance, marriage, and initiation. It is these loose associations, as well as the social relations and institutions that organize and give structure to them, that students reproduce and innovate on in their own peer groups.

BOBBY BROWN, COMPUTER BEAT, AND LOVER BOY: MALE SIGNIFIERS OF YOUTH CULTURE

One way to explore this core set of beliefs is to look further at how students talk about their interests, including how they use idioms of kinship and land to engage in conversations with metropolitan centers. A popular student hangout was a "disco club" located along the main tarmac road in Ndala Village. Inspired by the scenes students saw on music videos (which wealthier students had access to), the club was the height of entertainment for students searching for some escape. Students talked about it with great enthusiasm, as is evident in their essays.

> Chagga's tribe like Reggae sang by Bob Marley, Lucke Dube, Peter Tosh and Gregrory Isaac. When you pass this village you may see many people dance. You can confuse what is the problem.
>
> In my village every Sunday they dance each types of music and they enjoyed it. They say music is small key of life and they like especially Bluez sang by Judith Boucher, Lionel Rich and SuperWoman. And *mayenu* and *kwasakwasa* sang by Kanda Bongo Man and Pepe Kale.
>
> Our mothers and fathers on our village like to listen bluez only but they dislike to dance it. They say that is youth music.
>
> Schoolgirl, Form 3

My parents will never dance bleuzi. It is not their tradition. They get embarrassed to be youth in the village.

Schoolboy, Form 3

The villages around our school have a few cassettes they like and they know to dance Reggae only and listen Christian religion songs and *taarabu* [a coastal Swahili style of music]. And many students who come from that villages around our school they don't know what is cassette, which is reggae music, funk, bluez, *nzawisa*, *mayenu* and *kwasakwasa*, even how to dance it and to listen.

Schoolgirl, Form 3

Girls and boys who went to the club would flaunt the latest clothes that they had bought in Moshi or Arusha, and they would compete with one another to master the moves they had seen Kanda Bongo Man and Bobby Brown make.[7] Most who danced were secondary schoolboys who performed for schoolgirls and other youth in the village, yet occasionally girls danced in concert with boys, attracting the shouts and encouragement of school friends. The dancers themselves demonstrated virtual sex, hips moving in rapid gyrations. One schoolboy, for instance, acquired the name "M.C. Bobby," not only because he was the "Microphone Controller of Bobby Brown," but because he could dance in the manner students found sexually alluring about Bobby Brown's movements in music videos. Another boy was nicknamed "Lover Boy," after the American pop music group of this same name. And another, Computer Beat, was so named for his abilities to dance rapidly and rhythmically. Lover Boy and Computer Beat were popular in their own right, but M.C. Bobby stole the show with his dancing and charisma.

Like the American singer Bobby Brown, M.C. Bobby wore "cool pants" that were all the rage—baggy and big with the crotch hanging down. He walked the walk, talked the talk, and made his moves with the girls as he saw Bobby Brown do on video. M.C. Bobby won first place in a dance competition in Moshi Town—an award that earned him several hundred shillings, which he used to buy more clothes and music cassettes—and he performed occasionally with a group of other students at weddings and confirmations in Ndala Village. Bobby Brown's *Don't Be Cruel* (MCA label 1988) and *Bobby* (MCA label 1992) were among students' favorite recordings; Tupac Shakur (an American singer killed in a 1996 shooting), was in 1996 their favorite rapper. A music video produced by Kanda Bongo Man provided students with hours of entertainment. And I once observed M.C. Bobby and other boys and girls repeatedly view certain segments of a Bobby Brown video in which he danced and sang about love and romance; students looked intently on and repeated the lyrics and dance moves.

Schoolgirls' and schoolboys' fascination with Bobby Brown stemmed from what many saw as his subversive yet respectable qualities. Brown sang openly about romance and love—taboo subjects for most adults. He expressed himself through provocative, hip-thrusting movements that, although not unlike Chagga initiation dances in that they accentuated the lower portion of the body, were nonetheless recognized as sexually arousing and distinctly "American." Stories had it that Brown owned three houses in the United States and that he was building a fourth for his mother. It was this—and the fact that he allegedly took care of his children and wife, Whitney Houston—that students said earned him their respect. For central to many girls' and boys' ideals about fame and fortune was that upwardly mobile and successful people—whether living in the United States or on Mount Kilimanjaro—ought to retain connections with their natal families. Brown, to these students, was managing success in an appropriately gendered way. He was providing for his wife and family and promoting values of kinship and patrilineality. In building a new home, Brown signaled to students, much as Mama Daudi, who had bought the bananas at the graduation auction, had signaled to some people in the audience (Chapter 2), that he was remaining socially and emotionally close to home. In short, he was reproducing what many students had come to see as "traditional" qualities of Chagga society, even as he was contesting some of the rigid norms by singing about love and sex.

Students' fascination with Bobby Brown challenged adult ideas that *kijana* were developmentally immature and too young to dance suggestively and dress fashionably. In most teachers' views, the singer was a bad influence on students' characters—a person culturally "foreign" to Tanzanian values and practices, and "too adult" for still-formative youth. Indeed, his popularity provoked teachers to react against students' self-proclaimed authority and to demand adherence to school rules. In many teachers' views, students' fascination with Brown and other musicians inverted the structures of authority defined and policed at school. It affronted the ideal that teachers were socially, economically, and culturally "worth" more than their students (in the sense that teachers were older and therefore supposed to have acquired greater command over external influences than their juniors). And it made a mockery of the promise of schooling to offer students better lives *after* they graduated, by prematurely rewarding students with the signs of success that, when compared with the material wealth and sophistication of their teachers, made their teachers look comparatively poor and provincial.

Students' fascination with international figures is easy enough to explain in terms of the symbolic inversion of authority—students simply do what teachers and adults think that they should not. But what about the fact that mostly boys participated in this form of popular culture? Asante, a Form 3 student, argued that girls were not supposed to dance to the alluring rhythms of certain music:

> [G]irls are not supposed to dance the bluez or do any of the *kwasakwasa* that boys do. This is due to our tradition. Girls are not allowed to be promiscuous. This is against our culture and family rules. Some of them go out and dance the bluez but they have no respect.

Asante's cultural assumptions about gender differences were certainly not shared by all. The Form 3 schoolgirl quoted above went on to say that she "enjoyed" dancing. Her essay conveyed her sense of expertise and pride at being able to do what her parents did not, and her boldness in stepping into the center of the dance stage had earned her the nickname Mama Bluezi.

Yet even among girls who wrote about dance, "too much" dancing was often described as risky and offensive. One student wrote that dancing girls could be called "prostitutes" who "asked for trouble." Her essay captured the tone of some others: scorn and concern for the girls who went to the disco and "showed off." "People say that those girls are going to get raped and pregnant before they are married," Stellah's friend Angela later told me. "They are the ones, people say, who get pregnant and then drop out of school. That's why I never dance the blues." Even Stellah, who more than once danced blues and *kwasakwasa*, said she sometimes felt dirty (*mchafu*) and despised by others afterward.

One consequence of the uneven social and sexual connotations of dancing was that boys in this context came to stand metonymically for the entire "youth culture." Even girls who danced the blues with boys were seen by some as leaning toward masculinized forms. "Who do those girls think they are that they should go out and flaunt their bodies like this?" Angela's mother asked. Her implication, like that of others, was that these girls were "too big for themselves" and trying to be like important men. Bibi Muro, for instance, as we have seen earlier, blamed the school for encouraging girls to become more like men. She said that because most girls "these days" were not ritually circumcised "the way we were in the past," their "private parts" were unnaturally large; they were "climbing up just like men's."

The association between dancing and sexuality provided some students with the cultural tools for revising the puerile signs of youth culture and schooling. By working against what was expected of them, they could redefine themselves as "powerful youth." They could do what many of their parents and teachers could not—embody the worldly signs of commercial pop culture—and in so doing could make a claim to an adult status uniquely identified with their schooling. Education—particularly schooling—came into students' arguments about why they, and not teachers or parents, danced. "Educated people know this dancing is okay," was a common argument, the implication being that those who scorned it were culturally ignorant. Even more than this, students developed a language to describe themselves in contrast to elders. Whereas they gave specific nicknames to individuals, many called themselves, as a social group, "wise old men."

THE SHIFTING AND UNCERTAIN STATUS OF YOUTH: WAZEE WAZIMA

Wazee wazima—literally, wise old men (the singular is *mzee mzima*)—refers to youth who regarded themselves as detached from elders' authority and who were fully caught up in the project of socially refining themselves by buying and consuming imported commodities. The term was used derogatorily by some adults and students (that is, by those who did *not* self-identify as *wazee wazima*), but it was embraced playfully by students who considered themselves "of the present" and "in the know."

Wazee wazima are a particular incarnation of what Kerner has described as three character types popular in the early and mid-1980s: Check Rap, Check Bob, and TX Kubwa (Kerner 1988:320–328).[8] They are linguistic references (rarely used as direct forms of address) that characterize strategies for upward mobility. Much as Check Rap, Check Bob, and TX Kubwa were used by youth in the early and mid-1980s to parody the dominant culture of the adult world, the term *wazee wazima* is used in the 1990s to express youths' social distance from their "traditional" and "out-of-date" elders.

What distinguishes *wazee wazima* from youth culture of just a decade and a half ago is the particular emphasis on health and fitness symbolized in their name, as well as the comparatively greater extent to which they are integrated into the market economy. Whereas in the late 1980s people considered it unusual that youth (*vijana*) could have access to cash-and-carry items, now nearly every secondary school student is culturally connected to the global market through fashionable commodities of one kind or another. Shoes, hairstyles, music, dance styles—all reflect students' ostensible social orientations away from the cultural economy of the lineage and toward the economy of world markets.

Even the name *wazee wazima* reflects youths' social precociousness. The term *wazee* usually refers to old men of the village upon whom is bestowed the greatest respect and authority, but in the case of *wazee wazima*, students are not chronologically "old," but socially mature and wise, at least presumably. They do not assume that they are subordinate to their elders' authority in matters of consumer culture, and they do not presume to defer to their parents about what to buy, listen to, or watch in the way of imported music videos. Instead, they hold themselves up as masters of their own ways—and yet they frame their new ways in familiar terms.

Wazee itself is a masculinizing concept, one that implies that the pinnacle of health and fitness is male. In contemporary discourse, both girls and boys aspire to be "wise old men." But the emphasis on "health" (*wazima*) as a descriptor of cool, hip youth stands in stark contrast to some adults' concerns. Some students' parents and grandparents believe students are susceptible to sexually transmitted diseases, including AIDS. *Wazima* refers to (among other things) "healthy people" believed to be HIV-negative. When used to modify "people" (*watu*), *wazima* indicates in the conventional use that these people are physically fit, that they are at the pinnacle of performance, and that there are no risks in interacting with them.

Students who call themselves *wazee wazima* believe that they are healthy (*wenye afya na wazima*) and mentally fit. They are not passé in the

10. A secondary school student whom classmates identified as a *mzee mzima.*

way culture and custom are sometimes portrayed in the curriculum, nor are they marginal or dangerous in the way students who study too much are sometimes seen (Stambach 1998). *Wazee wazima* believe that they manage to avoid the ossification they see in elders' "tradition" and the dangers their elders associate with the fast pace of youth culture. Although old and mature in the sense of being "wise," *wazee wazima* are not obsolete—at least not (as they see it) if they continue to consume the commodities that they associate with education and modernity.

As Masolo notes in the course of talking about the ethnophilosophical work of Alexis Kagame, the word "*Uzima* in Kiswahili means life, biological life" and "*mtu mzima* may sometimes mean something more than or different from just a 'live person.' It may mean a mature person or one who is judged capable of exercising correct mental activities expected of adulthood" (Masolo 1994:90). The association of -*zima* with mental stability is important for thinking again about the ways students portray themselves as strong and able to deal with the possible dangers of too much schooling. The opposite of *wazima* is "rendered in *wazimu*, which means 'out of right mind,' 'incapable of good reasoning,' 'mad,' etc." (Masolo 1994:90). *Kupandwa na wazimu* means to be mounted by the ancestors, to be possessed or overcome with a form of madness that is even more devastating than being cursed (*kulaaniwa*), being toyed with mentally (*kuchezewa akili*), or being a person who suffers from madness (*kichaa*). *Wazee wazima* are not mad or confused; they are not disoriented from studying too much. Nor are they in danger of bursting their brains or falling into a panic from the pressures of secondary school. Indeed, *wazee wazima* hardly study at all; that is not the focus of what they are doing in school. Instead, their interest lies in acquiring the signs of adult status that will lead to upward mobility. Their health and fitness are symbolized in the term that is applied to them as a group, and their rapid progression from "youth" to "adulthood" is accelerated through accumulation.

Mzima also has a physical meaning that, in addition to referring to the health or age of a person or thing, refers to the wholeness or completeness of an object. *Nzima* can be used to modify the "whole house" (*nyumba nzima*), a "whole loaf of bread" (*mkate mzima*), the "whole body" (*mwili mzima*), the "whole city" (*mji mzima*), and so on.[9] When used in the form *mtu mzima* (literally "whole person"), *mzima* can be used to refer to the "full growth" or maturity of a person and to the attainment of the ideal state of personhood (Masolo 1994:90–91). Applied to *wazee wazima*, who position themselves as the most successful and fit products of the school experience, the ideal state of personhood is reflected in their personal control of cassettes, clothes, videos, and the like. Their ability to consume luxury items in general is an expression of their full social integrity.

People in Machame hold many views about the implications of this new *wazee wazima* group. From some perspectives, *wazee wazima* attest to positive social development and to students' success at removing themselves from having to work on the land. From other perspectives, *wazee wazima* are anomalies that schooling has created and that it must somehow now socially re-create, this time more acceptably. It is difficult to attribute one view or the other to any particular group, for many people hold both views concurrently, without any apparent contradiction. For example, a mother of a secondary school student complained that students these days "show off" (*kuringa*) in front of their elders. She saw it as particularly offensive that students walked through the village wearing fashionable clothes (*nguo za kisasa*) and that they danced to commercial music. To her these were signs that students did not know their proper place in the community, that they were acting older than their positions properly allowed, and that even though they *thought* they were *wazima*—healthy and grown-up—they were to her still socially immature and in need of adult supervision. At the same time, however, she pointed to the stereo cassette player and the pile of cassettes lying on a table as indications that her children (two of whom were secondary school students) were socioeconomically better off than their unschooled neighbors. The electronic equipment belonged to one of her sons, who had acquired it from his older (employed) brother. And she praised the fact that one of the main graduation events had been a "disco" performance in which several students got up and danced to a song by an American singer; this, she said, was worthy evidence of what students learned in school.

EDUCATIONAL OUTCOMES AND SOCIAL TRANSFORMATIONS

Wazee wazima, as a social group, then—like city sisters and stay-at-home mothers—represents a particular cultural locus in the picture of possible education outcomes. It is a masculinized counterpart to big city sisters and the symbolic opposite of what school failures, by students' terms, look like (Stambach 1998). While no single student fits the category precisely, the category reflects what people think education can in part do. It has meaning in relation to other categories, not in and of itself. By integrating international personalities with local values about family and lineage, and by abstracting and interpreting outside influences in ways that combine with local norms, students enact novel social possibilities within the constantly changing parameters of "men" and "old age." They combine cultural ideas about "the other" with local values about authority and power, and they demonstrate their educated, adult status in terms that are different from their parents.

Students are not the only actors who redefine and redeploy the signs of age and authority, but they are an important part of the social picture. They combine the highly localized symbols of cultural activity with more widely distributed beliefs and practices. In this regard, they overshadow what is typically thought to be male lineage members' integrative abilities. In the past, chiefs, subchiefs, and male lineage leaders combined highly localized beliefs and practices with transregional symbols of cultural activity, including trade. Ordinary adults, children, and youth were dependent on them for symbolically revitalizing the community by bringing rain, regulating irrigation channels, and sustaining political-economic order (S. F. Moore 1986). But today, school students assume this revitalizing and socially integrative function with greater and greater authority and independence. Their self-proclaimed capacity to control the signs of power and consumerism has prompted many living on Mount Kilimanjaro to comment with mixed approval on students' command of international culture. For some, students' wherewithal is an indicator of educational achievement. It is testament to the fact that Tanzanians can appropriate the signs of international power. For others, it is a sign of loss to the community and an indication that youth are "moving too far." It signifies the emasculation of "traditional culture" and the disruption of the hierarchical nature of gender relations characteristic of local life.

These various interpretations are indicative of a shift in power from elders to youth that has been going on for several decades. To pick up on a point that Sally Falk Moore made in her work on customary law on Mount Kilimanjaro (S. F. Moore 1986), schooling confers a disproportionate degree of authority on particular people within localized lineages. In *Social Facts and Fabrications*, Moore described twentieth-century transformations in political authority in terms of a shift in power from chiefs to localized patrilines. The political authority of chiefs, she argued, gradually diminished as commoner lineages gained greater autonomy and economic strength during colonial and postcolonial times. Whereas the courts redirected authority from chiefs to commoners, schooling did so from adults to youth in a process that some people saw as emasculating. In both cases cultural understandings of authority have changed substantially, yet in both cases the shift is top-down (from chief to commoner, from adult to youth): commoners revitalized the local community by internalizing the external influences of bureaucratic administration and coffee production in the early to mid-twentieth century; secondary school students have done so by internalizing the external influences of consumer culture.

Thinking about schooling in terms of students' appropriation of foreign culture approximates standard modernization theories, yet it also differs from them. It approximates them by acknowledging that schooling promotes the expansion of local economies into world markets, as I discussed in Chapter 1, and gives educated persons a "boost up" from one socioeconomic level to another. Yet it departs from them in that upward-oriented social and economic motion comes about through a process of internal elaboration interacting with external forces, not through a series of externally imposed measures to modernize a people. Thus to say that schooling in Africa involves the transmission of Western values into African culture (or its currently more prevalent formulation, that schooling "violates" an indigenous cultural system) attributes the problem to only one side—the external. It overlooks how external factors are first objectified and then given meaning from within.

All of this is a way of illustrating how two competing strands of thought in the theoretical literature are integrated culturally, at least in this particular area of Tanzania if not also in other places. Two observations have been made regarding the outcomes of schooling in Africa: one, that schooling contributes positively to social and economic problems and to technological change (e.g., Lave 1977:178; Serpell 1993:155–165); and two, that the organizing principles of schooling are so disjunct from African values that "neither writing nor schooling [has] made any significant difference to the basic organizing principles governing the evaluation of knowledge" (Bloch 1993:106). The first observation suggests that schooling *changes* the ways people act and behave; the second, that it does not. The first suggests that the learning environment and curriculum can be designed (and in some cases *has* been designed) to effect social and cultural change; the second suggests that it cannot, or at least that in some cases it *has not*. The two observations are not mutually exclusive, nor are they described as such in the above-cited literature, yet seldom are they treated together explicitly in any one analysis.

Considering that in Machame people identify schooling with material innovations and change *without* necessarily always seeing schooling as eroding the underlying principles of social organization, it would seem that the school is used to transform social relations within limits. People here in general appear to regard schooling as a means for addressing social and economic problems and as a means for preserving basic relationships. In this regard, the outcomes of schooling are less totalizing, less thoroughgoing, than some education planners have envisioned, yet schooling does have an influence—a profound one—on the ways people think about themselves and their worlds.

7

"Mountains Never Meet But People Do"

RELATIONSHIPS BUILT THROUGH SCHOOLING

I BEGAN this study with the aim of eliciting how the sociocultural dimensions of secondary schooling in Machame relate to values and beliefs about education in the wider society and, vice versa, how some of the organizing principles of social life on the mountain contribute to secondary schooling. I end with some reflections on the social ties schooling is endowed with creating, namely, new relations between seemingly different people and seemingly different cultures and societies.

When I left Machame in 1993, after having conducted research for nearly a year and a half, my farewells were marked by conversations about the need to stay in touch. I departed promising to write and send photos and to return as soon as I could, and several friends and I made arrangements for them to visit the United States. The farewells were difficult, for despite best-laid plans, no one really knew when or how our paths would meet again. As a way of making the parting easier, people would frequently console themselves and me with the saying "mountains never meet but people do." The saying conveys, in a prosocial way, the optimistic notion that people's paths will cross again.[1] I was not surprised to hear some people say that their own schooling would keep us in touch. Several Form 4 students who had just performed well on their national examinations and who were planning to continue with Forms 5 and 6 and then college, anticipated that they would someday study in Canada or the United States or that they would be involved in educational exchanges. Although, sadly, few of these plans have come to pass—usually money has been the obstacle—the optimism and enthusiasm that had been growing around education, spurred by new opportunities on the mountain for secondary school students, culminated in these sentiments about the possibility for schooling to bridge social worlds. One lesson students and parents seemed to have learned from schooling, indeed from my presence in their lives as a field researcher studying education, was that schooling sometimes took people to faraway places. If it did not exactly make mountains move, it brought people into closer proximity. Unfairly, in my view, it was easier for me to travel than for the vast majority of Tanzanians; however, many Tanzanians appeared to have learned that the road to travel and mobility began with access to schooling.

When I left again after my visit in 1996, this sentiment was greatly amplified. In the interim it had become even easier for Tanzanians to get foreign currency and passports, and although the United States Embassy had stiffened its criteria for granting Tanzanians visas, Canada remained a hope-inspiring entryway for people looking to study in North America. It had also become apparent that secondary school opportunities in the Machame area were predictable and growing, and that more people thought that they might qualify for placement into secondary schools and, from there, get into international programs. Again, few of these plans ever came to fruition, yet this did not stop the flow of applications. I left Tanzania in 1996 with several forms to mail to U.S. programs and with requests to forward more information about schooling in North America.

I mention this mood of enthusiasm because it struck me as one of the most powerful forces motivating and constraining many people, particularly students, during the period in which I conducted field research. Even though the vast majority of school students performed poorly on national exams and had little practical chance of continuing beyond Form 4,[2] the possibility of higher education and of international travel held great allure for many. In some cases, I could see that it was not educational programs alone that caught students' fancies but access to the material culture they had come to identify with "cool, hip" (safi, wa) life and to associate with an educated Western culture. Whether or not students in the end moved anywhere beyond their natal homes, their expectations, anticipations, and general social perceptions were that schooling would somehow, sometime, and in some way take them far. One school student who was about to board

a car on her way to secondary school captured the perception with a linguistic combination of Kiswahili and English. "*Wana*accelerate [they
accelerate]," she said of the other students who were already packed into
the back seat of a Mercedes-Benz.

And yet the enthusiasm for travel associated with schooling was marked
with a tenor of disappointment. Some of the most ardent advocates of secondary schooling, who saw state education as a means for bettering their
lives, had given up hope that their school education would produce the
lifestyle changes they had anticipated. Recent female school graduates in
particular were feeling the pull from two directions simultaneously. Many
had apparently not foreseen or understood the difficulty they would have
moving away from the village or from natal homes. Nor had they calculated
that the backlash against secondary-schooled women would reach the inten-
sity that it occasionally did. In several areas I visited in 1996, women said
they had to hide the fact that they had been school educated. They did so by
making sure they spoke only Kimachame and not Kiswahili or English—
both "school languages"—when they were in the village, and by wearing
clothes they associated with *mama wa nyumbani,* so as not to attract attention to what villagers might consider to be their schooled pretentions. Some
women told me that they trusted only other secondary school graduates with
their children and that they did not feel fully confident that less schooled village women would not curse or emotionally try to defeat them. In this
context, traveling became not only an opportunity for more schooling but a
chance to break out of the patrilineal and age-hierarchical model that social
relationships and structures on the mountain seemed to perpetuate.

I do not mean to suggest that many people rejected the tenets of formal
schooling (although some did), but rather that most failed to anticipate
fully the transformations with which secondary schooling would become
associated and the contentions these transformations would spawn. On the
one hand, secondary schooling was almost universally seen as the single
most transformative institution on the mountain, yet on the other hand,
people were of many minds about the ends to which schooling should be
put. The debate about the pros and cons of schooling appeared to be churn-
ing on and on. If any aspect had shifted since the early 1990s, it had to do
with schools' permanency. Whereas the financial basis and social fate of private secondary schools were uncertain in 1990, by 1996 and on into the
next millennium, private secondary schools now appeared certain to stay.

THE CULTURAL DYNAMICS OF EDUCATION

Many anthropological studies have examined the ways schooling defines and reshapes "local traditions." This work provides a better understanding of the ways local practices and beliefs define and shape "modernity." On Mount Kilimanjaro, to look at school students dancing to imported music or wearing some of the latest fashions they have seen in *Vogue* magazines (available for sale in urban centers), one might get the impression that schooling has changed village life into "modern things." One might also get the impression that schooling engineers these social changes by introducing students to new lessons. But what I hope to have shown is that "the modern" is made in no small part from within—from the dynamic interaction of social life on the ground, in concert with school-produced categories.

The question of what "the modern" is has been widely debated in social theory. As I noted in the introduction to this work, it has typically been discussed either in connection with tradition as a "foundational order" (Habermas 1979; Weber 1968) or with postmodernity as an eclectic pastiche of traditional themes and their variations (Benhabib 1992; Rabinow 1986; cf. S. F. Moore 1996b:603). I have kept these debates to a minimum in my analysis, preferring to foreground instead how modernity emerges through the social and political organization of social life. In doing so, I have chosen to emphasize what others by and large have not: that *the school* is an institution through and around which collective notions of modernity and tradition emerge. In northern Tanzania, the "modernity of schooling" is formulated in connection with "traditional forms" through the deep dialectical interplay of the organizational principles of everyday life (which stress age-hierarchy and patrilineality), and the narratives of schooling (which formulate tradition as a technologically backward form, and which have been shaped in part through the formulation of "culture" and "education" in colonial ethnography). The question I have been interested in is not whether or not—or even how—schools produce new modern subjects. Instead, I have been curious to know the terms by which people themselves have come to see schools' productive efforts as "modernity."

As secondary schools have become more permanently fixed on the landscape of Mount Kilimanjaro, people's tendency to identify the school as the main source of social change has made it increasingly difficult to break out of the deterministic language of policy. The very model that some policy planners hold—that schooling can engineer and promote social change—is increasingly the language in which people oppose and defend the operations of state-regulated education. Because secondary schooling calls for collective and personal redefinition, it is linked to the constitution of new cultural values and, in the end, to the seeming erosion of the practices and beliefs that school curricula and policies, and people themselves, have come to objectify as "Chagga tradition."

Alex Inkeles (1998) has asked whether or not the apparent global trend toward cultural convergence and toward an apparent uniformity of social life, marked by demographic shifts toward wage labor, bureaucratic management, and nuclear families, is a consequence of the operations of state-run schooling. His analysis, which leads him to conclude that some aspects of societies converge and others diverge, is too removed in my assessment from the microprocesses of everyday life to enable us to adequately understand how, and how unevenly, broad social institutions such as schools effect social change. On the surface, schooling appears to be culturally homogenizing. It supplies the trappings of an educated identity—a cultural taste for certain kinds of dress and entertainment (cf. Bourdieu 1984); a language for communicating widely, including increasingly across the Internet (notably, however, not in Machame where virtually no one has a computer or access to the Internet; indeed, where the electricity is unpredictable). It sometimes even provides employment opportunities, although in Tanzania this has not been the case for the majority (Malekela 1991). However, when we move our analyses beyond the school institution and look at the cultural practices and values that inform various local meanings of "education," we can begin to see that the similarity of outward forms does not always tell us about the heterogeneity of underlying organization. Much as the world system is a "rational expression of relative cultural logics" (Sahlins 1994:416), so are schools institutional forms that reveal a web of contingent and often contradictory understandings about how to structure and organize society. Classrooms and textbooks may appear the same, but the relationships embedded in and meanings read into them are often suprisingly unique and different.

I have argued in this book that schools are culturally endowed with the capacity to effect social change, not that policies or educational curricula are themselves transformative in the first instance. This argument challenges much of the accepted wisdom of the role of schools in development. Any effect that state-run education has had on social life and its organization has necessarily occurred in historically, spatially, and socially determined circumstances and in conjunction with local beliefs and practices. School curricula and classrooms, the banana grove and lineage lands, as we have seen, are some of the most salient sites where "education" is perceived as being culturally produced. The pedagogic messages imbued through banana grove farming, or through the lessons of ritual circumcision and initiation are seen by some—mostly those of older generations—as a means of instilling a sense of historical and cultural Chagga consciousness. In contrast, the lessons of schooling—especially those learned from peers and not necessarily (although also) from teachers in classrooms—is seen by others, mostly by students themselves, as a means for social advancement and upward mobility.

Taken together, the banana grove and school begin to structure alternative temporal and spatial terrains and, by extension, categories of people associated with tradition and modernity. Stay-at-home mothers versus city sisters, *wazee wazima,* and the charismatic qualities of some individuals— M.C.Bobby, Lover Boy, and Computer Beat, for instance, whom I introduced in Chapter 6—all convey the sense that there are distinct and different identities associated with tradition and modernity. There is nothing particularly unique about the phenomenon of differentiating old and new. When state-sponsored "improving institutions" such as schools objectify people's lifeways and call them "culture" or "tradition," local people almost always engage in a cultural renarration in an effort to join the political unit of perceived (and sometimes forcibly imposed) political power and to receive the economic benefits it promises. This is what appears to have happened in colonial days on the mountain (Lawuo 1984) and what is happening today in other places—parts of Mexico (Levinson, forthcoming), Nepal (Skinner and Holland 1996), and post-Soviet eastern Europe (Kozakiewicz 1992)—all in connection again with state-organized education.

IMPLICATIONS FOR THE STUDY OF GENDER AND GENERATION

Having analyzed in this work some of the institutions and practices that are identified with Chagga culture and marked with pedagogic qualities—initiation, marriage, and inheritance have been my primary focus—we can now ask how this adds to our understanding of gender and generation and the transformative role of schools. First and most significant, it is important to note that schools are not themselves instilling a set of principles and definitions by which all students the world over are becoming, in their gendered expressions and as newly schooled generations, more and more alike. Rather, changes people observe among school-educated students, and between young men and women, are increasingly attributed to the operations of schools and to the perceived effects of state-organized education. This is obviously a subtle distinction but one that moves beyond deterministic analyses that suggest that schools, if radically reformulated, can teach girls "women's ways of knowing" (Belenky et al. 1986). Schools in some cases do "teach gender," as when the Tanzanian syllabus instructs on Mothercraft, or when a religious instructor tells male students to "preserve your bullets; girls, lock your boxes." Sometimes, too, the social organization and structures of schools are imbued with masculinist beliefs and symbols, as when the mostly male teaching staff at Mkufi operates from a patrilineal position of adult male authority, or when schooling is equated with banana grove inheritance, a typically male prerogative.

However, the point to retain is that the kind of gendered and generational transformations associated with schools emerge through a dialectal interrelation of school practices with local culture. Thus the kind of "gendered knowing" schools produce is not culturally universal;[3] school-educated women who are thought by elders to be becoming more and more like Chagga men are neither women anticipated in the official policies nor those that hold in most versions of Western feminist ideals. Instead, they are a product of the interaction and mutual effects of the structures and principles of formal schooling and of social life on Mount Kilimanjaro. The ways in which school and home are perceived and are perceived to be acted upon are a complex process involving individual agency and the mobilization of collective forces behind social norms. Thus secondary school students and graduates formulate marital and employment alternatives in terms of extended families. Building a house on purchased land and having a child through whom to pass an inheritance independent of a husband are ideals that are expressed in terms of schools' opportunities *as they are produced in relation to and out of* the social structures and values of life on Mount Kilimanjaro.

In a sense, then, what schooling has done is to have helped to make people their own ethnographers. For even as ethnographers have sometimes felt they themselves have enjoyed the position of being able to speak about culture and tradition, schooling has provided school-goers the language for objectifying social practices and for contrasting seemingly different lifeways with one another. This as a phenomenon is one of the most interesting points of inquiry within an anthropology of education. How it is played out in terms of gender and generation has been a main focus of my inquiry.

On this point, and second, objectifications of age and gender are occurring in concert with political, economic, social, cultural, and demographic changes throughout the region. This creates formidable social tension that for some people turns "cultural changes" into "cultural loss." The rapid expansion of secondary school opportunities, combined with privatization and an increasing emphasis on democracy and individual freedom (S. F. Moore 1996b), adds grist to the mills of public perception that liberal democratic institutions such as schools lead to moral decay among youth, particularly young women. Consumed with thinking about converting their banana groves and grove products into cash for school fees, some people are overwhelmed with frustration to the point that they blame changes on women and youth. "Our daughters come back and think they can rule the roost," said Mama Angela, quoted at the beginning of this work. Joshua Makia and Mzee Lema, also quoted in the beginning, note that they have sold "our land and cows to send our children to secondary school" and that they have "given up everything so that our sons—even our daughters!— can go to school." Women and youth become the collectively marked categories around which people debate and direct social change.

Finally, efforts to institutionalize gender and age—as schools do through grade ranking and course programming (for example, home economics versus agricultural science as female and male orientations within the curriculum) typically trigger degrees of dissent. Educational policies and programs rarely go without some amount of social commentary. As a result, a dialogue of sorts develops between educators, policy-makers and curriculum planners, on the one hand, and parents, students, and villagers, on the other, who object to the version of social organization that the state is attempting to institutionalize. Gender and age become marked categories within this debate. They are categories typically spotlighted in educational interventions and, as such, are the focus of intense scrutiny and argument.

In Machame, one line of thinking within popular discourse was marked by an explicit comparison between schooling and initiation. So-called traditional practices were seen as more effective in producing stable social conditions than were the seemingly frivolous and risk-producing actions associated with (for girls) home economics. As Bibi Muro in Chapter 3 illustrated for us, home economics was responsible for stimulating (or at least not curbing, as circumcision and initiation were thought by some people to do) girls' sexual desires. These desires were, in turn, indicative of gendered relations gone awry: schoolgirls' risky behavior, the argument went, jeopardized social relations of production and reproduction once associated with extended lineages living on banana groves. In extreme cases, these schoolgirls were blamed for the spread of HIV.

Another line of thinking—not the exact opposite of this but one held by younger generations—was that schooling and initiation contrasted radically and that schooling provided the avenue for social and geographic mobility. City sisters and *wazee wazima* were the embodiment of this particular sentiment, for it was they who challenged institutional norms of the curriculum by pushing school lessons beyond the realm of teachers' control. Ongoing, individualized expressions of the self, of students' identities as individuals, bent, twisted, and manipulated the meanings of "self" once embedded in the policy Education for Self-Reliance (Nyerere 1967). Even though ESR was no longer on the front burner of educational planning and policy, students' continued reference to it and their refusal many times to abide with school rules outside classrooms, hardened perceptions that students did "things with socks" and otherwise toyed with gendered and generational codes. To many students, this was a terrific benefit that they thought came automatically with schooling—being granted the institutional space and freedom to play with social relations and to remake "culture" to their own ends. To others, particularly the oldest in the community, many of whom had had little or no school education, students' self-proclaimed abilities to call themselves *wazee wazima* or city sisters were nothing short of defiant and socially damaging.

In the foregoing pages, then, I have taken up others' challenges to describe and isolate the inside dynamics of local culture and education (e.g., Maurice Bloch 1993:106; Foley 1990:165–168; Willis 1990; Wulff 1995:1–2), and I have illustrated how culturally specific beliefs and practice contribute to what is particular about Chagga schools. As I noted at various points in this work, it would be misleading to imply that everything I portray here is unique to Chagga culture and society on Mount Kilimanjaro. Many pedagogic techniques and curricular emphases are characteristic of education and schooling in other parts of Africa (e.g., Bledsoe 1992; Bloch 1993; Foster 1965; Serpell 1993; Talis 1985), if not throughout the world (e.g., Hurtig 1998; Levinson, forthcoming; Swatridge 1985). Yet there is a core, if nebulous, set of beliefs that people from Mount Kilimanjaro identify as "Chagga." It is these loose associations, as well as the conceptual operations of patrilineality and hierarchy that connect them, that I hope to have illustrated in relation to schooling.

In formulating a description of the inside dynamics, I have drawn upon a wealth of African ethnography. My intention in previous pages has been to extend analyses of what might loosely be classified as anthropological studies of African knowledge, history, ritual, and power (among them Beidelman 1993; Bloch 1993; Comaroff and Comaroff 1992; Devisch 1993; Feierman 1990; Guyer 1995; Lambek 1993) by combining an analysis of culture and society on Mount Kilimanjaro with an examination of Tanzanian school curricula and policy. Additionally, I have sought to bring into discussions about African education a specific consideration of how "what goes on in schools" relates to the broader world and society. Except for a few works on generational transformations and ritual (most of which look at initiation, e.g., Kratz 1994; Richards 1956), there are to my knowledge no systematic studies in the anthropological literature on Africa of the rituals and activities of schooling or of the cultural assumptions that inform curricula. I have suggested in this cultural analysis of schooling that there are fundamental disjunctures between policy and practice, and I have illustrated how the official curriculum is valorized in relation to local ideals.

Finally, I have also explored how transformations in ideas about "education" reflect changes in what constitutes "community." In doing so, I have tried to convey that there is no one particular "Chagga community," but that multiple and often conflicting views about what is "Chagga" coexist. Differences are objectified in a range of cultural types—among them "cool, hip youth," "big sisters of the city," "stay-at-home mothers," even "farmers." I hope to have conveyed that these types are at once ephemeral yet enduring; that they reflect the particular events of the time yet speak to underlying tensions that give rise to change.

11. Mount Kilimanjaro, with Kibo peak located to the west, Mawenzi to the east.

ON THE TRANSFORMATIVE QUALITIES
OF ETHNOGRAPHY AND EDUCATION

In closing, I would like to reflect again on the adage about people and mountains. Like the adage I introduced at the beginning of this work—"a person living in a foreign place should not question the things she sees but upon returning to her own household, may comment all she wants"—the saying about mountains captures the sentiment that relationships are created through movements of people and the news they carry. The adage resonated on Mount Kilimanjaro with a story about two mountain peaks named Kibo and Mawenzi who "met again." According to the story, Kibo and Mawenzi, the two most prominent peaks on Mount Kilimanjaro, were sisters (see Illustration 11). When Mawenzi's fire went out, she begged an ember and some food from Kibo. Kibo granted Mawenzi this request, and Mawenzi returned home with food and an ember. Mawenzi was careless, however; she ate the food, and dropped the ember. She returned a second time to Kibo, and Kibo accommodated her, but again, Mawenzi ate the food and dropped the ember before arriving home. At the third request, Kibo got angry, picked up a wooden spoon, and beat her sister black and blue.

Two points are usually drawn from this story: one, that this is why Kibo is physically smooth and Mawenzi is jagged; two, that had Mawenzi recognized that "people" meet again, she might not have treated Kibo's gifts so glibly and might yet be in Kibo's favor. The story, like the adage, conveys the ideal that although people move—even though they grow up or go to school, or, as in my case with field research, they come, conduct research, and then move away—they very possibly meet again. *Unlike* mountains, they run into one another, and unless they are respectful and forward-thinking, as in the story Mawenzi was not, they jeopardize the quality of later interactions. They risk being ostracized and left out. Like Mawenzi, they are out in the cold.

This adage, in combination with the one I introduced in Chapter 1 on "strangers," provides insight into the cultural production of ethnography and of education. Both reflect Chagga cultural precepts about the wisdom of contemplating carefully the events and activities that one sees. The adage about strangers, as we have seen, speaks to specific situations in which would-be "wise people" would do well to remain silent: times when recently married Chagga women find themselves living amidst newly acquired affines; times when Chagga men are tempted to criticize their neighbors but must wait until they are beyond earshot; and times when anthropologists visiting "another place" wish to comment but must refrain until they "return home," and then must do so responsibly.

I hope to have remained true these sayings and to have neither revealed too much nor presented what I have said in a facile or irresponsible way. Whether or not I am successful, of course, depends not only on how I have conveyed and analyzed what I have seen, but also upon who will read this work and how they will interpret it. For reading, like writing ethnography, is a matter of engaging one's "self" in a cultural "other" (Boyarin 1993) and like research—and, indeed, like education itself—is a multiply configured process that changes everyone involved. In a study about education and schooling it is only fitting that I should anticipate (or more fittingly, humbly hope) that some people in Machame will read a portion or all of these pages. Indeed, several people have read and commented on earlier versions and have been instrumental in my reformulations. In continuing this exchange, I must come to terms ultimately with who is "a stranger" and what constitutes "home."

One answer, I suspect, lies in recent thinking in cultural anthropology: that schooling and other transnational processes "deterritorialize" local experiences by multiplying the "imaginative resources" people use to make sense of their changing lives (Appadurai 1991:196; Liechty 1995:188). Another—the same really, just differently configured in relation to other pieces of wisdom and values—takes us back to the Chagga saying about people and places, that "mountains never meet but people do." This saying illustrates how social relations emerge through the movements and communications of people. It points to the difficulties of isolating discrete communities and separating "one culture" from any other. Like the adage about "strangers" and "homes," it summarizes what I have sought to elicit in this work: that the cultural dimensions of schooling produce multiple ways of configuring social relations; that understandings of what constitutes education shift in the face of changing social and historical contexts; and that among the many other things schooling produces (whether at schools or colleges in the United States or at secondary institutions in Machame) is the recognition that, in the end, one is never entirely a "stranger" who can completely, unchanged, "return home."

NOTES

CHAPTER 1: "WHAT EDUCATED YOUTH DO THESE DAYS"

1. Stellah Mbasa, like Mkfui Secondary School and most proper names in this work, is a pseudonym. Following anthropological convention, I have sought to protect human subjects' rights and interests by not revealing the specifics of human subjects' identities. In some cases this has involved more than the use of pseudonyms to include modifying other markers of their identity, such as names of villages, birth orders within families, or the particularities of subjects' jobs. I have struggled a great deal with the ethics and methodology of this, though ultimately, as I describe later in this chapter, I found some resolution through the lessons I learned while living on Mount Kilimanjaro. I have come in the end to recognize that—despite the insistence of many people with whom I worked on the mountain who wanted to see their names in this work—retaining some degree of anonymity is essential for averting misinterpretation and unintended criticism.

2. It is typical for women who are mothers to be called by the first name of their firstborn child. In this case, Mama Elimbora's oldest biological daughter was named Elimbora. Mama Neema, quoted in this chapter's opening excerpts, had a firstborn child whose name was Neema. The same holds true for fathers, such that Elimbora's father was known among members of the community as Baba Elimbora. It does not matter if the firstborn child is male or female. In either case, parents will take children's names.

3. Unless otherwise noted, italicized translations are in Kiswahili, in this chapter and throughout this work. Kiswahili is the national and official language of Tanzania. The locally spoken dialect is Kimachame.

4. I mention Mr. Mbasa's father's brother's son, rather than his *uncle's* son, to draw attention to the culturally significant point that this is a cousin on Mr. Mbasa's paternal side, and thus an agnatic kin. As I discuss in the next chapter, agnatic kin, by customary practice, share rights over land and lineage wealth.

5. The Tanzanian school system comprises seven years of primary school (Standards I through VII), four years of secondary school (Forms 1 through 4) and two years of high school (Forms 5 and 6). Students seven years or older may enroll in Standard I.

6. Based on a survey I conducted of 375 households in Machame in 1992.

7. This group made up about 2 percent of the community, according to my household survey.

8. My thanks to J. P. Leary for helping me clarify this point.

9. It puts this Frazerian notion to the test insofar as schools are sufficient in providing what Frazer had in mind as adequate information for rational thinking.

10. Examples are too numerous to cite exhaustively, but for a glimpse of the iceberg, see Burke 1996; Hakansson 1988; Kratz 1994; Stoller 1989; Weiss 1996.

11. Most recently by Anderson-Levitt, Bloch, and Soumaré 1998; Bloch 1993; Bledsoe 1990, 1992; Hollos 1998; Mbilinyi 1998. See also Masemann 1974 and Weis 1979.

12. In comparative education, many write in general about the reconceptualization of African women as a socially constructed category (e.g., Kalu 1996; Wakoko and Lobao 1996). But few address the gendered constructions of male and female identities or the sociocultural processes (including everyday and extraordinary rituals) that define and create gendered differences. Biraimah (1989), for instance, posits that Nigerian girls are exposed to greater disadvantages than boys through the differential distribution of knowledge in elementary schools, but she bypasses discussion of how boys and girls are socially created, or how various social interactions get variously identified as male and female. Elliott and Kelly, in a special edition of the *Comparative Education Review* (1980), look at the inequities of achievement and of resources directed to schoolgirls and boys. But they do not examine the ways gender is multiply constructed in schools and other arenas of everyday life, including people's relationship to land, to one another (as sexual and nonsexual partners), and to their local and global material worlds.

13. Behar and Gordon 1995; Belenky et al. 1986; Noddings 1993; Harding and Hintikka 1983.

14. Machame is located on the southwestern slopes of Mount Kilimanjaro, approximately thirteen miles northwest of Moshi, the regional capital, and approximately thirty miles east of Arusha. The area—roughly fifty-five square miles—ranges in elevation from 1,000 to 5,000 feet above sea level.

15. At least this is the way many people described the transition to independence to me: that is, as a process of *giving up* autonomy rather than gaining greater independence. For the colonial system was remembered in the 1990s by some people living on Mount Kilimanjaro as having provided a political-economic structure for the advancement of Chagga ideals and plans. It was not necessarily (or only) seen as an authoritarian system administered by '"foreigners" that violated indigenous cultural norms (although it certainly was for some).

16. This number is figured at an annual growth rate of 2.8 percent and is based on my own calculations of census figures (the United Republic of Tanzania 1988:301–303) for the official administrative districts that correspond to the area known conventionally on the mountain as Machame.

17. This figure is based on information found in the "Development Notebook" (*Daftari ya Wilaya Kodi ya Maendeleo*) provided by the Ndala Village Chairman's Office.

18. *Ukoo,* or clan, refers to all levels of patrilineal kin—in other words, to all women and men who are related patrilineally. Context indicates which group is intended. See S. F. Moore 1986:17.

19. The Assembly of God was founded in the early 1990s in Machame by a group of evangelists from the United States.

20. The distinction between "government" and "private" schooling in Tanzania is different from that in the United States. Government schools in Tanzania are generally more prestigious than private counterparts primarily because selection to government schools is competitive and limited. Private schools are easier to get into, assuming one can afford to pay school fees, and assuming there is a private secondary school in one's village or nearby. In Machame, there were six private and one government secondary schools at the time of my stay.

21. During the first five years, admissions to Mkufi increased tenfold, from thirty students in 1988 to more than 300 in 1993. In 1993, 60 percent of the student body was girls. By 1996, enrollment was 450, and girls' and boys' enrollment had reached approximate parity. In 1992, expansion from a four-year secondary school to a five-year high school earned Mkufi Secondary School greater prestige by attracting students from different regions of Tanzania, including Iringa, Bukoba, Pwani, and Mbeya. Even though the overall regional representation of the student body stayed approximately the same, the fact that Mkufi drew even a dozen students from other regions supported an impression that Ndala was up and coming.

22. Ministry of Education and Culture 1992b, 1995b.

23. Several who asked if I was a Peace Corps volunteer were skeptical of the U.S. State Department's recent decision to suspend its Tanzanian mission, arguing that the international activities that precipitated the suspension were the doings of high-level organizations, not of the local people who benefited from Peace Corps work.

24. The Carter administration is remembered—fondly, for the most part—for having imported tons of corn to Kilimanjaro Region during drought years. Even many young children born well after the Carter years know this former president's name.

25. *Wazungu* is a generic term for people of phenotypically apparent European ancestry. *Mzungu* is the singular form.

26. Most universities, including all that I have been affiliated with, require researchers to obtain approval from research participants. Part of this process includes submitting a Human Subjects' Rights statement to the university sponsoring the research.

27. *Kite kikamfika masaleni nlyo kikomaa* in Kimachame; *Mtu muoga akiwa sehemu geni haongei, lakini akifika kwao ndio anaanza kupiga kelele* in Kiswahili.

28. Compare with Jackson 1998.

29. Including a Danish-sponsored project on land management in western Tanzania.

CHAPTER 2: SCHOOLING, INHERITANCE, AND BANANA GROVES

1. Bruno Gutmann long ago noted the significance of the banana grove for connecting the living and the dead, and for symbolizing gendered relations on Mount Kilimanjaro (Gutmann 1926; 1932). Gutmann inspired a veritable lineage of scholars of Chagga culture to think about land. Raum (1940 [1967]), writing about Chagga childhood and the life course on Mount Kilimanjaro, argued that each stage of the life cycle was marked ritually with reference to the banana grove. S. F. Moore (1986), in her study of Chagga law and custom, used Raum's and Gutmann's insights to observe how jural rights were negotiated and maintained in terms of the *kihamba* (Kimachame). More recently, Kerner (1995) has noted how ritual objects provide an exegesis of the Chagga body politic in terms of the grove, and Setel (1995) has pointed out how the banana grove provides a heuristic for modeling demographic change.

2. Middle sons were described as less fortunate siblings whose chances of acquiring land depended on their own abilities to convince their fathers or brothers to give them a grove or on their successes in staking out land in uninhabited territories and establishing residence there. A land reform bill, passed by the Tanzanian National Assembly on February 11, 1999, has partly superceded customary practices, yet people living on Mount Kilimanjaro continue to reckon land along lines that are independent of the bill.

3. A veritable web of irrigation channels threads across Mount Kilimanjaro. Filled year-round with waters from the melted snow peak, the major channels have followed the same routes for generations and have been a key resource for people on the mountain.

4. Many varieties grow on the mountain. Among them are: *mishare nlelembwe* (Kimachame; a tree that produces a thin, sweet banana that cooks quickly and is sometimes used for making beer); *nshonova* (Kimachame; a tree that produces thicker, heartier bananas, good for cooking with beans); *itoki* (Kimachame; a tree that produces bananas that are boiled with meat and considered suitable for roasting and making *mbege*); *msusu* (Kimachame; a tree that produces good roasting bananas); *ikonosi* (Kimachame; a tree that produces sweet bananas that are roasted and used for brewing beer); *inanambo* (Kimachame; a banana tree that produces fruit for roasting and making soup); and *mafanaia, nduya, ilalyi,* and *finangwa* (Kimachame; each considered excellent trees for producing bananas for brewing beer).

5. This comparison alludes to a Chagga saying: *Ikororo lyiseka isaa foo* (Kimachame)—"a banana bast that has not yet dried out should not laugh at the one that has"—which is often used to admonish children who speak out against adults' authority.

6. Vavrus 1998:292.

7. *Kite nkikuuya uwen fo* in Kimachame; literally, "a dog does not die in a foreign land."

8. As explained to me by a young Chagga man, who identified himself as a Lutheran Christian, many Chagga in Machame (the majority of whom self-identify as Lutheran) view the growing Muslim population on the mountain as a social

threat. This is why some people refer to aggressive go-getters as "Palestinians"—because they challenge the status quo. Christian-Muslim rivalries on the mountain date to colonial times, although many Christians believe today that the tensions have been recently mounting. See also Chapter 5 for another example of how and why some people refer to go-getters—especially Chagga women—as "Palestinian."

9. Compare with Ortner (1966:33)

10. See, for examples, Horn and Arriagada 1986; Lewis and Wanner 1979; World Bank 1991.

CHAPTER 3: "SHOULD WE DRINK BANANA BEER OR COCA-COLA?"

1. Jocelyn Mtei may have been speaking colloquially here. *Amepata jiko* (Kiswahili), "he got a hearth," is used interchangeably with *ameoa*, "he got married." She may have been saying that *marriage* makes the lineage.

2. Students and teachers use "domestic science" and "home economics" interchangeably, as I do in this chapter.

3. It is interesting that the syllabus stops with parenthood, for it suggests that the social value of women as mothers stops when their children themselves start to parent.

4. There is a large and interesting anthropological literature on dress practices in Africa. See, for instance, Renne 1995.

5. A distinction that, as Miller (1981), among others, has shown, is linked to the development of commercial culture.

6. As with, in the very interesting cases today, movements for same-gender marriages in the United States.

7. By my household survey, less than 1 percent had gas stoves, though these were generally households with the highest levels of schooling.

8. In McRobbie's words, "full identities are never achieved" (1994:192).

9. On Mount Kilimanjaro, as in many areas of eastern and southern Africa, marriage is not a matter simply of transferring rights from one lineage to another or of changing status as a consequence of the passage of beer prestations and other wealth, as a classical literature on kinship and marriage described it (Evans-Pritchard 1951; Fortes 1962). Rather, it involves a number of steps that include different kinds of heterosexual partnerships that extend along a continuum, ranging from the casual and fleeting to the ritualized and extended.

John Comaroff's (1980b) discussion of the processual nature of Tswana marriages, and of the difficulty in distinguishing affinal from agnatic relationships by virtue of the ambiguities surrounding the creation and categorization of heterosexual unions, is valuable for understanding the Chagga case. Heterosexual relationships in Machame, as among the Barolong boo Ratshidi, are almost always regarded as potential marriages, even though all elements that constitute the most elaborated form of union may not always be formally realized. The point that agnation and affinity are often indistinguishable pertains to the Chagga case even though Chagga, unlike Tswana, do not allow any forms of cousin marriage. Indeed it would seem from Chagga marriages that even in a case where exogamic proscriptions are well entrenched, affinity and agnation are nonetheless ambiguously and processually defined. On Mount Kilimanjaro, marriage is ideally exogamous and virilocal. See also Bledsoe 1980; Guyer 1994:234–235.

10. In the Kimachame dialect, this exchange is called *waghi wa isale*.

11. Banana trees in the past were sometimes called "milk trees" (Gutmann 1926:294), though I did not hear them called this in Machame.

12. See S. F. Moore (1986:197–209) for discussion of Chagga disputations involving marriage negotiations and women.

13. Suspicions of poisoning are routine in this process: the uncertainty and ambiguity of the visit and the unusual insinuation that someone is interested in claiming the lineage "fruits" of the land provoke mistrust of the people who come offering unsolicited gifts of banana beer.

14. *Waghi wa iporomwa ngagha* (Kimachame).

15. *Waghi wa mwanamaye wa nndu* (Kimachame).

16. *Waghi wa harambee* (Kimachame).

17. The order of distribution of *ndafu* (in Kimachame, roasted goat) at the public ceremony replicated the birth order of lineage agnates: senior men received the first and largest share of the meat; less senior agnates the second and smaller share. Pieces of meat were taken home, again according to social rank. The *kidari* (in Kimachame, the breastbone and surrounding meat) was reserved for the most senior male; and the *ngari* (in Kimachame, the middle ribs and rump) were reserved for the second rank of men in hierarchy (see also S. F. Moore 1986:340–341, fn. 10).

18. She is referring to the amoebic dysentery associated with the use of unboiled water.

19. Chagga men also learned *mbyaa* during initiation, though I am referring here to *mbyaa tya waniini*, lessons of the couch, that girls learn during female initiation.

20. *Kusheereyaa indan ikato mau nyinrine, ndoo nyinrine, lyo maata wakelema vana, ee, watiri na vana. Aata yen nshelema bibi. Yee! Nshelema aten. Yee, yee, veengi mbalemy. A lee, nkitiri maana ki ro bibi? Yee? Nkitiri maana ki yerinwa? Nkikasha. Nkikasha? Hee. Kikasha nyindo weerinwa nyeli walelema laalu. Ee. Weefo wo walelema te. Ee, watiri na weefu. Ee. Yee. Kweekyo nkikasha? Hee. Ulaalu ata ara kwarinwa mwana nafu se? Laalu maata wakelema. Wakelema? Yee, watiri na vana. Aa. Yee, wakelema irinwa. Ahaa. Yeese nkikasha lulatye lukarinwa. A le bibi le, nkiki elyi vandu warina? Ni nkimila. Nkimila? Ee. Ahaa. Kweekyo nkimila baasi. Alafu wai vandu mbo waambaa le, mwana wa kikaile, nlazima arinwa lyo ara kushaangaika, yaangaika na vomi. Mm. Yee, vandu mbalelema den.* (Kimachame)

21. Which were as high as the equivalent of $250 that year (1992). To give some perspective, a teacher's monthly salary was about $30.

22. So too, according to Bibi Muro, green dresses were to initiands what green dresses (*lati* in Kimachame) were to brides (*mbashaa na ta kijani washaa nato*

wokakuja, kama nyeupe za aarusi [Kimachame and Kiswahili]): both were a special kind of dress associated with a rite of passage.

CHAPTER 4: "EDUCATION IS MY HUSBAND"

1. Richards speculated that initiation was possibly a form of "ordeal or oracle magic" (Richards 1956:123) and suggested that teachers were testing initiands to see if they were ready to become adults. But she also said—and this is a point Victor Turner (1967) later elaborated—that Bemba spoke about initiation as though specialists in charge of the ceremony were catalyzing changes within initiands. She noted that Bemba believed initiation instructors were "changing an alarming condition to a safe one," and that they were securing the transition from unproductive childhood to a potentially dangerous yet productive adulthood (Richards 1956:125).

2. This is a frequent phenomenon in anthropological research. See Emerson, Fretz, and Shaw 1995.

3. November 1, 1991. Unlike Bibi Eshimuni's comments, which I have translated from the Kiswahili, above, Mr. Ngowi conveyed all of this in English.

4. In colonial times, primary schooling went through Standard VIII, not through Standard VII, as it does today.

5. My own sample size is small, yet the trend appears to be wide and growing. Of the twenty Form 4 secondary school girls and six recent graduates whom I asked directly, nine said they wanted to set up a household and have children independent of men. Their visions should be seen as changing *preferences*, not necessarily as changing *practices*.

6. Conventionally, younger brothers wait for older sisters to marry. This used to be because goats and cattle transacted from sister's husband's lineage to her father's would then provide the necessary bridewealth for younger sons to use in their own marriage. These days, however, bridewealth is not circulated in so literal a way, although marriage order among siblings continues in many cases to follow this convention.

7. The relationships Caroline Bledsoe (1990) and Karen Tranberg Hansen (1998) describe between schoolgirls and sugar daddies in Sierra Leone and Zambia, respectively, are similar to those I observed in Tanzania.

8. This finding is also reported by the Tanzania Gender Networking Programme 1993; Tumbo-Masabo and Lijeström 1994; and Rwebangira and Lijeström 1998.

9. Luise White (1991) discusses social biases that independent women living in East Africa face. See also Senkoro 1982.

10. This is a phrase that comes up a lot among secondary school students and graduates. It often appears on school announcement boards and posters and is used by teachers to remind students that they alone are responsible for doing their own work.

11. Such a view is often associated with the work of Pierre Bourdieu (1977, 1984). See Reed-Danahay (1996:26–29) and Levinson and Holland (1996:6) for discussions of Bourdieu's work on this subject.

12. Janise Hurtig (1998) presents a similar interpretation of Venezuelan school-girl's histories. I am grateful to Hurtig for helping me think, through her own analysis, about Emi's situation.

CHAPTER 5: "BOYS, PRESERVE YOUR BULLETS; GIRLS, LOCK YOUR BOXES"

1. For example, age and gender categories are sometimes counteracted through teachers' structuring of classroom activities or by the ways that students organize themselves into social groups on the basis of material culture and social values.

2. For a selection of recent ethnographic accounts of education, gender, and to a lesser extent, age, in the United States, France, and England, see Luttrell 1997; Mac an Ghaill 1994; Proweller 1998; Raissiguier 1994; Thorne 1997.

3. Included in this number are more than fifty classes I observed at Mkufi Secondary School.

4. This ratio was high compared to some other places in sub-Saharan Africa. Stromquist reports (1998:31) that in 1993, women constituted about 44 percent of all secondary school students in sub-Saharan Africa. Studies by Kathryn Anderson-Levitt, Marianne Bloch, and Aminata Maiga Soumaré (1998) and Josephine Beoku-Betts (1998) document girls' underrepresentation in West African schools.

5. As a reminder, Mount Kilimanjaro is located 3 degrees south of the equator.

6. Most of the more than fifty classes I observed at Mkufi Secondary School were not being evaluated yet exhibited these characteristics. I was a regular presence at Mkufi and trust that after several months my observing had little bearing on teachers' styles.

7. This does not mean that students' behavior was always in line with the unwritten codes of acceptable conduct at schools. Students spent a great deal of time overturning school rules and questioning teachers' authority (see Chapter 6). But student "unruliness" usually occurred when teachers were absent and students sat unattended—not during times of directed instruction, at least not as I observed them.

8. For examples of this media genre and of the popular Western argument that girls' schooling in Africa is problematic, see the *New York Times*, March 8, 1995, p. 12; The White House, Office of the Press Secretary, March 24, 1998.

9. To be sure, Mount Kilimanjaro is an exception in that it has a history of schooling girls as well as boys, yet as an exception it should not be overlooked. Nor is it the only one. Other areas, notably Upare, Bukoba, and Mbeya in Tanzania, as well as other areas of sub-Saharan Africa (see Hakansson 1994; Ngula 1996) also share this history.

10. This passage is a reconstruction from notes I took while observing the lesson. I was not able to photocopy the text at the time and was later told by Macmillan Publishers in Chicago that the text is out of print.

11. The idea of building the nation through education is an official policy objective, as I noted in previous chapters. In making reference to "building the nation," Mr. Uroki here is framing the goal of education within an official nationalist discourse.

12. See again Chapter 2, Note 8. Mr. Uroki's attribution of aggression to Chagga schoolgirls paints school-educated women as cold-blooded.

13. This is Raum's editorial insert.

14. Cf. Bledsoe 1992; Stambach 1998. To be sure, some students also look to women for blessings, though as stated by students and adults, it is male elders who predominantly confer blessings.

15. With the exception of those that are for girls and women only—e.g., female initiation.

16. See di Leonardo 1991; Lutkehaus 1995:10; Yanagisako and Collier 1987.

17. Certainly this is a marital preference that needs to be researched in the future: How are school-educated girls' marital preferences actually *realized* in practice?

18. The pastor I observed at Mahali repeated his lesson at other Lutheran-sponsored secondary schools. At public schools (called "government schools" in Tanzanian English), pastors, priests, and sheiks led moral instruction for students of any religious identification. In the course of my work, I observed four lessons on moral instruction at three different schools. In three of these lessons, the subject of gendered sexuality was the focus of the lecture.

19. PASTOR: *Lakini, sasa tumesema kwamba tunamalizia kipindi ambacho tulikuwa tumeshaanza kuhusu dini. Ebu tusome wote.*

STUDENTS: *Usafi wa Maisha ya Kijana.*

PASTOR: *Sasa awe kijana Mwislamu au kijana Mkristo, ni jinsi gani aisafishe njia yake? Na sasa ndio maana waraka wa mtume Paulo waraka wa Yohana wa kwanza na mlango wa pili na mstari ule wa kumi na nne ndio unasema "nimewaandikia nyinyi vijana kwa sababu mna nini? Mna nguvu na neno la Mungu linakaa ndani yenu." Si ndiyo?*

STUDENTS: *Ndiyo.*

PASTOR: *Ok. Tukaangalia tukajifunza kwa kutumia Bibilia jinsi ambavyo uhusiano wa mvulana na msichana ni mzuri. Au kunapokuwa na nguvu ya mvutano ile tunasema ni neema ya Mungu. Si ndiyo?*

STUDENTS: *Ndiyo.*

PASTOR: *Halafu, nikasema kwamba kama hakuna nguvu hiyo, mpeleke mahali kupimwa kwa sababu yawezekana una nini?*

STUDENTS: *A problem.*

PASTOR: *Ndiyo, kama uhusiano huu hautatunzwa, na kama nguvu hii iliyoko ndani ya mwanandamu haitatunzwa vizuri, ifanyike kwa wakati wake na mahali pake, ni rahisi sana jambo hili kukumba watu na ndiyo maana unaona kwamba dunia inakumbwa na jambo hili. Ndio ukaona vijana wamejisikia hivyo basi wanakwenda ovyo ovyo kama wanyama. Lakini linalodaiwa hapa ni nini?*

STUDENTS: *Kutawala.*

PASTOR: *Kujitawala. Lakini sawa tunasema kwamba kujitawala kijana ili kuepekana na baa hili. Kutawala nguvu maanake tuliifananisha na nini?*

STUDENTS: *Na moto.*

PASTOR: *Uhusiano wa mvulana na msichana si mbaya. Sawa? Lakini uhusiano huu uwe katika misingi ya neno la nani?*

STUDENTS: *Ya neno la Mungu.*

PASTOR: *Kwamba mawazo yenu yawe safi mnapokuwa na uhusiano wa namna hii. Msiwashe moto ovyo ovyo. Kuwasha ovyo ovyo tutakuita kichaa. Kilicho muhimu ni kujitawala ilil moto huu uwe kitu kizuri.*

20. *Unakuwa na busara unapoweza kuyatawala mawazo yakawa safi. Unapoweza kuwa mtulivu bila kuhangaika hangaika na vitu visivyofaa. Wewe nakushauri kwamba kama ni hivyo basi wewe hifadhi—wewe hifadhi risasi zako ndani ya seli.*

21. Flora Mbasha Popenoe is a Machame-born woman who helped me translate and transcribe this tape-recorded lesson from Kiswahili.

22. Passive and active forms of this verb are also used in the local dialect to differentiate "married women" from "marrying men."

23. On Chagga views of family planning, see Vavrus 1998. Birth control pills were available free of charge at most clinics in Machame.

24. *Unakula madawa ya sijui ni ya kuharibu nini, mimba siji ni ya kuzuia mimba, sijui nini. Hata ukiona mwenzako anakuangalia we unasema, "Amenionaje?" Watu wengine utakuta wengine kwa sababu ya hiyo hofu masanduku yao yana kufuli lile la "OB." Yaani anaimarisha mtu mwingine asije akachungulia ndani aone kilichomo ndani. Funga vizuri.*

25. Popenoe, pers. comm.

26. In rough analogy, the pastor's emphasis on birth control parallels a demographic emphasis on regulating girls' fertility. One line of argument in population studies is that schooling and fertility rates are inversely related: higher levels of schooling correlate with lower rates of fertility, and lower rates of fertility with higher living standards (Adamchak and Ntseane 1992; Ainsworth, Beegle, and Nyamete 1995; Jejeebhoy 1995). For the application of anthropological theories of marriage and the life cycle to the interpretation of demographic data in Africa, see Bradley 1995; Bledsoe and Pison 1994; Hollos 1998; Johnson-Kuhn 1996. The pastor's views seem to differ from the conventional precepts of population studies. For he seems to imply that birth control *leads* to sexual desire, and that sexual desire itself leads to increased rates of fertility—not that birth control pills themselves help students manage reproduction.

27. PASTOR: *Tusome wote.*

STUDENTS: *Ulevi ni hatari.*

PASTOR: *Unajua ujinga huu wa kucheza na sex unanyima watu maendeleo. Huwezi kuendelea bwana! Kabisa. Kweli ukinywa, utakunywa, baadaye utakuawa pombe.. Sasa kichanganyike hiki, kichanganyike ulevi maendeleo yatatoka wapi? Ulevi ni?*

STUDENTS: *Hatari.*

PASTOR: *Ni nini?*

STUDENTS: *Hatari.*

PASTOR: *Someni jamaani.*

STUDENTS: *Ulevi ni hatari.*

PASTOR: *Ubongo huwa haufanyi kazi. Mimi nimewaambia tangu mwanzoni sio kwamba zinaa na ulevi si zinaondoa ufahamu, zinawaondolea maarifa. Ule uwezo wa kupokea maarifa hautakuwepo.*

28. Janise Hurtig (1998) makes a similar point about gender regimes in Venezuelan secondary schools.

28. Absent teachers were often working second jobs, which many needed to supplement their low salaries.

CHAPTER 6: "THINGS WITH SOCKS"

1. Transcribed by Karen Peterson, Abdul Rahman Ally, and Nassor Ali Hilal. My thanks to them for making this text available to me.

2. See Lévi-Strauss 1962:16–36.

3. A gendered component of heterosexual unions, as we have seen, is expressed in the terms "to marry" (*kuowa*) and "to be married" (*kuoloewa*). The active form is typically used to describe men's marital agency, the latter form is typically used to describe women's passive married state—see Chapters 3 and 5. My argument here is that these marital terms express deep structural relations between men and women, and that girls' ambiguous usage of socks—male items—put this passive-active relationship on edge.

4. Teachers who engaged in quid pro quo harassment were frowned upon and when discovered, were sanctioned—though rarely were cases uncovered. For discussions of student harassment in other parts of sub-Saharan Africa, see Bledsoe 1990, Cabral 1998.

5. For excellent collections of essays on generational views of students' dilemmas, see *Chelewa, Chelewa: The Dilemma of Teenage Girls*, edited by Zubeida Tumbo-Masabo and Rita Lijeström and *Haraka, Haraka . . . Look Before You Leap: Youth at the Crossroads of Custom and Modernity*, by Magdalena K. Rwebangira and Rita Lijeström.

6. Including MacLaren's 1993 work on the political economy of a Canadian Catholic high school, Peshkin's 1991 study of race and community in central California, Vered Amit-Talai's 1995 work on dislocation and friendship in a Quebec high school, and Shane J. Blackman's 1998 analysis of resistant female youth culture in the south of England.

7. Kanda Bongo Man is a Zairian musician who resides most of the time in London; Bobby Brown is a Los Angeles-based musician who was wildly popular among students at Mkufi.

8. Check Rap, Check Bob, and TX Kubwa were distinguished by the degree to which they were connected to the consumer economy. Check Rap engaged in petty trade, often on the black market, and had no steady source of income. Check Bob were white-collared businesspeople who preferred, although could not always

afford, imported goods. TX Kubwa had international tastes (TX was, and remains, the prefix for European-owned expatriate car license plates) and were members of elite social clubs.

9. In Kiswahili, adjectives such as -zima are modified to agree with the object they are describing. Agreement is formed by attaching a prefix (such as m-, n-, or wa-), as in *mzima, nsima, wazima.*

CHAPTER 7: "MOUNTAINS NEVER MEET BUT PEOPLE DO"

1. Some people said this was an age-old Chagga adage, others, that it was a pan-African phrase. I had seen the saying in a primary school textbook and I have since heard it in connection with social life in Namibia. This adage is also nicely discussed in the preface to Kerner 1988.

2. More than 70 percent of students who took National Form IV examinations in 1994, for instance, scored below the passing mark that would qualify them for entry into government Form 5 schools (Ministry of Education and Culture 1995b).

3. Nor are they simply the opposite: culturally relative. For an excellent discussion of the necessary interrelation of these two conceptualizations, the universal and the relative, see Strathern 1995.

REFERENCES

Abernethy, David B. 1969. *The Political Dilemma of Popular Education: An African Case*. Stanford, CA: Stanford University Press.

Abu-Lughod, Lila. 1990. The Romance of Resistance: Tracing Transformations of Power through Bedouin Women. *American Ethnologist* 17(1):41–55.

Adamchak, Donald J., and Peggy Gabo Ntseane. 1992. Gender, Education, and Fertility: A Cross-National Analysis of Sub-Saharan Nations. *Sociological Spectrum* 12:167–182.

Ainsworth, Martha, Kathleen Beegle, and Andrew Nyamete. 1995. *The Impact of Female Schooling on Fertility and Contraceptive Use: A Study of Fourteen Sub-Saharan Countries*. Washington, DC: World Bank.

Althusser, Louis. 1971. Ideology and Ideological State Apparatuses. In *Lenin and Philosophy and Other Essays*. Translated by Ben Brewster. New York: Monthly Review Press.

Amit-Talai, Vered. 1995. The Waltz of Sociability: Intimacy, Dislocation, and Friendship in a Quebec High School. In *Youth Cultures: A Cross-Cultural Perspective*. Edited by Vered Amit-Talai and Helena Wulff. New York: Routledge.

Amit-Talai, Vered, and Helena Wulff, eds. 1995. *Youth Cultures: A Cross-Cultural Perspective*. New York: Routledge.

Anderson, Benedict. 1983. *Imagined Communities: Reflections on the Origin and Spread of Nationalism*. London: Verso.

Anderson-Levitt, Kathryn M., Marianne Bloch, and Aminata Maiga Soumaré. 1998. Inside Classrooms in Guinea: Girls' Experiences. In *Women and Education in Sub-Saharan Africa: Power, Opportunities, and Constraints*. Edited by Marianne Bloch, Josephine A. Beoku-Betts, and B. Robert Tabachnick. Boulder, CO: Lynne Rienner Publishers.

Appadurai, Arjun. 1991. Global Ethnoscapes: Notes and Queries for a Transnational Anthropology. In *Recapturing Anthropology: Working in the Present*. Edited by Richard G. Fox. Seattle: University of Washington Press. School of American Research Advanced Seminar Series.

———. 1996. *Modernity at Large: Cultural Dimensions of Globalization*. Minneapolis: University of Minnesota Press.

Apple, Michael. 1993. *Official Knowledge: Democratic Education in a Conservative Age*. New York: Routledge.

Asayehgn, Desta. 1979. *The Role of Women in Tanzania: Their Access to Higher Education and Participation in the Labour Force*. Paris: International Institute for Educational Planning.

Behar, Ruth, and Deborah Gordon. 1995. *Women Writing Culture*. Berkeley: University of California Press.

Beidelman, Thomas O. 1993. *Moral Imagination in Kaguru Modes of Thought*. Bloomington: Indiana University Press.

Belenky, Mary Field, Blythe McVicker-Clinchy, Nancy Rule Goldberger, and Jill Mattuck Tarule. 1986. *Women's Ways of Knowing: The Development of Self, Voice, and Mind*. New York: Basic Books.

Bendix, Reinhard. 1964. *Nation Building and Citizenship: Studies of Our Changing Social Order*. New York: Wiley.

Benhabib, Seyla. 1992. *Situating the Self*. New York: Routledge.

Beoku-Betts, Josephine A. 1998. Gender and Formal Education in Africa: An Exploration of the Opportunity Structure at the Secondary and Tertiary Levels. In *Women and Education in Sub-Saharan Africa: Power, Opportunities, and Constraints*. Edited by Marianne Bloch, Josephine A. Beoku-Betts, and B. Robert Tabachnick. Boulder, CO: Lynne Rienner Publishers.

Biraimah, Karen. 1989. The Process and Outcomes of Gender Bias in Elementary Schools: A Nigerian Case. *The Journal of Negro Education* 58(1):50–67.

Blackman, Shane. 1998. 'Poxy Cupid!' An Ethnographers and Feminist Account of Resistant Female Youth Culture: The New Wave Girls. In *Cool Places: Geographies of Gender*. Edited by Tracey Skelton and Gill Valentine. New York: Routledge.

Bledsoe, Caroline. 1980. *Women and Marriage in Kpelle Society*. Stanford, CA: Stanford University Press.

———. 1990. School Fees and the Marriage Process for Mende Girls in Sierra Leone. In *Beyond the Second Sex: New Directions in the Anthropology of Gender*. Edited by Peggy Reeves Sanday and Ruth Gallagher Goodenough. Philadelphia: University of Pennsylvania Press.

———. 1992. The Cultural Transformation of Western Education in Sierra Leone. *Africa* 62(2):182–202.

Bledsoe, Caroline, and Gilles Pison. 1994. Introduction to *Nuptiality in Sub-Saharan Africa: Contemporary Anthropological and Demographic Perspectives*. Edited by Caroline Bledsoe and Gilles Pison. Oxford: Clarendon.

Bledsoe, Caroline, and the National Research Council (U.S.), Committee on Population, eds. 1999. *Critical Perspectives on Schooling and Fertility in the Developing World*. Washington, DC: National Academy Press.

Bloch, Marianne, and Frances Vavrus. 1998. Introduction to *Women and Education in Sub-Saharan Africa: Power, Opportunities, and Constraints*. Edited by Marianne Bloch, Josephine A. Beoku-Betts, and B. Robert Tabachnick. Boulder, CO: Lynne Rienner Publishers.

Bloch, Maurice. 1993. The Uses of Schooling and Literacy in a Zafimaniry Village. In *Cross-Cultural Approaches to Literacy*. Edited by Brian V. Street. New York: Cambridge University Press.

Bourdieu, Pierre. 1977. *Outline of a Theory of Practice*. Translated by Richard Nice. Cambridge: Cambridge University Press.

————. 1984. *Distinction: A Social Critique of the Judgement of Taste*. Translated by Richard Nice. Cambridge, MA: Harvard University Press.

Bourgois, Philippe. 1996. Confronting Anthropology, Education, and Inner-City Apartheid. *American Anthropologist* 98(2):249–258.

Boyarin, Jonathan. 1993. Introduction to *The Ethnography of Reading*. Edited by Jonathan Boyarin. Berkeley: University of California Press.

Bradley, Candice. 1995. Women's Empowerment and Fertility Decline in Western Kenya. In *Situating Fertility: Anthropology and Demographic Inquiry*. Edited by Susan Greenhalgh. Cambridge: Cambridge University Press.

Burke, Timothy. 1996. *Lifebuoy Men, Lux Women: Commodification, Consumption and Cleanliness in Modern Zimbabwe*. Durham, NC: Duke University Press.

Cabral, Zaida. 1998. Issues in Girls' Education in Mozambique. Paper presented at the Tenth World Congress of WCCES, Cape Town, South Africa.

Carnoy, Martin, and Joel Samoff, with Mary Ann Burris, Anton Johnston, and Carlos Alberto Torres. 1990. *Education and Social Transition in the Third World*. Princeton, NJ: Princeton University Press.

Collier, Jane, Michelle Z. Rosaldo, and Sylvia Yanagisako. 1997. Is There a Family? In *The Gender/Sexuality Reader: Culture, History, Political Economy*. Edited by Micaela di Leonardo and Roger N. Lancaster. New York: Routledge.

Comaroff, Jean. 1986. *Body of Power, Spirit of Resistance: The Culture and History of a South African People*. Chicago: University of Chicago Press.

Comaroff, Jean, and John Comaroff. 1993. Introduction to *Modernity and Its Malcontents: Ritual and Power in Postcolonial Africa*. Chicago: University of Chicago Press.

Comaroff, John. 1980a. Introduction to *The Meaning of Marriage Payments*. Edited by John Comaroff. London: Academic Press.

————. 1980b. Bridewealth and the Control of Ambiguity in a Tswana Chiefdom. In *The Meaning of Marriage Payments*. Edited by John Comaroff. London: Academic Press.

Comaroff, John, and Jean Comaroff. 1992. Homemade Hegemony. In *Ethnography and the Historical Imagination*. Boulder, CO: Westview.

Cooksey, Brian, George A. Malekela, and J. Lugalla. 1993. *Parents' Attitudes Toward Education in Rural Tanzania*. Tanzania Development Research Group (TADREG). Research Report Number 5.

Corrigan, Philip, and Derek Sayer. 1985. *The Great Arch: English State Formation as Cultural Revolution*. Oxford: Basil Blackwell.

Crapo, Richley H. 1996. *Cultural Anthropology: Understanding Ourselves and Others*. Fourth Edition. Dubuque, IA: Times Mirror Higher Education Group.

Daftari ya Wilaya Kodi ya Maendeleo. 1992. Machame: Hai District, Tanzania.

Davies, Bronwyn. 1989. *Frogs and Snails and Feminist Tales: Preschool Children and Gender*. Sydney, Australia: Allen and Unwin.

Devisch, René. 1993. *Weaving the Threads of Life: The Khita Gyn-Eco-Logical Healing Cult among the Yaka*. Chicago: University of Chicago Press.

di Leonardo, Micaela. 1991. Introduction to *Gender at the Crossroads of Knowledge: Feminist Anthropology in the Postmodern Era*. Edited by Micaela di Leonardo. Berkeley: University of California Press.

Dore, Ronald. 1976. *The Diploma Disease: Education, Qualification and Development*. Berkeley: University of California Press.

Dundas, Charles. 1924. *Kilimanjaro and Its Peoples: A History of the Wachagga, Their Lands, Customs, and Legends Together with Some Account of the Highest Mountain in Africa*. London: H.F. & G. Witherby.

Eckert, Penelope. 1989. *Jocks and Burnouts: Social Categories and Identity in the High School*. New York: Teachers College Press.

Elliott, Carolyn M., and Gail P. Kelly. 1980. Introduction: Perspectives on the Education of Women in Third World Nations. *Comparative Education Review*. 24(2):S1–S12.

Emerson, Robert M., Rachel I. Fretz, and Linda L. Shaw. 1995. *Writing Ethnographic Fieldnotes*. Chicago: University of Chicago Press.

Erikson, Erik H. 1950 [1963]. *Childhood and Society*. New York: Norton.

Evans-Pritchard, Edward. 1951. *Kinship and Marriage among the Nuer*. Oxford: Clarendon.

Feierman, Steven. 1990. *Peasant Intellectuals: Anthropology and History in Tanzania*. Madison: University of Wisconsin Press.

Feldman, S. Shirley, and Glen R. Elliott, eds. 1990. *At the Threshold: The Developing Adolescent*. Cambridge: Harvard University Press.

Foley, Douglas. 1990. *Learning Capitalist Culture: Deep in the Heart of Tejas*. Philadelphia: University of Pennsylvania Press.

Fortes, Meyer. 1962. Introduction to *Marriage in Tribal Societies*. Edited by Meyer Fortes. Cambridge: Cambridge University Press.

Foster, Philip J. 1965. *Education and Social Change in Ghana*. Chicago: University of Chicago Press.

Frazer, James George. 1890. *The Golden Bough: A Study in Magic and Religion*. London: Macmillan.

Freud, Anna. 1937. *The Ego and Mechanisms of Defense*. London: Hogarth Press.

Fuller, Bruce. 1991. *Growing Up Modern: The Western State Builds Third-World Schools*. New York: Routledge.

Gaitskell, Deborah. 1988. Race, Gender, and Imperialism: A Century of Black Girls' Education in South Africa. In *Benefits Bestowed? Education and British Imperialism*. Edited by J. A. Mangan. Manchester, UK: Manchester University Press.

Gay, John, and Michael Cole. 1967. *The New Mathematics and an Old Culture: A Study of Learning among the Kpelle of Liberia*. New York: Holt, Rinehart, and Winston.

Geertz, Clifford. 1973. *The Interpretation of Cultures: Selected Essays*. New York: Basic Books.

———. 1994. The Uses of Diversity. In *Assessing Cultural Anthropology*. Edited by Robert Borofsky. New York: McGraw-Hill.

Giddens, Anthony. 1979. *Central Problems in Social Theory: Action, Structure and Contradiction in Social Analysis*. Berkeley: University of California Press.

Goffman, Erving. 1977. The Arrangement between the Sexes. *Theory and Society* 4(3):301–331.

Greenhalgh, Susan. 1995. Introduction to *Situating Fertility: Anthropology and Demographic Inquiry*. Edited by Susan Greenhalgh. Cambridge: Cambridge University Press.

Grindal, Bruce T. 1972. *Growing Up in Two Worlds: Education and Transition among the Sisala of Northern Ghana*. New York: Holt, Rinehart, and Winston.

Grosz-Ngaté, Maria. 1997. Introduction to *Gendered Encounters: Challenging Cul-*

tural Boundaries and Social Hierarchies in Africa. Edited by Maria Grosz-Ngaté and Omari H. Kokole. New York: Routledge.

Gutmann, Bruno. 1926. *Das Recht der Dschagga*. Munich: Beck'sche Verlagsbuchhandlung. Translated by A.M. Nagler. Human Relations Area Files. New Haven, CT: Yale University Press.

———. 1928. Aufgabender Gemeinschaftsbildung in Afrika. *Africa* 1:42a–45, English summary, pp. 511–515.

———. 1932. *Die Stammeslehren der Dschagga, Volume 1*. Munich: C.H. Beck'sche Verlagsbuchhandlung. [Translated from the German by Ward Goodneough and Dorothy Crawford. 1958. Human Relations Area Files. New Haven: Yale University Press.]

———. 1935a. *Rasse un Mission*. Lutherisches Missionjahrbuch:8–26.

———. 1935b. The African Standpoint. *Africa* 8:1–17.

———. 1935c. *Die Stammeslehren der Dschagga, Volume 2*. Munich: C.H. Beck'sche Verlagsbuchhandlung.

———. 1938. Die Stammeslehren der Dschagga, Volume 3. Munich: C.H. Beck'sche Verlagsbuchhandlung.

Guyer, Jane I. 1994. Lineal Identities and Lateral Networks: The Logic of Polyandrous Motherhood. In *Nuptiality in Sub-Saharan Africa: Contemporary Anthropological and Demographic Perspectives*. Edited by Caroline Bledsoe and Gilles Pison. Oxford: Clarendon.

———. 1995. Wealth in People as Wealth in Knowledge: Accumulation and Consumption in Equatorial Africa. *Journal of African History* 36:91–102.

Habermas, Jürgen. 1979. *Communication and the Evolution of Society*. Translated by Thomas McCarthy. Boston, MA: Beacon Press.

Hakansson, Thomas. 1988. *Bridewealth, Women, and Land: Social Change among the Gusii of Kenya*. Stockholm: Uppsala University.

———. 1994. The Detachability of Women: Gender and Kinship in Processes of Socioeconomic Change among the Gussi of Kenya. *American Ethnologist* 21(3): 516–538.

Hall, G. Stanley. 1904. *Adolescence: Its Psychology and Its Relations to Physiology, Anthropology, Sociology, Sex, Crime, Religion, and Education*. New York: D. Appleton and Company.

Hall, Kathleen. 1995. There's a Time to Act English and a Time to Act Indian: The Politics of Identity among British-Sikh Teenagers. In *Children and the Politics of Culture*. Edited by Sharon Stephens. Princeton, NJ: Princeton University Press.

Hansen, Karen Tranberg. 1992. Domesticity in Africa. In *African Encounters with Domesticity*. Edited by Karen Tranberg Hansen. New Brunswick, NJ: Rutgers University Press.

———. 1997. *Keeping House in Lusaka*. New York: Columbia University Press.

———. 1998. Dressing Dangerously: Miniskirts in the Time of AIDS in Zambia. Manuscript.

Harding, Sandra G., and Merrill B. Hintikka, eds. 1983. *Discovering Reality: Feminist Perspectives on Epistemology, Metaphysics, Methodology, and Philosophy of Science*. Boston, MA: Kluwer.

Harter, Susan. 1990. Self and Identity Development. In *At the Threshold: The Developing Adolescent*. Edited by S. Shirley Feldman and Glen R. Elliott. Cambridge, MA: Harvard University Press.

Heath, Shirley Brice. 1983. *Ways with Words: Language, Life, and Work in Communities and Classrooms.* Cambridge: Cambridge University Press.

Henry, Jules. 1965. *Culture Against Man.* New York: Vintage Books.

Hodgson, Dorothy L., and Sheryl McCurdy. 1996. Wayward Wives, Misfit Mothers, and Disobedient Daughters: "Wicked" Women and the Reconfiguration of Gender in Africa. *Canadian Journal of African Studies* 30(1):1–9.

Holland, Dorothy C., and Margaret A. Eisenhart. 1990. *Educated in Romance: Women, Achievement, and College Culture.* Chicago: University of Chicago Press.

Hollos, Marida. 1998. The Status of Women in Southern Nigeria: Is Education a Help or a Hindrance? In *Women and Education in Sub-Saharan Africa: Power, Opportunities, and Constraints.* Edited by Marianne Bloch, Josephine A. Beoku-Betts, and B. Robert Tabachnick. Boulder, CO: Lynne Rienner Publishers.

Horn, R. and A.M. Arriagada. 1986. *The Educational Attainment of the World's Population: Three Decades of Progress.* Washington, DC: World Bank, Education and Training Department.

Hornsby, George. 1964. German Educational Achievement in East Africa. *Tanganyika Notes and Records* 62(3):83–90.

House-Midamba, Bessie. 1990. Class Development and Gender Inequality in Kenya, 1963–1990. Lewiston, NY: Edwin Meller.

Hunt, Nancy Rose. 1992. Colonial Fairy Tales and the Knife and Fork Doctrine in the Heart of Africa. In *African Encounters with Domesticity.* Edited by Karen Tranberg Hansen. New Brunswick, NJ: Rutgers University Press.

Hurtig, Janise. 1998. *Gender Lessons: Schooling and the Reproduction of Patriarchy in a Venezuelan Town.* Doctoral Dissertation, Department of Anthropology, University of Michigan.

Inkeles, Alex. 1998. *One World Emerging? Convergence and Divergence in Industrial Societies.* Boulder, CO: Westview.

Inkeles, Alex, and David H. Smith. 1974. *Becoming Modern: Individual Change in Six Developing Countries.* Cambridge, MA: Harvard University Press.

Institute of Curriculum Development. 1988. History Syllabus. Ministry of Education and Culture. Dar es Salaam, Tanzania.

Jackson, Michael. 1998. *Minima Ethnographica: Intersubjectivity and the Anthropological Project.* Chicago: University of Chicago Press.

Jacoby, Russell. 1994. *Dogmatic Wisdom: How the Education and Cultural Wars Have Misled America.* New York: Doubleday.

Jejeebhoy, Shireen J. 1995. *Women's Education, Autonomy, and Reproductive Behavior: Experience from Developing Countries.* Oxford: Clarendon.

Johnson-Kuhn, Jennifer A. 1996. The Mother and the Virgin: Catholicism, Education, and Reproduction in Southern Cameroon. Manuscript. Department of Anthropology, Northwestern University.

———. 1999. Describing the First Space. Paper presented at the Center for Demography and Ecology. University of Wisconsin, Madison.

Kalu, Anthonia C. 1996. Women and the Social Construction of Gender in African Development. *Africa Today* 43(3):269–288.

Kerner, Donna O. 1988. The Social Uses of Knowledge in Contemporary Tanzania. Doctoral Dissertation, Department of Anthropology, City University of New York.

———. 1995. Chaptering the Narrative: The Material of Memory in Kilimanjaro, Tanzania. In *The Labyrinth of Memory: Ethnographic Journeys*. Edited by Marea C. Teski and Jacob J. Climo. Westport, CT: Bergin and Garvey.

King, Elizabeth M., and M. Anne Hill. 1993. *Women's Education in Developing Countries: Barriers, Benefits, and Policies*. Baltimore, MD: Johns Hopkins University Press.

Knight, John B., and Richard H. Sabot. 1990. *Education, Productivity, and Inequality: The East African Natural Experiment*. New York: Published for the World Bank, Oxford University Press.

Kondo, Dorrine K. 1990. *Crafting Selves: Power, Gender and Discourses of Identity in a Japanese Workplace*. Chicago: University of Chicago Press.

Kozakiewicz, Mikolaj. 1992. Educational Transformation Initiated by the Polish Perestroika. *Comparative Education Review* 36(1):91–100.

Kratz, Corinne A. 1994. Affecting Performance: Meaning, Movement, and Experience in Okiek Women's Initiation. Washington: Smithsonian Institution Press.

Lacey, Colin. 1970. *Hightown Grammar: The School as a Social System*. Manchester, UK: Manchester University Press.

LaFontaine, J.S., ed. 1978. *Sex and Age as Principles of Social Differentiation*. London: Academic Press.

Lambek, Michael. 1993. *Knowledge and Practice in Mayotte: Local Discourses of Islam, Sorcery, and Spirit Possession*. Toronto: University of Toronto Press.

Lave, Jean. 1977. Cognitive Consequences of Traditional Apprenticeship Training in West Africa. *Anthropology and Education Quarterly* 8(3):177–180.

Lave, Jean, and Etienne Wenger. 1991. *Situated Learning: Legitimate Peripheral Participation*. Cambridge: Cambridge University Press.

Lawuo, Z.E. 1984. *Education and Social Change in a Rural Community: A Study of Colonial Education and Local Response among the Chagga between 1920 and 1945*. Dar es Salaam: University of Dar es Salaam Press.

Leach, Edmund Ronald. 1965. *Political Systems of Highland Burma*. Boston: Beacon Press.

Lema, Alex O.J. 1969. The Role of the Machame Chiefdom in the Politics of the Wachagga Since the 1930s. Africana Library, manuscript. University of Dar es Salaam.

Levinson, Bradley A. 1998. The Moral Construction of Student Rights: Discourse and Judgement among Mexican Secondary School Students. *Journal of Contemporary Ethnography* 27(1):45–84.

———. In Press. *We Are All Equal: The Play of Student Culture at a Mexican Secondary School and Beyond*. Durham, NC: Duke University Press.

Levinson, Bradley A., and Dorothy C. Holland. 1996. Introduction to *The Cultural Production of the Educated Person: Critical Ethnographies of Schooling and Local Practice*. Edited by Bradley A. Levinson, Douglas E. Foley, and Dorothy C. Holland. Albany: State University of New York Press.

Lévi-Strauss, Claude. 1962. *The Savage Mind*. Chicago: University of Chicago Press.

———. 1969. *The Elementary Structures of Kinship*. Translated by James Harle Bell, John Richard von Sturmer, and Rodney Neeham, editor. Boston: Beacon Press.

———. 1971. The Family. *Man, Culture, and Society*. Edited by Henry L. Shapiro. London: Oxford University Press.

Lewis, Lionel S., and Richard A. Wanner. 1979. Private Schooling and the Status Attainment Process. *Sociology of Education* 52(2):99–112.

Liechty, Mark. 1995. Media, Markets, and Modernization: Youth Identities and the Experience of Modernity in Kathmandu, Nepal. In *Youth Cultures: A Cross-Cultural Perspective*. Edited by Vered Amit-Talai and Helena Wulff. London: Routledge.

Lutkehaus, Nancy C. 1995. Feminist Anthropology and Female Initiation in Melanesia. In *Gender Rituals: Female Initiation in Melanesia*. Edited by Nancy C. Lutkehaus and Paul B. Roscoe. New York: Routledge.

Luttrell, Wendy. 1997. *School-Smart and Mother-Wise: Working-Class Women's Identity and Schooling*. New York: Routledge.

Luykx, Aurolyn. 1999. *The Citizen Factory: Schooling and Cultural Production in Bolivia*. Albany: State University of New York Press.

Mac an Ghaill, Máirtín. 1994. *The Making of Men: Masculinities, Sexualities and Schooling*. Buckingham, UK: Open University Press.

Malekela, George A. 1991. Educated Youth Unemployment in Tanzania. In *Social Problems in East Africa*. Edited by C.K. Omari and L.P. Shaidi. Dar es Salaam: University of Dar es Salaam Press.

Malekela, George A., D. Ndabi, and Brian Cooksey. 1990. *Girls' Educational Opportunities and Performance in Tanzania*. Tanzania Development Research Group (TADREG). Research Report Number 2.

Maliyamkono, T.L. 1980. The School as a Force for Community Change in Tanzania. *International Review of Education* 26(3):335–347.

Mang'enya, Erasto. 1984. *Discipline and Tears: Reminiscences of an African Civil Servant in Colonial Tanganyika*. Dar es Salaam: Dar es Salaam University Press.

Marealle, Petro Itosi. 1965. Chagga Customs, Beliefs, and Traditions. Translated by R.D. Swai. *Tanganyika Notes and Records*. 64:56–61.

Masemann, Vandra. 1974. The "Hidden Curriculum" of a West African Girls' Boarding School. *Canadian Journal of African Studies* 8(3):479–494.

Masolo, D.A. 1994. *African Philosophy in Search of Identity*. Bloomington: Indiana University Press.

Mauss, Marcel. 1967. *The Gift*. Translated by Ian Cunnison. London: Cohen and West.

Mbilinyi, Marjorie. 1972. The "New Woman" and Traditional Norms in Tanzania. *Journal of Modern African Studies* 10(1):57–72.

———. 1973. Education, Stratification, and Sexism in Tanzania: Policy Implications. *The African Review* 3(2):327–340.

———. 1998. Searching for Utopia: The Politics of Gender and Education in Tanzania. In *Women and Education in Sub-Saharan Africa: Power, Opportunities, and Constraints*. Edited by Marianne Bloch, Josephine A. Beoku-Betts, and B. Robert Tabachnick. Boulder, CO: Lynne Rienner Publishers.

McFadden, Mark G. 1995. Resistance to School and Educational Outcomes: Questions of Structure and Agency. *British Journal of Sociology of Education*. 16(3):293–309.

McLaren, Peter. 1993. *Schooling as a Ritual Performance: Towards a Political Economy of Educational Symbols and Gestures*. London: Routledge.

McRobbie, Angela. 1994. Different, Youthful, Subjectivities: Towards a Cultural

Sociology of Youth. In *Post-Modernism and Popular Culture*. A collection of essays by Angela McRobbie. New York: Routledge.

Mead, Margaret. 1928 [1973]. *Coming of Age in Samoa*. New York: American Museum of Natural History.

———. 1970. Letter from Peri-Manus II. In *Applying Cultural Anthropology: An Introductory Reader*. Edited by Aaron Podolefsky and Peter J. Brown. Mountain View, CA: Mayfield Publishing.

Meekers, Dominique. 1994. Education and Adolescent Fertility in Sub-Saharan Africa. *International Review of Modern Sociology* 24(1):1–43.

Meyer, John W., David H. Kamens, and Aaron Benavot, with Yung-Kyung Cha and Suk-Ying Wong. 1992. *School Knowledge for the Masses: World Models and National Primary Curricular Categories in the Twentieth Century*. Washington, DC: Falmer Press.

Miller, Michael B. 1981. *The Bon Marché: Bourgeois Culture and the Department Store, 1869-1920*. Princeton, NJ: Princeton University Press.

Ministry of Education and Culture. 1988. History Syllabus. Dar es Salaam: Institute of Curriculum Development.

Ministry of Education and Culture. 1992a. English Language Teaching Support Project. Phase II. Project Monitoring Report. Edited by Catherine Kivanda, Coelestrina Kazaura, Paul Simonds. Dar es Salaam.

———. 1992b. *Basic Education Statistics in Tanzania*. Dar es Salaam, Tanzania.

———. 1995a. *Girls' Secondary Education Support: Pilot Design*. Dorothy A.S. Mbilinyi and Alphonse G. Mduda. Dar es Salaam.

———. 1995b. *Basic Education Statistics in Tanzania*. Dar es Salaam, Tanzania.

Ministry of National Education. 1977. *Applied Sciences Secondary School Syllabus*. Dar es Salaam: United Republic of Tanzania.

Mitchell, Timothy. 1988. *Colonising Egypt*. Cambridge: Cambridge University Press.

Moore, Henrietta. 1994. *A Passion for Difference: Essays in Anthropology and Gender*. Bloomington: Indiana University Press.

Moore, Sally Falk. 1976. The Secret of Men: A Fiction of Chagga Initiation and Its Relation to the Logic of Chagga Symbolism. *Africa* 46(4):357–370.

———. 1986. *Social Facts and Fabrications: "Customary" Law on Kilimanjaro 1880–1980*. Cambridge: Cambridge University Press.

———. 1996a. Introduction to *Chaga Childhood: A Description of Indigenous Education in an East African Tribe*. Hamburg, Germany: LIT Verlag. Distributed by Transaction Publishers, Rutgers University.

———. 1996b. Post-Socialist Micro-Politics: Kilimanjaro. *Africa* 66(4):587–606.

Mudimbe, V.Y. 1988. *The Invention of Africa: Gnosis, Philosophy, and the Order of Knowledge*. Bloomington: Indiana University Press.

New York Times. 1995. U.S. to Help Girls in Poor Lands [or Countries] Stay in School. March 8, p. 12.

Ngula, Alex. 1996. Girls' Education in Namibia. Paper presented at conference on Education, Knowledge, and Culture. Joensuu, Finland.

Noddings, Nel. 1993. *Educating for Intelligent Belief or Unbelief*. New York: Teachers College Press.

Nyerere, Julius. 1967. Education for Self-Reliance. In *Freedom and Socialism/Uhuru* na Ujamaa: A Selection from Writings and Speeches, 1967-1967. Edited by Julius K. Nyerere, 1968. Dar es Salaam: Oxford University Press.

Omari, I.M. 1991. Innovation and Change in Higher Education in Developing Countries: Experiences from Tanzania. *Comparative Education* 27(2):181–205.

Oppong, Christine. 1981. *Middle Class African Marriage: A Family Study of Ghanaian Senior Civil Servants*. London: George Allen and Unwin.

Ortner, Sherry B. 1974. Is Female to Male as Nature Is to Culture? In *Woman, Culture and Society*. Edited by Michelle Zimbalist Rosaldo and Louise Lamphere. Stanford, CA: Stanford University Press.

———. 1996. *Making Gender: The Politics and Erotics of Culture*. Boston: Beacon Press.

Parsons, Talcott. 1959. The School Class as a Social System: Some of Its Functions in American Society. In *Schools and Society: A Unified Reader*. Second Edition. Edited by Jeanne H. Ballantine. Mountain View, CA: Mayfield.

Peshkin, Alan. 1972. *Kanuri Schoolchildren: Education and Social Mobilization in Nigeria*. New York: Holt, Rinehart and Winston.

———. 1991. *The Color of Strangers, The Color of Friends: the Play of Ethnicity in School and Community*. Chicago: University of Chicago Press.

Porter, Karen.1996. The Agency of Children, Work, and Social Change in the South Pare Mountains. In *On the Backs of Children: Children and Work in Africa*. Edited by Karen A. Porter. Published by the Society for the Anthropology of Work, American Anthropological Association. Summer and Fall.

Project Proposal. 1989. Mkufi Secondary School Mission Statement.

Proweller, Amira. 1998. *Constructing Female Identities: Meaning Making in an Upper Middle Class Youth Culture*. Albany: State University of New York Press.

Psacharopoulos, George. 1995. Returns to Investment in Education: A Global Update. *World Development* 22(9):1325–1343.

Psacharopoulos, George, and William Loxley. 1985. *Diversified Secondary Education and Development: Evidence from Colombia and Tanzania*. Baltimore, MD: Johns Hopkins University Press.

Rabinow, Paul. 1986. Representations are Social Facts: Modernity and Post-Modernity in Anthropology. In *Writing Culture*. Edited by James Clifford and George E. Marcus. Berkeley: University of California Press.

Radway, Janice A. 1984. *Reading the Romance: Women, Patriarchy, and Popular Literature*. Chapel Hill: University of North Carolina.

Raissiguier, Catherine. 1994. *Becoming Women, Becoming Workers: Identity Formation in a French Vocational School*. Albany: State University of New York Press.

Raum, Otto Friedrich. 1940 [1967] *Chaga Childhood: A Description of Indigenous Education in an East African Tribe*. New York: Oxford University Press.

Read, Margaret. 1960. *Children of Their Fathers: Growing Up among the Ngoni of Nyasaland*. New Haven, CT: Yale University Press.

Reed-Danahay, Deborah. 1996. *Education and Identity in Rural France: The Politics of Schooling*. Cambridge: Cambridge University Press.

Renne, Elisha P. 1995. *Cloth That Does Not Die: The Meaning of Cloth in Búnu Social Life*. Seattle: University of Washington Press.

Resnick, Idrian N. 1968. Introduction to *Tanzania: Revolution by Education*. Edited by Idrian Resnick. Arusha: Longmans of Tanzania.

Richards, Audrey Isabel. 1956 [1982]. *Chisungu: A Girl's Initiation Ceremony among the Bemba of Zambia*. New York: Tavistock.

Rosaldo, Michelle Zimbalist. 1974. Woman, Culture and Society: A Theoretical Overview. *Woman, Culture and Society*. Edited by Michelle Zimbalist Rosaldo and Louise Lamphere. Stanford, CA: Stanford University Press.

Rwebangira, Magdalena K., and Rita Lijeström. 1998. *Haraka, Haraka . . . Look Before You Leap: Youth at the Crossroad of Custom and Modernity*. Stockholm: Nordiska Afrikainstitutet.

Sahlins, Marshall. 1994. Cosmologies of Capitalism: The Trans-Pacific Sector of "The World System." In *Culture/Power/History: A Reader in Contemporary Social Theory*. Edited by Nicholas B. Dirks, Geoff Eley, and Sherry B. Ortner. Princeton, NJ: Princeton University Press.

Samoff, Joel. 1993. The Reconstruction of Schooling in Africa. *Comparative Education Review* 37(2):181–222.

Schultz, Theodore William. 1963. *The Economic Value of Education*. New York: Columbia University Press.

Senkoro, F.E.M.K. 1982. *The Prostitute in African Literature*. Dar es Salaam: University of Dar es Salaam Press.

Serpell, Robert. 1993. *The Significance of Schooling: Life-Journeys in an African Society*. Cambridge: Cambridge University Press.

Setel, Philip W. 1995. Bo'n Town Life: Youth, AIDS, and the Changing Character of Adulthood in Kilimanjaro, Tanzania. Doctoral Dissertation, Department of Anthropology, Boston University.

Shann, G.N. 1956. The Early Development of Education among the Chagga. *Tanganyika Notes and Records* 45:21–32.

Shire, Chenjerai. 1994. Men Don't Go to the Moon: Language, Space, and Masculinities in Zimbabwe. In *Dislocating Masculinity: Comparative Ethnographies*. Edited by Andrea Cornwall and Nancy Lindisfarne. London: Routledge.

Skinner, Debra, and Dorothy Holland. 1996. Schools and the Production of the Educated Person in a Nepalese Hill Community. *The Cultural Production of the Educated Person: Critical Ethnographies of Schooling and Local Practice*. Edited by Bradley A. Levinson, Douglas E. Foley, and Dorothy C. Holland. Albany: State University of New York Press.

Stahl, Kathleen. 1964. *History of the Chagga People of Kilimanjaro*. London: Mouton & Co.

Stambach, Amy. 1998. "Too Much Schooling Makes Me Crazy": School-Related Illnesses on Mount Kilimanjaro. *Comparative Education Review* 42(4):497–512.

———. In press. *Kutoa Mimba*: Debates about Schoolgirl Abortion in Northern Tanzania. In *The Sociocultural and Political Context of Abortion from an Anthropological Perspective*. Edited by Alaka Basu. Oxford: Clarendon.

Steele, R.C. 1966. A Check-List of the Trees and Shrubs of the South Kilimanjaro Forests. *Tanzania Notes and Records* 66:183–186.

Stein, Howard. 1992. Economic Policy and the IMF in Tanzania: Conditionality, Conflict, and Convergence. In *Tanzania and the IMF: The Dynamics of Liberalization*. Edited by H. Campbell and H. Stein. Boulder, CO: Westview.

Stephens, Sharon. 1995. Introduction, *Children and the Politics of Culture*. Edited by Sharon Stephens. Princeton, NJ: Princeton University Press.

Stoller, Paul. 1989. *Fusion of the Worlds: An Ethnography of Possession among the Songhay of Niger.* Chicago: University of Chicago Press.

Strathern, Andrew. 1995. Universals and Particulars: Some Current Contests in Anthropology. *Ethos* 23(2):173–186.

Stromquist, Nelly. 1998. Agents in Women's Education: Some Trends in the African Context. In *Women and Education in Sub-Saharan Africa: Power, Opportunities, and Constraints.* Edited by Marianne Bloch, Josephine A. Beoku-Betts, and B. Robert Tabachnick. Boulder, CO: Lynne Rienner Publishers.

Swantz, Marja-Liisa. 1985. *Women in Development: A Creative Role Denied? The Case of Tanzania.* New York: St. Martin's Press.

Swatridge, Colin. 1985. *Delivering the Goods: Education as Cargo in Papua New Guinea.* London: Manchester University Press.

Talis, Sarah Joan. 1985. Education for Self-Reliance: An Ethnographic Study of Tanzanian Secondary School Students. Doctoral Dissertation, Rutgers University, School of Education.

Tanzanian Demographic Health Survey (TDHS) 1991/1992. 1993. Edited by Sylvester Ngallaba, Saidi Hussein Kapiga, Ireneus Ruyobya, and J. Ties Boerma. Bureau of Statistics, Planning Commission, Dar es Salaam, Tanzania. Macro International Inc., Columbia, Maryland.

Tanzanian Gender Networking Programme. 1993. *Gender Profile of Tanzania.* University of Dar es Salaam, Dar es Salaam, Tanzania.

Thompson, A.R. 1976. Historical Survey of the Role of the Churches in Education from Precolonial Days to Post-Independence. In *Church and Education in Tanzania.* Edited by Allan J. Gottneid. Nairobi: East African Publishing House.

Thorne, Barrie. 1997. *Gender Play: Girls and Boys in School.* New Brunswick, NJ: Rutgers University Press.

Tripp, Aili Mari. 1997. *Changing the Rules: The Politics of Liberalization and the Urban Informal Economy in Tanzania.* Berkeley: University of California Press.

Tsing, Anna Lowenhaupt. 1993. *In the Realm of the Diamond Queen: Marginality in an Out-of-the-Way Place.* Princeton: Princeton University Press.

Tumbo-Masabo, Zubeida, and Rita Lijeström, eds. 1994. *Chelewa, Chelewa: The Dilemma of Teenage Girls.* Uppsala, Sweden: The Scandinavian Institute of African Studies.

Turner, Victor. 1967. Betwixt and Between: The Liminal Period in *Rite de Passage.* In *The Forest of Symbols: Aspects of Ndembu Ritual.* Ithaca, NY: Cornell University Press.

United Republic of Tanzania. 1988. *Population Census, Regional Profile, Kilimanjaro.* Dar es Salaam: Bureau of Planning and Statistics.

Valentine, Gill, Tracey Skelton, and Deborah Chambers. 1998. Cool Places: An Introduction to Youth and Youth Cultures. In *Cool Places: Geographies of Youth Cultures.* Edited by Tracey Skelton and Gill Valentine. New York: Routledge.

Varenne, Hervé, and Ray McDermott, with Shelley Goldman, Merry Naddeo, and Rosemarie Rizzo-Tolk. 1998. *Successful Failure: The School America Builds.* Boulder, CO: Westview.

Vavrus, Frances K. 1998. Schooling, Fertility, and the Discourse of Development: A Study of the Kilimanjaro Region of Tanzania. Doctoral Dissertation, Department of Curriculum and Instruction, University of Wisconsin, Madison.

Wakoko, Florence, and Linda Lobao. 1996. Reconceptualizing Gender and Reconstructing Social Life: Ugandan Women and the Path to National Development. *Africa Today* 43(3):307–322.

Walkerdine, Valerie. 1990. *Schoolgirl Fictions*. London: Verso.

Watts, Michael. 1992. Capitalisms, Crises, and Culture: Notes Toward a Totality of Fragments. In *Reworking Modernity: Capitalisms and Symbolic Discontent*. Edited by Allan Pred and Michael Watts. New Brunswick, NJ: Rutgers University Press.

Weber, Max. 1968. *Economy and Society: An Outline of Interpretive Sociology*. Edited by Guenther Roth and Claus Wittich. New York: Bedminster Press.

Weis, Lois. 1979. Education and the Reproduction of Inequality: The Case of Ghana. *Comparative Education Review* 23(1):41–51.

Weiss, Brad. 1996. *The Making and Unmaking of the Haya Lived World: Consumption, Commoditization, and Everyday Practice*. Durham, NC: Duke University Press.

Wexler, Philip, with the assistance of Warren Crichlow, June Kern, Rebecca Martusewicz. 1992. *Becoming Somebody: Toward a Social Psychology of School*. Washington, DC: Falmer Press.

White House Press Release. Remarks by President Clinton to the Community of Kisowera School, Uganda. March 24, 1998.

White, Luise. 1991. *The Comforts of Home: Prostitution in Colonial Nairobi*. Chicago: University of Chicago Press.

Willis, Paul E. 1977. *Learning to Labor: How Working-Class Kids Get Working-Class Jobs*. New York: Columbia University Press.

———. 1990. *Common Culture: Symbolic Work at Play in the Everyday Cultures of the Young*. With Simon Jones, Joyce Canaan, and Geoff Hurd. San Francisco: Westview.

Winter, Jurgen Christoph. 1979. *Bruno Gutmann, 1876–1966: A German Approach to Social Anthropology*. Oxford: Clarendon.

World Bank. 1988. *Education in Sub-Saharan Africa: Policies for Adjustment, Revitalization, and Expansion*. Washington, DC: World Bank.

———. *World Development Reports*. Washington, DC: World Bank.

Wulff, Helena. 1995. Introducing Youth Culture in Its Own Right: The State of the Art and New Possibilities. In *Youth Cultures: A Cross-Cultural Perspective*. Edited by Vered Amit-Talai and Helena Wulff. New York: Routledge.

Yanagisako, Sylvia J., and Jane F. Collier. 1987. Toward a Unified Analysis of Gender and Kinship. In *Gender and Kinship: Essays Toward a Unified Analysis*. Edited by Jane F. Collier and Sylvia J. Yanagisako. Stanford, CA: Stanford University Press.

INDEX

abortion, 105
adolescence
    as portrayed in education policies,
        142–143
    as portrayed in home economics
        syllabus, 54–56
    teachers' and students' views of,
        139–145
adulthood, 142
affines, 93, 172
age-mates, 36
agnatic kin, 175n.4
agricultural production
    at school, 41–44
    of banana groves, 33–34
    social relationships generated
        through, 41
    see also land
agricultural science curriculum, 42–44
AIDS
    perceived susceptibility of students
        to, 74, 154
    song about, 137
    see also HIV infection
alcohol, *see* beer, drunkenness
Althusser, Louis, 59
aphorisms
    about "a person living in a foreign
        place," 24–26, 172–173,
        177n.27
    about "mountains never meet but
        people do," 161, 171–173

about "returning home to die," 37,
    178n.7
    as means of indirect expression, 28
authority,
    student challenges to, 136–137
    teachers' 124

banana groves
    and inheritance, 30–38
    as expression of collective cultural
        life, 31–32, 131
    as expression of moral character, 34,
        35
    as outmoded symbol of social life, 36
    as seen in relation to schooling,
        32–33, 35–38, 39, 44–47,
        165–166
    cultivation of, 33, 34
    references to in marriage process,
        65, 69
    selling, 30, 35
    students' care of, 144
bananas
    and beer production, 35
    sale of, 37–38
    varieties of, 34–35
beer
    as contrasted in symbolic value with
        Coca-Cola products, 61, 69,
        70–72
    brewing as sign of uneducated
        status, 61